Teen Finance Series

Financial Independence Information
For Teens, First Edition

Teen Finance Series

Financial Independence Information For Teens, First Edition

Tips for a Successful Financial Life

Including Facts about Financial Literacy, Teen
Employment, Internships, Budgeting, Basic Banking,
Tax Education, Managing Expenses, and Credit Scores

OMNIGRAPHICS
615 Griswold, Ste. 901
Detroit, MI 48226

Bibliographic Note
Because this page cannot legibly accommodate all the copyright notices, the Bibliographic Note portion of the Preface constitutes an extension of the copyright notice.

* * *

OMNIGRAPHICS
Angela L. Williams, *Managing Editor*

* * *

Library of Congress Cataloging-in-Publication Data

Title: Financial independence for teens.

Description: 1st edition. | Detroit, MI : Omnigraphics, [2019] | Series: Teen finance series | "Angela L Williams, Editorial Manager." | Includes index.

Identifiers: LCCN 2018049167 (print) | LCCN 2018050656 (ebook) | ISBN 9780780815827 (ebook) | ISBN 9780780815810 (hardcover : alk. paper)

Subjects: LCSH: Teenagers--Finance, Personal. | Financial literacy.

Classification: LCC HG179 (ebook) | LCC HG179 .F4623 2019 (print) | DDC 332.02400835--dc23

LC record available at https://lccn.loc.gov/2018049167

Table of Contents

Preface

Part One: Determining When a Teen Is Ready to Be Independent

Chapter 1——Financial Capability and Literacy 3

Chapter 2——Assessing Yourself and Your Future 7

Chapter 3——Planning for Independence 11

Chapter 4——Parent and Teen Guidance to Ensure Success 19

Chapter 5——Teen Embarkment on the Journey to
Independence 23

Chapter 6——Minor Emancipation Laws 27

Chapter 7——Teens with Disabilities 31

Chapter 8——Barriers for Foster Care Teens 35

Part Two: Teen Employment

Chapter 9——Work and Age Restrictions Requirement for
Employment 39

Chapter 10—Know the Rules 45

Chapter 11—Data on Teen Participation in the Workforce 51

Chapter 12—Exploring Your Career Path 55

Chapter 13—Internships: Previewing a Profession 61

Chapter 14—Job Opportunities 65

Chapter 15—Networking for Teens 69

Chapter 16—Creating a Résumé 73

Chapter 17—What Is a Cover Letter? 77

Chapter 18—Finding a Job 79

Chapter 19—Jobs for Disabled Teens 83

Chapter 20—Workplace Skills 89

Chapter 21—Workplace Ethics 93

Chapter 22—Workplace Stress 97

Chapter 23—Work–Life Balance 101

Chapter 24—Workplace Hazards 107

Chapter 25—Workers' Rights and Safety 111

Chapter 26—Self-Employment 117

Part Three: Creating and Living within a Budget

Chapter 27—Budgeting 127

Chapter 28—Avoiding Common Mistakes with Money 135

Chapter 29—Basic Facts about Banks and Banking 141

Chapter 30—How to Save and Invest 147

Chapter 31—Essential Money Management 151

Chapter 32—Fine-Tuning Your Money Management 161

Chapter 33—Financial Empowerment 167

Chapter 34—Taxes and Tax Benefits for Education 179

Chapter 35—Working with Financial Professionals 183

Part Four: Living on Your Own

Chapter 36—Renting an Apartment or House 191

Chapter 37—Renter's Guide: Ten Tips
        for Tenants 197

Chapter 38—Sharing Rooms and Related Agreements 201

Chapter 39—Landlord Requirements 211

Chapter 40—Landlord–Tenant Responsibilities 215

Chapter 41—Cosigning Requirements for Young
                           Renters 221

Chapter 42—Managing Renters' Insurance 225

Chapter 43—Transportation Needs 229

Chapter 44—Managing Expenses 233

Chapter 45—Electronic Banking 237

Chapter 46—Finding and Applying for a Scholarship 241

Chapter 47—Financial Aid for Studying Abroad 245

Part Five: Planning for the Future

Chapter 48—Future Financial Goals 251

Chapter 49—How to Become an Entrepreneur 253

Chapter 50—Deciding Your Career 257

Chapter 51—Protecting Your Credit Score 267

Chapter 52—Your Credit Score and Why It Matters 275

Chapter 53—How to Rebuild Your Credit Score 279

Chapter 54—How to Dispute Credit Report Errors 287

Chapter 55—Educational Goals and Responsibilities 293

Chapter 56—How to Have a Higher Earning Potential 297

Chapter 57—Day Trading 301

Chapter 58—Ways to Make Money Online 305

Chapter 59—Things You Can Do to Avoid Fraud 311

Part Six: If You Need More Information

Chapter 60—Online Money Management Tools 317

Chapter 61—Financial Independence Information
          for Disabled Teens...321

Chapter 62—Resources for Financial Independence 337

Index **353**

Preface

About This Book

The U.S. Bureau of Labor Statistics (BLS) reports the number of youth working, from the age of 16–24 years have increased from 2 million to 20.9 million from April to July 2018. With the technology boom and information at finger tips, the way teens earn, shop, and live have drastically changed. A proven fact, teens want to have a certain degree of financial independence and a guaranteed way to be able to achieve that independence is a job. Work always gives financial security and help meet needs. However, the challenge here for any teen is to find the right job and choose a career path that would benefit them in future.

Financial Independence Information For Teens, First Edition provides insights on knowledge related to financial capability and literacy for teens. It gives the reader information on labor laws, teen workforce participation, age requirements, various kinds of employment available in the market, job search and résumé preparation, self-assessment, career planning, apprenticeship, internships, etc. It also explains the necessary management skills needed at a workplace, basic workers' right, and work-life balance. Information on budgeting, saving, investing, money management, and taxes, and importance of working with professionals is also included. It discusses about housing options and legal formalities related to it, transportation, and opportunities to study abroad, financial aid for education, etc. The book concludes with a list of online money management tools and a directory of resources for financial information.

How to Use This Book

This book is divided into parts and chapters. Parts focus on broad areas of interest; chapters are devoted to single topics within a part.

Part One: Determining When a Teen Is Ready to Be Independent begins with a brief insight on the emotional and physical factors determining whether a teen is ready to be financially independent, the barriers they face, and how parents can guide and ensure their success. It also provides information on minor emancipation laws, how teens with disabilities can experience financial independence, and the barriers faced by teens in foster care to achieve financial independence.

Part Two: Teen Employment deals with the process of getting employment. It begins with an overview of legal requirements for getting employed, laws pertaining to child labor, statistics of teens in the nation's workforce, the types of employment available for teens, including internships, opportunities, and hazards related to the workplace. It also offers information on tools essential for job search such as networking, job search strategies, workplace ethics, workplace stress, balancing work and life, and concludes with rights and safety aspects for teen workers. Additionally, it deals with jobs for disabled teens and self-employment opportunities.

Part Three: Creating and Living within a Budget focuses on budgeting, saving, investments, financial knowledge, financial empowerment, and taxes and tax benefits for education. It also presents basic facts about banks and banking, managing money, and how to work with financial professionals.

Part Four: Living on Your Own focuses on housing options for teens who prefer to lead an independent life, besides legal issues related to renting, maintenance, and sharing responsibilities. It also discusses about sharing room, landlord requirements, landlord and tenant responsibilities, managing expenses, and details about finding and applying for a scholarship and financial aid for studying abroad.

Part Five: Planning for the Future dwells upon future financial and educational goals, career decisions, ways to protect and rebuilt credit score. Additionally, it deals with day trading, earning potential, options for earning online, and fraud prevention.

Part Six: Additional Information offers resources for financial independence.

Bibliographic Note

This volume contains documents and excerpts from publications issued by the following U.S. government agencies: Centers for Disease Control and Prevention (CDC); Consumer Financial Protection Bureau (CFPB); Federal Deposit Insurance Corporation (FDIC); Federal Trade Commission (FTC); Internal Revenue Service (IRS); National Institute for Occupational Safety and Health (NIOSH); National Resource Center for Youth Development (NRCYD); Occupational Safety and Health Administration (OSHA); Office of Housing and Community Development (OHCD); Office on Women's Health (OWH); TreasuryDirect; USA.gov; U.S. Bureau of Labor Statistics (BLS); U.S. Department of Education (ED); U.S. Department of Homeland Security (DHS); U.S. Department of Labor (DOL); U.S. Department of the Treasury (USDT); U.S. General Services Administration (GSA); U.S. Small Business Administration (SBA); U.S. Social Security Administration (SSA); and Youth.gov.

It may also contain original material produced by Omnigraphics.

The photograph on the front cover is © Real Deal Photo/Shutterstock.

Part One
Determining When a Teen Is Ready to Be Independent

Chapter 1

Financial Capability and Literacy

What Is Financial Capability and Literacy?

Financial capability and literacy are defined as "the capacity, based on knowledge, skills, and access, to manage financial resources effectively." This set of skills can help youth achieve financial well-being that happens when they can fully meet current and ongoing financial obligations, feel secure in their financial future, and are capable of making decisions that allow them to enjoy life. Financial education is how youth can learn these skills through a variety of resources and programming.

Financial capability is the ability of individuals "to understand, assess, and act in their best financial interest." It is the combination of the financial knowledge needed to make good choices, the ability to apply that knowledge in day-to-day life, and the necessary access to financial products and services.

(Source: "A Financial Empowerment Toolkit for Youth and Young Adults in Foster Care," National Resource Center for Youth Development (NRCYD), U.S. Department of Health and Human Services (HHS).)

Youth face a financial marketplace that is more complex than the one faced by previous generations. A study found that millennials have greater financial concerns than older generations:

- 55 percent of millennials with student debt worry that they will not be able to pay off their debt, and

About This Chapter: Text under the heading "What Is Financial Capability and Literacy?" is excerpted from "Financial Literary," Youth.gov, April 28, 2016; Text under the heading "Why Is Knowledge of Financial Capability Important?" is excerpted from "Facts about Youth Financial Knowledge and Capability," Youth.gov, April 28, 2016.

- Almost 50 percent are concerned that they have too much debt in general (i.e., credit cards).

Financial capability is knowing how to spend wisely, manage credit, and plan for the future. Financial capability is an effective way to help youth, no matter their circumstances, avoid common financial vulnerabilities and build economic stability. Youth should be educated about finances early in life and at pivotal points in their development and financial lives. Having a higher financial literacy early in life is associated with:

- Less credit card debt

- Higher savings rates

- Fewer personal bankruptcies

As they approach high-school graduation, students and their caregivers will make important decisions about whether to pursue higher education and, if so, how to face the reality of paying for it. Additionally, youth who do not attend college or trade school directly after high school will more quickly face financial responsibilities as adults. These early choices can have a long-lasting impact on their financial well-being.

Why Is Knowledge of Financial Capability Important?

Learning financial capability is important because youth are increasingly facing higher levels of debt:

- The average debt of students when they graduated from college rose from $18,550 (in 2004) to $28,950 (in 2014), an increase of 56 percent.

- From 2004 to 2009, the median credit card debt among college students increased 74 percent.

Unfortunately, many youth have not received either formal or informal guidance on financial matters. So, they may not be ready to make sound financial choices:

- A survey of 15-year-olds in the United States found that 18 percent of respondents did not learn fundamental financial skills that are often applied in everyday situations, such as building a simple budget, comparison shopping, and understanding an invoice.

- A report on the results of a financial literacy exam found that high-school seniors scored on average 48 percent correct, showing a strong need for more comprehensive financial education for youth in high school.

- According to the 2008 results of the National Longitudinal Survey of Youth (NLSY), only 27 percent of youth knew what inflation was and could do simple interest-rate calculations.

Financial illiteracy is more common among low-income individuals because they typically do not have wide access to accurate financial information. With such illiteracy, youth in low-income households can fall victim later as adults to scams, high-interest-rate loans, and increasing debt. Training low-income individuals in financial management can be an effective way to improve their knowledge in five areas:

- Predatory lending practices

- Public and work-related benefits

- Banking practices

- Savings and investing strategies

- Credit use and interest rates

Young people often learn about money informally through socialization, such as observing and listening to their caregivers, influential adults, and peers. Youth are not consistently introduced to more formal instruction on money matters—for example, through a classroom curriculum or other training on saving, spending, allowances, and the importance of focusing on short-term goals (i.e., purchasing an item, saving money, paying off a debt) to be able to get to long-term financial goals (i.e., saving for college, buying a house).

Distinguishing what youth do not understand about financial topics is important. It is also beneficial to understand the specific concerns that youth have when it comes to money.

A survey of a diverse group of youth and adults regarding what they wanted to learn about finance found that concerns among youth differed within youth groups depending on their background. The survey also found a disconnect between what adults thought youth should learn and what youth prioritized, for example:

- Pregnant or parenting teens and teens in the juvenile justice system or on probation were most concerned about learning how to save money for a home, but migrant teens and teens in school were most interested in learning how to save money for college.

- Almost 70 percent of adults in the survey felt that teens should learn about how to complete and file a tax return form, but only 39 percent of the teens were interested in learning about this topic.

- However, more than half of the teens in the juvenile justice system or on probation and almost half of the migrant teens showed an interest in learning how to complete and file a tax return.

- Although a majority of teens wanted to learn about money, more than half wanted to learn in an easy way. This could include strategies that are convenient, utilize technology, and are not time-consuming for youth.

Chapter 2

Assessing Yourself and Your Future

Humans aren't really very good at assessing themselves. So, often, when we need to make decisions about our own future, we have trouble doing so. However, we're often faced with the need to make important, potentially life-altering decisions, such as what college to attend, what major to choose, and what career to pursue. And, in those cases, the best way to proceed is to conduct an honest assessment of our talents, past performance, values, and interests in order to make informed choices. Fortunately, you don't have to do it alone. There are a number of avenues of assistance available, both formal and informal, to help you conduct a meaningful self-assessment.

How Assessment Can Help

A self-assessment is a guide that helps an individual make a decision. It provides insight and gives you a roadmap as you plan for and think about the future.

Some benefits of assessment include:

- Help identify your skills and areas of interest

- Highlight your learning style and the way you do your best work

- Point out areas where you need more training or experience

- Help you learn about educational or occupational opportunities that will suit you best

- Get you to consider new courses of study or career paths

About This Chapter: "Assessing Yourself and Your Future," © 2017 Omnigraphics.

Self-assessment not only helps identify educational programs and careers that align with your talents and interests, but also pinpoints areas for improvement and guides you toward programs and occupations that you might want to pursue.

On the other hand, don't expect assessment to:

- Guarantee that a given educational or career path will be open to you

- Ensure that you'll like any given program or occupation

- Predict how well you'll succeed

Getting Started

To begin a self-assessment there are a few questions you can ask yourself that might help get you the process:

What Am I Good At?

Often, we think we know what we can do, but sometimes we overlook skills we've developed through the years. To help jog your memory, ask yourself such questions as:

- In which classes do I get the best grades?

- In what parts of specific classes (such as labs or team projects) do I do best?

- At what extracurricular activities do I think I excel?

- How good am I at tasks that require manual dexterity?

- How well do I envision and implement solutions to problems?

- Have I gotten good responses to oral presentations?

What Do I Enjoy?

To help determine your areas of interest, ask yourself questions such as:

- What classes do I like?

- What do I do well?

- When I'm reading or watching TV, what topics draw my attention?

- What types of things am I doing when I lose track of time?

- How do I spend my spare time?

- Among people I know, who do I think has the most interesting job?

What Is Important to Me?

In addition to areas where you excel or those you enjoy, don't forget to take into account things that you feel strongly about. Some items to consider:

- Do I feel best when I work alone or with a group?

- Do I prefer difficult challenges or more frequent accomplishments?

- How much time do I invest in physical activity?

- Am I a risk-taker, or do I prefer security?

- Does competition drive me or discourage me?

- Is it important for me to be a leader?

Assessment Tools

The above series of questions is just a way of beginning to think about the assessment process. The best way to proceed is to complete a series of questionnaires and exercises specifically developed by experts to identify skills, personality types, values, areas of interest, and other factors that go into decision-making. Some of these include:

- **Myers–Briggs Type Indicator.** This well-known 93-question test, which has been around for many years, helps identify your basic personality type, which can be useful in choosing an educational or career path.

- **Strong Interest Inventory.** Developed by a psychologist named Strong, this inventory consists of almost 300 items, to which you indicate the strength of your reaction. The results are then compared to those of people happily employed in various occupations, giving you an idea of areas to investigate further.

- **StrengthsQuest.** This 30-minute online assessment helps identify your current strengths in a variety of areas—and the personal characteristics behind them—and relates them to the development of educational and career strategies.

Today, most schools have computerized assessment programs available that can help point you to information about degree programs, financial aid, and career paths. Check with your guidance counselor for details.

But these tools are just some of the more well-known tips of the iceberg. There are numerous other formal assessment tools, some of which may be more appropriate for you. A school guidance counselor or career counselor can help you explore other means of conducting an effective self-assessment. There are also a large number of online resources available to students planning their future educational or vocational paths, many of which can be found on college and university websites. Exploring some of these may provide some extra insight and trigger some ideas.

References

1. "Assessing Yourself and Exploring Career and Educational Options," University of Minnesota Duluth (UMD), 2007.

2. "Career Choice Requires Self-Assessment," SchoolGuides.com, n.d.

3. Pelusi, Nando, Ph.D. "Assessing Yourself, Honestly," *Psychology Today*, June 9, 2016.

4. "Researching Occupations," College of the Rockies, n.d.

Chapter 3

Planning for Independence

Thinking about Moving Out

Imagine that you have just finished school and you have your first full-time job in retail, as an associate at your favorite clothing store. You make $1,500 per month (about $9.40/hr.), and take home about $1,200. You also get a monthly bonus of $400 if you meet your sales goals. You have about $600 in savings from your old part-time pizza job. Do you think you have enough to move out of your parents' house and get your own apartment, or even buy your own home? You think you might be ready to move out and get your own space. This chapter will talk about how to figure out if you are financially ready to do that and go over some things you might need to know.

Renting Your Own Space

How much do you think it costs to move into a house or apartment?

Costs to Move In

When you want to rent an apartment, landlords will typically ask for additional money, called a deposit, to assure that you will take care of their property and pay your rent on time. They will probably also ask you to sign a lease. This lease protects both of you by clearly stating the arrangement between you.

About This Chapter: This chapter includes text excerpted from "Module 8: A Roof over Your Head," Federal Deposit Insurance Corporation (FDIC), March 28, 2009.

A **lease** is a legal document. It states that the landlord agrees to provide a space for you to live and that it is in "livable" condition (free of bugs and mechanical defects). A lease also states that you agree to pay a certain amount for a set period of time for the apartment. The lease lists your responsibilities as a renter, such as keeping the apartment in good condition. You have certain rights as a renter; see the U.S. Department of Housing and Urban Development (HUD) site.

The costs of securing a rental property usually include:

- Security deposit.
- Payment of the first month's rent.
- Fees, including credit report fees and pet fees or deposits.
- Costs of connecting utilities (electric, phone, water) which may be required by the utility companies.

Security Deposit

A security deposit is money you put on deposit with the landlord when you sign the lease. It is held in an account by the landlord during the term of your lease. You may instead be asked to pay the deposit once your application is approved to reserve the unit, as it lets the landlord know that you are serious about moving in.

The deposit guarantees to the landlord that you will stay for the length of your lease term and not move out early or without notice. Some landlords may allow you to break your lease and walk away by paying a substantial fee. For example, if your rent is $600 per month and there are three months left on your lease when you move out, you may be legally obligated to pay the landlord $1,800. If your security deposit were $600, the landlord might take you to court to obtain the remaining $1,200. These details should be discussed with the landlord and written in the lease before you sign it.

The security deposit is also used when you move out to help pay for any damages to the property other than normal wear and tear. If there are no damages, the money is returned to you. The amount of a security deposit can vary, but it is usually equal to at least one month's rent. It may be based, in part, on your credit history.

Upfront Payments

Landlords usually require you to pay your first month's rent along with your security deposit when you sign a lease. They probably will also require you to pay for the remaining days in a month if you move in before the first of the month.

Additional Fees

Nonrefundable move-in fees are common in some areas. These cover the cost of preparing the apartment for your move-in. Some landlords may charge nonrefundable application or credit report fees to assess your eligibility to rent the apartment. These fees may be negotiable and restricted by law in some cities or states.

Utility Connection Fees

Utility companies (water, gas, electric, telephone, cable, etc.) usually charge a connection fee to begin service. Sometimes you have to pay the fees before your service is connected, and other times you can pay with your first bill. If a fee is charged, it can be anywhere from a few dollars to $60 or more. They may also ask for a security deposit in addition to connection fees. This is based on your credit and utility payment history, if you have one.

Paying for Your Space

Your income must cover your expenses for each month. The continuing costs of renting an apartment are:

- Rent and other fees (storage, pet fees, parking, etc.)
- Utilities
- Renter's insurance (usually optional)
- The possibility of rent increases

Rent and Fees

Some properties have fees in addition to the rent. Are you going to have a cat or dog? Many landlords charge extra fees and a deposit for pets, possibly including an upfront fee, and extra rent on top of that. You might also need storage or a parking space that can cost extra in some neighborhoods. A good rule of thumb is that no more than 30 percent of your gross income should be spent on rent. That means that if your gross income is $1,500, you should spend no more than $450 on rent. Then you have the remainder of your income for other expenses.

Utilities

You paid to have your utilities connected, but you still have to pay for the service every month. Depending on your apartment, your utilities may be included. Ask before you rent; you might save some money! And watch out: utility bills can vary with the seasons, and they can be very expensive. Many companies have a budget plan so that you pay the same amount throughout the year.

Renters' Insurance

Renters' insurance protects you against the loss or destruction of your possessions in the event your property is stolen or damaged, such as through a fire or burglary. It also covers your living expenses if you are unable to live in your apartment because of a fire or other covered peril. Renters' insurance also provides liability protection if, for example, someone is injured at your home while visiting. Other types of coverage like earthquake or flood insurance may be available at an additional cost. Renters' insurance is usually optional, although some landlords may require you to obtain coverage when you move in.

Rent Increases

The cost of everything rises; even your rent. Your landlord is not allowed to raise the rent during the term of your lease. For example, if you sign a one-year lease, your rent payment will be the same for that year. But at the end of your lease, the landlord may raise your rent. Some communities may have rent-control laws that govern these rent increases; others do not. Be prepared. Look for an apartment that charges less than what your income allows. That way, if you stay after your lease expires, you will have some financial room to cover rent increases.

Sharing Space: Roommates

In order to keep the costs affordable, many young people share an apartment with one or more roommates. In exchange for sharing common areas like a living room, bathroom, and kitchen, you also share all the costs of renting.

Buying a Home

A mortgage is a loan, provided by a financial institution to buy a house or condo. Homes can be expensive and are often not affordable for a person just starting off in life who has yet to accumulate savings and build a credit history. Mortgages are large sums of money. Mortgage payments are made over long periods of time, usually 15–30 years. There are many different types of loans that will meet the needs of people in different situations.

Costs of a Mortgage

Mortgages are not free; in addition to paying them back, you have to pay additional money to obtain one. The costs involved in buying a home include:

- **Closing costs:** Closing costs are fees associated with buying and settling, or finalizing, your loan. They can include property taxes, broker and attorney fees, inspection fees, title insurance, and many other items.

- **Taxes and insurance:** You will probably have to pay some taxes upfront. The locality (usually county and state) where you live will charge taxes on the property, which are generally paid upfront at first and then either monthly with your mortgage payment or separately by you once or twice a year. They can amount to several thousand dollars per year, depending on the value of your house and the state where you live. You also need homeowner's insurance, in case your house catches on fire, the basement floods in a storm, or a window breaks due to your next door neighbor's son's baseball. You may also obtain other insurance, such as flood or earthquake insurance.

- **Interest over the course of the loan:** Interest is money that the bank charges you to borrow money. A portion of every mortgage payment goes toward interest.

The Mortgage Payment
What Makes up a Mortgage Payment?

A mortgage payment is more than just paying back the amount you owe on a home loan. The two parts of the mortgage that pay back the loan are the principal and the interest.

1. Principal is the amount applied to the outstanding balance of the loan. This part is the loan itself.

2. Interest is the amount that the lender, or financial institution, charges for borrowing money.

Escrow

Taxes and homeowner's insurance are paid using a system called escrow. An escrow is a special bank account held by a financial institution for the purpose of paying taxes and insurance. When the bank calculates your mortgage payment, they include 1/12th of your taxes and 1/12th of your homeowner's insurance. When you pay your mortgage, the lender takes this part of the payment and deposits it into the escrow account. Then the financial institution pays the taxes on your behalf to the government and pays your insurance premiums.

In some cases, private mortgage insurance is required to protect the lender if the buyer does not pay the loan. Although this is paid with the mortgage, it is also deposited into the escrow account and paid to the mortgage insurance company.

You can pay taxes and insurance separately. But then you have to remember to save the money each month to pay at the end of the year when the taxes and insurance are due. If you don't, you could have some large bills, maybe several thousand dollars, which you owe but can't pay. Paying separately keeps your mortgage low, but you have to be disciplined enough to save.

Renting versus Buying

There are many advantages and disadvantages of renting and owning a home.

Advantages of Renting

When you rent:

- Property maintenance is the responsibility of the landlord.

- You are only under a rental contract for one year or less.

- You do not have other costs associated with owning a home, such as property taxes or homeowner's insurance.

Renter's insurance can be obtained from the same companies as homeowner's insurance. Renter's insurance is generally cheaper than homeowner's insurance.

Disadvantages of Renting

When you rent:

- You are not the owner of your home.

- Your rent might increase.

- You might not be able to renew your rental contract and then you will have to find a new place to live.

- You are essentially paying your landlord's mortgage.

- You will not obtain a federal tax deduction for your rent payments, while mortgage interest is tax deductible.

As a homeowner, you can enjoy several benefits of ownership:

- You can build equity. Equity refers to the value of the home minus the debt you owe on it. As you pay down the loan and your home value increases, you build up equity.

- One of the benefits of equity is that you can borrow against it for many purposes, usually at a relatively low interest rate. But, remember you could lose your home if you don't pay back the loan.

- Homes have traditionally increased in value over time; so many people consider a home to be an investment.

- Once your mortgage is paid in full, the home is yours.

- Home ownership may reduce the amount of income tax you owe since mortgage interest and property taxes are deductible.

Costs of Owning a Home

When you own a home, property maintenance and upkeep are your responsibility. You are also responsible for the additional costs of:

- Homeowner's insurance

- Real estate taxes

- Mortgage interest

- Homeowner's/condominium association fees, in some cases. These fees pay for maintenance of the common areas and the exterior of the buildings and grounds.

- Maintenance or repair expenses

When you own a home, it is not as easy to move as it is when you rent. You will typically have to sell or rent your home before you can afford to buy or rent another one.

It is also important to understand that you can lose your home, and your investment in it if you do not make timely mortgage payments.

Chapter 4

Parent and Teen Guidance to Ensure Success

Parents often become less involved in your life as you enter the middle grades. But as a young adolescent, you need as much attention and love from them as they provided when you were younger. A good relationship with parents or other adults is the best safeguard you can have as you grow and explore. By the time you reach adolescence, you and your parent will have had years of experience with each other.

Your relationship with your parent may change—in fact, it almost certainly must change—however, as you develop the skills required to be a successful adult. These changes can be rewarding and welcome. As you make a mental and emotional leap, your conversations will grow richer. As your interests develop and deepen, you may begin to teach your parents—how to slug a baseball, what is happening with the city council or county board, or why a new book is worth reading.

America is home to people with a great variety of attitudes, opinions, and values. Americans have different ideas and priorities, which can affect how your parents choose to raise you. Across these differences, however, research has shown that parents can be effective with the following qualities:

- **Showing love.** When you behave badly, parents may become angry or upset with you. They may also feel miserable because they become angry or upset. But these feelings are different from not loving you. Young adolescents need adults who are there for them—people who connect with them, communicate with them, spend time with them, and show a genuine interest in them. This is how they learn to care for and love others.

About This Chapter: This chapter includes text excerpted from "Being an Effective Parent—Helping Your Child through Early Adolescence," U.S. Department of Education (ED), September 11, 2003.

According to school counselor Carol Bleifield, "Parents can love their children but not necessarily love what they do—and children need to trust that this is true."

- **Providing support.** Young adolescents need support as they struggle with problems that may seem unimportant to their parents and families. They need praise when they've done their best. They need encouragement to develop interests and personal characteristics.

- **Setting limits.** Young adolescents need parents or other adults who consistently provide structure and supervision that is firm and appropriate for age and development. Limits keep all children, including young teens, physically and emotionally safe. Carole Kennedy is a former middle-school principal, U.S. Department of Education's (ED) Principal-in-Residence (2000), and president of the National Association of Elementary School Principals (NAESP). She puts it this way: "They need parents who can say, 'No, you cannot go to the mall all day or to movies with that group of kids.'"

- **Being a role model.** Young adolescents need strong role models. Their actions speak louder than words. If they set high standards for themselves and treat others with kindness and respect, then the adolescents stand a better chance of following their parents' example. As adolescents explore possibilities of who they may become, they look to their parents, peers, well-known personalities, and others to define who they may become.

- **Teaching responsibility.** We are not born knowing how to act responsibly. A sense of responsibility is formed over time. As we grow up, we need to learn to take more and more responsibility for such things as:

  - Completing chores, such as doing yard work, cleaning their rooms or helping to prepare meals, that contribute to the family's well being;

  - Completing homework assignments without being nagged;

  - Taking on community activities;

  - Finding ways to be useful to others; and

  - Admitting to both the good and bad choices that they make.

- **Providing a range of experiences.** Adolescence is a time for exploring many areas and doing new things. You may try new sports and new academic pursuits and read new books. You may experiment with different forms of art, learn about different cultures and careers, and take part in community or religious activities. Your parents can open doors for you with whatever means they can. They can introduce you to new people and the world that you are still not exposed to.

- **Showing respect.** It is tempting to label all young adolescents as being difficult and rebellious. But these youngsters vary as much as children in any other age group. Parents need to be treated with respect, which requires your parents to recognize and appreciate your differences and to treat you as an individual. By treating you with respect, they can help you to take pleasure in good behavior.

There are no perfect parents. However, a bad decision or an "off" day (or week or month) isn't likely to have any lasting impact on you.

Chapter 5

Teen Embarkment on the Journey to Independence

When you are young, you can learn self-control and how to plan ahead, which are skills needed for a strong financial foundation. As you grow older, you will probably be increasingly exposed to advertising and peer influences. This makes your parent's role essential in developing responsible financial habits.

According to research, "during elementary and middle school, children start to become aware of different brands and make judgments about people based on the particular things they consume, suggesting that the early elementary grades may be a developmentally appropriate time to teach children to resist consumer culture."

Research shows that the preteen years are critical for developing an internal compass for what's important and what's not. Here are some examples of how you can learn important lessons from parents—even if they are just shopping for shoes.

Role of Parents

More and more preteens are exposed to advertising and peer pressure. Parents can help them with timely interventions.

Parents can help by instilling values such as frugality, thinking twice, and staying away from temptations. By asking a few questions, Jen's father was able to figure out that the brand name wasn't important to his daughter, which helped his daughter absorb an important lesson

About This Chapter: Text in this chapter begins with excerpts from "The Right Shoes and Common Sense Can Help Your Preteen Gain Financial Ground," Consumer Financial Protection Bureau (CFPB), September 3, 2015; Text under the heading "Experience Helps in Developing Financial Confidence" is excerpted from "The Teenage Years Are for Practicing Money Decisions in a Safe Space," Consumer Financial Protection Bureau (CFPB), October 16, 2015.

> ## Jen and Her Craving for Branded Shoes—A Case Study
> The father of nine-year-old Jen shared this story: "Last year when we were shopping, Jen was adamant about getting a specific brand of shoes. I didn't want to pay $100 for a pair of shoes that would be too small in a few months, so I asked her some questions. It turns out she just wanted a pair of high tops ($25) that her friends had, not specifically brand-name shoes. There's that dynamic where they're influenced by advertising or peers."

about value. Instead of just buying on impulse, Jen learned to take a step back and ask herself what she really wanted.

Another sneaker story comes from the parents of Tina, an eleven-year-old: "Tina got a pair of sneakers for the holidays. But when Tina wore them to school, her classmates teased her for not having the 'latest' brand, after she claimed she did. My daughter felt bad and didn't want to wear sneakers anymore. We sat down with Tina and did a little online scouting into sneaker fashions. It turns out that Tina's sneakers weren't the most expensive brand, but they were definitely one of the 'latest' versions of the sneaker."

So, Tina went back to school in her sneakers armed with the information they had found, and proud to tell her classmates that her sneakers were just fine. With a timely intervention from her parents, Tina learned a valuable lesson about peer influence.

Preteens Pick up Self-Control and Habits from Parents and Caregivers

During the preteen years, developmentally, it's a little early for you to handle your own money decisions. Instead, it's a great time for parents to intervene in key situations to talk about financial common sense. They can encourage you to ask yourself what you really want, or show you how to do research to find facts; they can help you create an internal yardstick to help you make your own decisions as you grow into adulthood. Being able to make decisions that make the most sense for you as an individual—and not just buying the trendiest thing even if it's just about shoes—is a skill that will serve you well throughout your financial life.

Experience Helps in Developing Financial Confidence

Hands-on experiences with managing finances help to promote your self-confidence and belief in your own ability to succeed. This is one of the key drivers for financial well-being in adulthood.

An important part of teenagers' development is taking the time to process and reflect on your money decisions—so you can learn from successful choices as well as mistakes. Whether you are learning from a class or afterschool program, a first job, or a decision you have made, parents and caregivers can act as sounding boards. As they do for younger children, parents and caregivers continue to play an important role in facilitating behaviors in your teenage years that lead to your financial well-being in adulthood.

Chapter 6

Minor Emancipation Laws

Your parent or legal guardian is obligated by law to feed, clothe, and educate you and to act in your best interests until you reach your state's "age of majority," or the age at which you are considered an adult. Some states allow minors to petition the court for emancipation, or independence, before they reach adulthood, though.

What Is Minor Emancipation?

Minor emancipation is the legal process by which a juvenile petitions the court to request legal independence. If the court grants you emancipation status, then you are released from the guardianship and custody of your parents or legal guardians. In most cases, this emancipation also terminates your parents or legal guardians from any obligation to provide you with

- Financial support, including child support

- Healthcare

- Housing

Emancipation laws vary by state, and some states have no emancipation statutes. Roughly half of the U.S. states do provide emancipation statues, however, and allow minors to petition the court for independence in accordance with these legal provisions.

How a Minor May Seek Emancipation Status

Juveniles who join the U.S. military, marry, or reach the age of majority are granted automatic juvenile emancipation. However, other juveniles who wish to live independently and

About This Chapter: "Emancipation Laws," © 2019 Omnigraphics.

enjoy the rights, privileges, and responsibilities of adulthood before reaching the legal age of majority must petition the court for emancipation in order to live independently.

Court-Approved Emancipation

State emancipation laws vary and often include a minimum age at which a juvenile may petition the court (usually at sixteen years of age). Some states also require juveniles to obtain parental permission to pursue legal emancipation. Hence, a crucial first step toward juvenile independence is to research the emancipation statutes of your state in order to determine if you qualify to apply for emancipation. You may be able to obtain this information through your own research, but some juveniles seek the expert advice and assistance of a family law attorney or legal aid organization.

Court Emancipation Requirements

Minors who wish to pursue emancipation and qualify to do so file a "declaration of emancipation." This document triggers the court to consider your request for independence and to take certain steps to determine your level of maturity and ability to live independently.

Because juvenile emancipation increases the likelihood that a minor will experience financial insecurity, homelessness, and impoverishment, the court will carefully consider your best interests before deciding to grant or deny emancipation. Minors seeking emancipation status due to abandonment, abuse, or domestic violence are especially vulnerable to impoverishment and homelessness following emancipation since emancipation leave juveniles solely responsible for providing their own food, shelter, clothing, transportation, healthcare insurance, and other needs.

When your emancipation petition is heard by the court, specific details will be considered in the course of the judge deciding whether minor emancipation is in your best interests. These considerations include whether you have:

- Demonstrated an ability to support yourself financially

- Made arrangements for housing

- Completed school and received a diploma

- Convinced the court that you are mature enough to function as an adult and make responsible adult decisions

Some states also consider whether your parents or legal guardians rely on your income for their survival.

What Rights, Privileges, and Responsibilities Are Granted to Emancipated Minors?

Emancipated minors are granted many specific rights, duties, and responsibilities that are otherwise limited to adults. If you are granted juvenile emancipation, then you will typically be granted the right to:

- Live independently
- Enroll in a school of your choice
- Obtain work permits
- Keep your own earnings
- Approve your own medical treatments and procedures
- Apply for public benefits
- Enter into leases and other contractual agreements
- Buy, sell, and inherit property
- File a lawsuit

Emancipated minors must still abide by other state or federal minimum-age laws, however, including the age at which you may legally purchase alcohol or tobacco, obtain a driver's license, marry, or vote.

References

1. Cataldo, Mayra Alicia. "Safe Haven: Granting Support to Victims of Child Abuse Who Have been Judicially Emancipated," *Family Court Review* 52:3, July 2014.

2. "Selected State Minor Emancipation Laws," FindLaw, December 13, 2005.

Chapter 7

Teens with Disabilities

A disability is any condition of the body or mind (impairment) that makes it more difficult for a person with the condition to do certain activities (activity limitation) and interact with the world around them (participation restrictions).

There are many types of disabilities, such as those that affect a person's

- Vision

- Movement

- Thinking

- Remembering

- Learning

- Communicating

- Hearing

- Mental health

- Social relationships

Although "people with disabilities" sometimes refers to a single population, this is actually a diverse group of people with a wide range of needs. Two people with the same type of

About This Chapter: Text in this chapter begins with excerpts from "Disability Overview," Centers for Disease Control and Prevention (CDC), August 1, 2017; Text under the heading "Financial Lives of People with Disabilities" is excerpted from "Working to Improve the Financial Lives of People with Disabilities," Consumer Financial Protection Bureau (CFPB), June 3, 2015; Text beginning with the heading "Ticket to Work Program" is excerpted from "About Ticket to Work," U.S. Social Security Administration (SSA), August 5, 2017.

disability can be affected in very different ways. Some disabilities may be hidden or not easy to see.

According to the World Health Organization (WHO), disability has three dimensions:

1. Impairment in a person's body structure or function, or mental functioning; examples of impairments include loss of a limb, loss of vision, or memory loss

2. Activity limitation, such as difficulty seeing, hearing, walking, or problem-solving

3. Participation restrictions in normal daily activities, such as working, engaging in social and recreational activities, and obtaining healthcare and preventive services

Financial Lives of People with Disabilities

Approximately 57 million Americans have a disability, and this number is increasing as the population ages. The most economically vulnerable population, including those with disabilities, are typically the hardest to reach and the most difficult to serve. They are more than twice as likely to be asset poor, and most likely to lack access to a bank or credit union account and use alternative financial services that may be less appropriate or costly.

Ticket to Work Program

Social Security's Ticket to Work program supports career development for Social Security disability (SSDI) beneficiaries ages 18 through 64 who want to work. The Ticket program is free and voluntary. The Ticket program helps people with disabilities progress toward financial independence.

The Ticket program is a good fit for people who want to improve their earning potential and are committed to preparing for long-term success in the workforce. Ticket to Work offers beneficiaries with disabilities access to meaningful employment with the assistance of Ticket to Work employment service providers called employment networks. If you are ready to go to work, there are people ready and waiting to help you!

The career-development services and support you need are unique to you. The Ticket program can connect you with the right mix of free employment-support services and approved service providers that will best fit your needs.

The Ticket program and work incentives allow you to keep your benefits while you explore employment, receive vocational rehabilitation services, and gain work experience. Your cash benefits and Medicaid or Medicare often continue throughout your transition to work, and there are protections in place to help you return to benefits if you find you are unable to continue working due to your disability.

Why Ticket to Work

If you receive disability benefits from Social Security, then you know that getting those benefits took time, energy, and patience. In determining your eligibility for disability benefits, Social Security found that you could not earn enough money to support yourself. With the right opportunities and supports, however, many people can earn a higher standard of living by going to work and leaving the benefit rolls.

Earning a living through employment is not something everyone can do, but it may be right for you. Many find that the rewards far outweigh the risks. Take the time to learn about the employment services and supports that Social Security offers beneficiaries with disabilities through the Ticket to Work program—you may be surprised!

How to Get Started

If you decide to participate, getting started is easy! First, call the Ticket to Work helpline at 866-968-7842/866-833-2967 (TTY) to verify your eligibility. Customer service representatives will explain to you how the program works and answer any questions or address any concerns you might have. They will also offer to mail you a list of service providers, or if you prefer, you can use the find help tool to get a customized list of providers that are available to help you.

The next step is deciding what service provider is right for you. You may work with either an employment network (EN) or your state vocational rehabilitation (VR) agency, depending on your needs. You may also receive services from your VR agency and then receive ongoing services from an EN.

Some ENs are also part of a state's public workforce system. These workforce ENs provide access to additional employment-support services, including training programs and special programs for youth in transition and veterans. A Ticket to Work participant who assigns their Ticket to a workforce EN will either work with a workforce EN directly or via other providers in the workforce system, including American job centers.

Once you and your service provider decide to work together, you will collaboratively develop a plan to help you reach your work goals. Your employment team will then help you make progress toward those goals and, eventually, a more financially independent future.

Making Timely Progress after You Assign Your Ticket

Your road to employment through the Ticket program is a two-way street: You receive free assistance from your service provider to prepare for, find, and keep a job, while you work your way toward financial independence. In return, you pledge to Social Security that you will take specific steps—determined by the plan you developed with your service provider—within specific timeframes set by Social Security to:

- Work at a specified earnings level or

- Complete educational or training requirements.

When you participate in the Ticket program, you are working with your EN or VR to reduce or eliminate your dependence on SSDI and/or Supplemental Security Income (SSI) cash benefits.

Taking the agreed-upon steps toward employment within Social Security's timeframes is called making "timely progress" toward:

- Receiving the education and training you need to succeed at work and your long-term career

- Becoming and staying employed

- Reducing your dependence on SSDI or SSI payments

- Earning your way off cash benefits, if possible

For you, the return for making "timely progress" is that you succeed in achieving a more financially independent life.

Chapter 8

Barriers for Foster Care Teens

Youth in foster care face a number of different barriers to becoming financially capable. The purpose of this table is to convey the correlation of the barrier with the promising practice.

Many young people do not understand the multi-faceted impacts of poorly managed finances. The immediate consequences may be felt by experiencing a loss of housing, transportation, food, etc. However, young people also need to have an understanding of how these circumstances can impact them in the future. Poor credit history and scores now, even if they are the result of identity theft that is not the youth's fault, can result in the inability to obtain safe and affordable housing, employment, car loans, insurance, and other assets for several years.

In today's complicated financial marketplace, young people face an array of financial products and services. Sorting through their options without some guidance and information is difficult. While regulated payday loan services, credit repair companies, debt settlement companies, auto title loans, check cashing services, rent-to-own stores, and other fringe services may tempt youth with aggressive marketing practices, however, mainstream options are often best. Young people need information about the terms of these fringe services to identify what financial products and services are best for them.

In addition to managing their personal finances in the present, young adults also need information and tools to prepare for the future. The responsibility for benefits such as retirement, and health and life insurance are also important considerations. While employers often offer these benefits, some require employee contributions. Understanding how these services or lack of these services can impact their lives over a lifetime is another area that needs discussion.

About This Chapter: This chapter includes text excerpted from "A Financial Empowerment Toolkit for Youth and Young Adults in Foster Care," National Resource Center for Youth Development (NRCYD), U.S. Department of Health and Human Services (HHS), 2014.

Young people whose employers do not offer health insurance and retirement benefits also need to know how to enroll in health insurance programs and individual retirement accounts on their own. For young people who are healthy and not necessarily thinking about retirement, which is decades away, convincing them of the importance of retirement savings and health-care can be difficult. While the implementation of the Affordable Care Act will create incentives for companies to offer health insurance and for uninsured individuals to purchase it, it is likely that the American public in general, and young people in particular, will have difficulty navigating the law and the healthcare exchanges.

Barriers to learning financial capability include:

- Young people in care often experience multiple placements leading to inconsistent financial role models.

- Foster parents or other role models do not share financial information with youth in their care, excluding them from any discussions involving money. As a result, youth transition from care with little knowledge or understanding of how the financial system operates.

- Young people in congregate care settings may have more limited opportunities to learn and use financial education skills because of program rules and requirements.

- States often do not have a mechanism for co-signing for youth under 18 to open checking or savings accounts.

- Young people who exit care often do not have the safety net of biological family or other support systems to assist them financially.

Part Two
Teen Employment

Chapter 9

Work and Age Restrictions Requirement for Employment

The U.S. Department of Labor (DOL) is committed to helping young workers find those positive and early employment experiences that can be so important to their development, but the work must be safe. The youth employment provisions of the Fair Labor Standards Act (FLSA) were enacted to ensure that when young people work, the work does not jeopardize their health, well-being or educational opportunities. Employers are subject to the youth employment provisions generally under the same coverage criteria as established for the other provisions of the FLSA.

It is an unfortunate fact that children do get injured, even killed, in the workplace. The National Institute for Occupational Safety and Health (NIOSH) estimates that 160,000 American children suffer occupational injuries every year—and 54,800 of these injuries are serious enough to warrant emergency room treatment.

Both federal and state laws govern the employment of young workers and when both are applicable, the law with the stricter standard must be obeyed.

The federal youth employment provisions do not:

- Require minors to obtain "working papers" or "work permits," though many States do;

- Restrict the number of hours or times of day that workers 16 years of age and older may be employed, though many states do;

- Apply where no FLSA employment relationship exists;

- Regulate or require such things as breaks, meal periods, or fringe benefits;

About This Chapter: This chapter includes text excerpted from "Child Labor Provisions of the Fair Labor Standards Act (FLSA) for Nonagricultural Occupations," U.S. Department of Labor (DOL), December 2016.

- Regulate such issues as discrimination, harassment, verbal or physical abuse, or morality, though other Federal and State laws may.

Minimum Age Standards for Employment

The FLSA and the youth employment regulations issued at 29 CFR, Part 570, establish both hours and occupational standards for youth. Children of any age are generally permitted to work for businesses entirely owned by their parents, except those under age 16 may not be employed in mining or manufacturing and no one under 18 may be employed in any occupation the Secretary of Labor has declared to be hazardous.

18—Once a youth reaches 18 years of age, she or he is no longer subject to the Federal youth employment provisions.

16—Basic minimum age for employment. Sixteen- and 17-year-olds may be employed for unlimited hours in any occupation other than those declared hazardous by the Secretary of Labor.

14—Young persons 14 and 15 years of age may be employed outside school hours in a variety of nonmanufacturing and nonhazardous jobs for limited periods of time and under specified conditions.

Under 14—Children under 14 years of age may not be employed in nonagricultural occupations covered by the FLSA. Permissible employment for such children is limited to work that is exempt from the FLSA (such as delivering newspapers to the consumer and acting). Children may also perform work not covered by the FLSA such as completing minor chores around private homes or casual babysitting.

Occupations Banned for All Minors under the Age of 18
The Hazardous Occupations Orders (HO)

The FLSA establishes an 18-year minimum age for those nonagricultural occupations that the Secretary of Labor finds and declares to be particularly hazardous for 16- and 17-year-old minors, or detrimental to their health or well-being. In addition, Child Labor Regulation No. 3 also bans 14- and 15-year-olds from performing any work prescribed by the HOs. There are currently 17 HOs which include a partial or total ban on the occupations or industries they cover.

- **HO 1.** Manufacturing or storing explosives—bans minors working where explosives are manufactured or stored, but permits work in retail stores selling ammunition, gun shops, trap and skeet ranges, and police stations.

- **HO 2.** Driving a motor vehicle or work as an outside helper on motor vehicles—bans operating motor vehicles on public roads and working as outside helpers on motor vehicles, except 17-year-olds may drive cars or small trucks during daylight hours for limited times and under strictly limited circumstances.

- **HO 3.** Coal mining—bans most jobs in coal mining.

- **HO 4.** Occupations in forest fire fighting, forest fire prevention, timber tract, forestry service, and occupations in logging and sawmilling operations—bans most jobs in: forest-fire fighting; forest fire prevention that entails extinguishing an actual fire; timber tract management; forestry services; logging; and sawmills.

- **HO 5.** Power-driven woodworking machines—bans the operation of most power-driven woodworking machines, including chainsaws, nailing machines, and sanders. *

- **HO 6.** Exposure to radioactive substances and ionizing radiation—bans employment of minors where they are exposed to radioactive materials.

- **HO 7.** Power-driven hoisting apparatus—bans operating, riding on, and assisting in the operation of most power-driven hoisting apparatus such as forklifts, nonautomatic elevators, skid-steers, skid-steer loaders, backhoes, manlifts, scissor lifts, cherrypickers, work-assist platforms, boom trucks, and cranes. Does not apply to chair-lifts at ski resorts or electric and pneumatic lifts used to raise cars in garages and gasoline service stations.

- **HO 8.** Power-driven metal-forming, punching and shearing machines—bans the operation of certain power-driven metal-working machines but permits the use of most machine tools.*

- **HO 9.** Mining, other than coal—bans most jobs in mining at metal mines, quarries, aggregate mines, and other mining sites including underground work in mines, work in or about open cut mines, open quarries, and sand and gravel operations.

- **HO 10.** Power-driven meat-processing machines, slaughtering and meat-packing plants—bans the operation of power-driven meat processing machines, such as meat slicers, saws, and meat choppers, wherever used (including restaurants and delicatessens). Also prohibits minors from cleaning such equipment, including the hand-washing of the disassembled machine parts. This ban also includes the use of this machinery on items other than meat, such as cheese and vegetables. HO 10 also bans most jobs in meat and poultry slaughtering, processing, rendering, and packing establishments.*

- **HO 11.** Power-driven bakery machines—bans the operation of power-driven bakery machines such as vertical dough and batter mixers; dough rollers, rounders, dividers, and sheeters; and cookie or cracker machines. Permits 16- and 17-year-olds to operate certain lightweight, small, portable, counter-top mixers and certain pizza dough rollers under certain conditions.

- **HO 12.** Balers, compactors, and power-driven paper-products machines—bans the operation of all compactors and balers and certain power-driven paper products machines such as platen-type printing presses and envelope die cutting presses. Sixteen- and 17-year-olds may load, but not operate or unload, certain scrap paper balers and paper box compactors under very specific guidelines. *

- **HO 13.** Manufacturing of brick, tile and related products—bans most jobs in the manufacture of brick, tile and similar products.

- **HO 14.** Power-driven circular saws, band saws, guillotine shears, chain saws, reciprocating saws, wood chippers, and abrasive cutting discs—bans the operation of, and working as a helper on, the named types of power-driven equipment, no matter what kind of items are being cut by the equipment.*

- **HO 15.** Wrecking, demolition, and ship-breaking operations—bans most jobs in wrecking, demolition, and ship-breaking operations, but does not apply to remodeling or repair work which is not extensive.

- **HO 16.** Roofing operations and work performed on or about a roof—bans most jobs in roofing operations, including work performed on the ground and removal of the old roof, and all work on or about a roof.*

- **HO 17.** Trenching and excavation operations—bans most jobs in trenching and excavation work, including working in a trench more than four feet deep.*

The regulations provide a limited exemption from HOs 5, 8, 10, 12, 14, 16, and 17 for apprentices and student-learners who are at least 16 years of age and enrolled in approved programs.

The term "operation" as used in HOs 5, 8, 10, 11, 12, and 14 generally includes the tasks of setting up, adjusting, repairing, oiling or cleaning the equipment.

Enforcement and Penalties

Investigators of the Wage and Hour Division who are stationed across the U.S. enforce the youth employment provisions of the FLSA. As the Secretary of Labor's representatives, they have the authority to conduct investigations and gather data on wages, hours, and other employment conditions or practices in order to assess compliance with all the provisions of the FLSA.

An employer that violates the youth employment provisions may be subject to civil money penalties (CMPs). The amount of the CMP assessment, which may not exceed a cap set by statute, depends upon the application of statutory and regulatory factors to the specific circumstances of the case.

- As a general matter, child labor CMP assessments will be higher if the violation contributed to the injury or death of the youth involved in the violation. The severity of any such injury will be taken into account in determining the amount of a CMP.

- CMP assessments may be decreased based on the size of the business.

- CMP assessments will reflect the gravity of the violation and may be doubled if the violation is determined to be willful or repeated.

A CMP assessment for a violation that causes the death or serious injury of a minor is subject to a higher statutory cap.

- An injury qualifies as a "serious injury" for this purpose if it involves permanent or substantial harm. Both the significance of the injury and the duration of recovery are relevant in determining whether an injury is serious.

- If more than one violation caused a single death or serious injury, more than one CMP may be assessed.

- CMP assessments based on the death or serious injury of a minor may be doubled up to a higher statutory cap if the violation is determined to be willful or repeated.

Chapter 10

Know the Rules

Before you start working, you should know what your employer can and cannot require of you. As a young worker, you are limited in the types of jobs and number of hours you can work. The rules are different for agricultural work. States also have rules, and employers must follow both.

Rules for Various Age Group

Rules vary by age group.

Rules for Workers under 14

Kids under 14 can gain valuable experience in working, but there are limits to what jobs you can do.

What Jobs Can Workers under 14 Do?

If you are under 14 you are only allowed to:

- Deliver newspapers to customers;

- Babysit on a casual basis;

- Work as an actor or performer in movies, television (TV), radio, or theater;

- Work as a homeworker gathering evergreens and making evergreen wreaths; and

About This Chapter: This chapter includes text excerpted from "Youth Rules—Know the Rules," *YouthRules!*, U.S. Department of Labor (DOL), May 8, 2012.

- Work for a business owned entirely by your parents as long as it is not in mining, manufacturing, or any of the 17 hazardous occupations.

Below is a list of 17 hazardous occupations banned for persons under the age of 18:

1. Manufacturing or storing of explosives;

2. Driving a motor vehicle or working as an outside helper on motor vehicles;

3. Coal mining;

4. Forest fire fighting and forest fire prevention, timber tract, forestry service, and occupations in logging and sawmilling;

5. Using power-driven woodworking machines;

6. Exposure to radioactive substances and ionizing radiation;

7. Using power-driven hoisting apparatus;

8. Using power-driven metal-forming, punching and shearing machines;

9. Mining, other than coal;

10. Using power-driven meat-processing machines, slaughtering, meat and poultry packing, processing, or rendering;

11. Using power-driven bakery machines;

12. Using balers, compactors, and power-driven paper-products machines;

13. Manufacturing brick, tile, and related products;

14. Using power-driven circular saws, band saws, guillotine shears, chain saws, reciprocating saws, wood chippers, and abrasive cutting discs;

15. Working in wrecking, demolition, and ship-breaking operations;

16. Roofing and work performed on or about a roof;

17. Trenching or excavating.

There are different rules for children under age 14 working in agriculture. States also have rules, and employers must follow both.

Rules for Workers Who Are 14 or 15

Fourteen and fifteen-year-olds are limited in what hours they can work and what jobs they can do.

What Hours Can Workers Who Are 14 or 15 Work?

All work must be performed outside school hours and you may not work:

- More than three hours on a school day, including Friday;

- More than 18 hours per week when school is in session;

- More than 8 hours per day when school is not in session;

- More than 40 hours per week when school is not in session; and

- Before 7 a.m. or after 7 p.m. on any day, except June 1st through Labor Day, when night-time work hours are extended to 9 p.m.

If you are home schooled, attend private school, or no school, a "school day" or "school week" is any day or week when the public school where you live while employed is in session. There are some exceptions to the hours' standards for 14 and 15-year-olds if you have graduated from high school, you are excused from compulsory school attendance, or you are enrolled in an approved work experience or career exploration program or work-study program.

What Jobs Can Workers Who Are 14 or 15 Do?

There are certain jobs you are allowed to do, including:

- Retail occupations;

- Intellectual or creative work such as computer programming, teaching, tutoring, singing, acting, or playing an instrument;

- Errands or delivery work by foot, bicycle, and public transportation;

- Clean-up and yard work which does not include using power-driven mowers, cutters, trimmers, edgers, or similar equipment;

- Work in connection with cars and trucks such as dispensing gasoline or oil and washing or hand polishing;

- Some kitchen and food service work including reheating food, washing dishes, cleaning equipment, and limited cooking;

- Cleaning vegetables and fruits, wrapping sealing, and labeling, weighing pricing, and stocking of items when performed in areas separate from a freezer or meat cooler;

- Loading or unloading objects for use at a worksite including rakes, hand-held clippers, and shovels;

- 14 and 15-year-olds who meet certain requirements can perform limited tasks in saw-mills and woodshops; and

- 15-year-olds who meet certain requirements can perform lifeguard duties at traditional swimming pools and water amusement parks.

If an occupation is not specifically permitted, it is prohibited for youth ages 14 and 15.

How Much Should Workers Who Are 14 or 15 Be Paid?

Although some exceptions may apply, in most circumstances you must be paid the federal minimum wage, $7.25 per hour. Your eligibility for the federal minimum wage depends on what you do and where you work.

If you are younger than 20 and eligible for the minimum wage, your employer may pay you as little as $4.25 per hour for the first 90 consecutive calendar days of your employment. This is not limited to your first employer. Each time you change jobs, your new employer can pay you this youth minimum wage.

There are different rules for 14 and 15-year-olds working in agriculture and states also have rules; employers must follow both.

Rules for Workers Who Are 16 or 17

Although there are no federal rules limiting the hours 16 and 17-year-olds may work, there are restrictions on the types of jobs you can do.

What Hours Can Workers Who Are 16 or 17 Work?

At 16 and 17 you may work unlimited hours.

What Jobs Can Workers Who Are 16 or 17 Do?

Any job that has not been declared hazardous by the Secretary of Labor is permissible for 16- and 17-year olds.

How Much Should Workers Who Are 16 or 17 Be Paid?

Although some exceptions may apply, in most circumstances you must be paid the federal minimum wage, $7.25 per hour. Your eligibility for the federal minimum wage depends on what you do and where you work.

If you are younger than 20 and eligible for the minimum wage, your employer may pay you as little as $4.25 per hour for the first 90 consecutive calendar days of your employment. This is not limited to your first employer. Each time you change jobs, your new employer can pay you this youth minimum wage.

There are different rules for 16 and 17-year-olds working in agriculture. States also have rules, and employers must follow both.

Rules for Workers Who Are 18

Once you turn 18, most youth work rules do not apply.

What Hours Can Workers Who Are 18 Work?

There are no limits to the number of hours 18-year-olds can work.

What Jobs Can Workers Who Are 18 Do?

Once you turn 18, you can perform any job.

How Much Should Workers Who Are 18 Be Paid?

Although some exceptions may apply, in most circumstances you must be paid the federal minimum wage, $7.25 per hour. Your eligibility for the federal minimum wage depends on what you do and where you work.

If you are younger than 20 and eligible for the minimum wage, your employer may pay you as little as $4.25 per hour for the first 90 consecutive calendar days of your employment. This is not limited to your first employer. Each time you change jobs, your new employer can pay you this youth minimum wage.

States also have rules, and employers must follow both.

Chapter 11

Data on Teen Participation in the Workforce

According to a report by the U.S. Bureau of Labor Statistics (BLS) from April–July 2018, the number of employed youths between 16 and 24 years old increased by 2–20.9 million. In 2018, 55 percent of young people were employed in July, with little changed from a year earlier. (The month of July typically is the summertime peak in youth employment.)

The unemployment rate for youth was 9.2 percent in July, also little changed from July 2017. Because this chapter focuses on the seasonal changes in youth employment and unemployment that occur each spring and summer, the data are not seasonally adjusted.

Facts
- Nearly all young people—98.6 percent—hold at least one job between the ages of 18 and 25.
- The average young person holds 6.3 jobs between 18 and 25.

(Source: "Employment," Youth.gov.)

Labor Force

The youth labor force—16- to 24-year-olds working or actively looking for work—grows sharply between April–July each year. During these months, large numbers of high school and college students search for or take summer jobs, and many graduates enter the labor market to

---

About This Chapter: This chapter includes text excerpted from "Employment and Unemployment among Youth Summary," U.S. Bureau of Labor Statistics (BLS), U.S. Department of Labor (DOL), August 16, 2018.

look for or begin permanent employment. During the summer of 2018, the youth labor force grew by 2.6 million, or 12.7 percent, to a total of 23.0 million in July.

The labor force participation rate for all youth was 60.6 percent in July, unchanged from a year earlier. (The labor force participation rate is the proportion of the civilian noninstitutional population that is working or looking and available for work.) The summer labor force participation rate of youth has held fairly steady since July 2010, after trending downward for the prior two decades. The summer youth labor force participation rate peaked at 77.5 percent in July 1989.

The July 2018 labor force participation rate for 16 to 24-year-old men, at 61.1 percent, was down 1.2 percentage points over the year. The rate for young women, at 60 percent, rose 1.2 percentage points during the same period, reducing the gap in labor force participation between young men and women. Whites had the highest youth labor force participation rate in July 2018, at 62.8 percent. The rate was 56.5 percent for Blacks, 43.3 percent for Asians, and 58 percent for Hispanics. Over the year, the labor force participation rate rose for Hispanics (+1.4 percentage points) and declined for Asians (-4.1 points). The decline among Asians offset a similar increase (+4.3 percentage points) between July 2016–2017. Labor force participation rates in July 2018 for Whites and Blacks were essentially unchanged from a year earlier.

Employment

In July 2018, there were 20.9 million employed 16–24-year-olds, about the same number as the summer before. Between April–July 2018, the number of employed youths rose by 2.0 million, in line with the change between April–July 2017. The employment-population ratio for youth—the proportion of the 16 to 24-year-old civilian noninstitutional population with a job—was 55 percent in July 2018, little changed from the prior year.

Employment-population ratios in July 2018 were higher than a year earlier for young women (54.8%), Whites (58%), and Hispanics (51.7%). The ratios declined for young men (55.2%) and Asians (39.7%). The ratio for Blacks, at 47.2 percent in July, was about unchanged from the summer before.

In July 2018, the largest percentage of employed youth worked in the leisure and hospitality industry (26%), which includes food services. An additional 18 percent of employed youth worked in the retail trade industry, and 11 percent worked in education and health services.

Unemployment

Unemployment among youth rose by 567,000 from April–July 2018, compared with an increase of 458,000 for the same period in 2017.

The youth unemployment rate, at 9.2 percent in July 2018, was little changed from July 2017. This represents the lowest summer youth unemployment rate since July 1966. The number of unemployed youths was 2.1 million in July 2018, little different from a year earlier. Of the 2.1 million unemployed 16 to 24-year-olds, 1.5 million were looking for full-time work in July 2018, also little changed from July 2017.

In July 2018, the unemployment rates for both young men (9.8%) and women (8.6%) were little changed from the summer before. The July 2018 rate for young Asians (8.4%) declined over the year, while the rates for young Whites (7.6%), Blacks (16.5%), and Hispanics (10.8%) showed little change over the year.

Chapter 12

Exploring Your Career Path

What do you want to be when you grow up? How about a writer or a medical researcher? An actor or an athlete? Whatever it is, you will learn that there are many paths to a career. After high school, you can choose to continue school or begin a career right away. Even though you are young, it's not too early to start thinking about your future educational and professional goals.

You probably know about people with such careers as teachers, doctors, actors, and lawyers. But did you know that there are thousands of other possibilities out there? You may be years away from deciding what you want to do as a career, but you should be open to exploring different options and thinking about what interests you.

Start Thinking about What You Want to Do after High School

Here are some helpful steps for planning for your future:

Think about classroom subjects that interest you. Then talk with your school counselor about the skills and training you will need to pursue your interests. You can look into more than one area!

- **Learn more about college and careers.** Ask your counselor to help you find books and websites on these topics as well as college and career fairs that you can go to. Talk with your family and people in your community about jobs and schools that interest you.

About This Chapter: Text in this chapter begins with excerpts from "Exploring Your Career Path," girlshealth. gov, Office on Women's Health (OWH), August 24, 2018; Text beginning with the heading "Start Thinking about What You Want to Do after High School" is excerpted from "Planning for Your Future," girlshealth.gov, Office on Women's Health (OWH), January 20, 2015.

- **Learn more about yourself.** Talk with your school counselor, parents or guardians, and doctor about your strengths and weaknesses. What are you good at and what do you need to practice? Then make some early choices with your counselor and parents or guardians about what might be the best path for you—going to college, working, both, or something else?

- **Ask someone who works in a field that interests you if you can visit them at work.** See if you can "job shadow," which means you watch what they do during a normal day on the job. You can also learn about a work mentoring program specifically for people with disabilities.

- **Make a list of possible goals and then break them into some manageable chunks.** You can check out a website for teens thinking about life after high school, www.youthhood. org. It offers a life map and other tools for learning about your options and deciding about your future.

If You Would Like to Work

In case you are interested to work then:

- **Learn about vocational programs offered in your high school and community.** Vocational programs teach you how to do certain kinds of jobs. There are many types of vocational careers, such as working as a dental assistant, working in hotels, and working with computers.

- **Work with a vocational rehabilitation counselor on skills you need to learn to do your job.** A counselor also can help you practice interviewing and figure out how you will get to work. If you don't already have a vocational rehabilitation counselor, ask about one at school. You also can look for your state vocational rehabilitation office online or in your phonebook in the state government listings section.

- **Gain work experience.** Get experience working by:
  - Taking on a summer or part-time job
  - Volunteering at your school or in the community
  - Doing chores around the house or for your neighbors

- **Check online resources.** Check out links to employment resources at www.abilityon-line.org, a website for young people with illnesses and disabilities. It also has a message forum where you can get employment tips.

- **Explore job banks and other resources.** The Americans with Disabilities Act (ADA) says that employers can't reject you for a job you are qualified for because of your disability.

Employers also have to provide "reasonable accommodations," which are changes to a job or workspace to help people with disabilities. Examples include a bigger computer monitor, a special chair, a quieter work area, or a more flexible schedule. The Job Accommodation Network (www.askjan.org) offers lots of help and information related to workers rights.

- **Learn whether supported employment is right for you.** Supported-employment programs help a person with a traumatic brain injury, a mental-health disorder, a learning disability, or another severe disability find a job and learn how to do it. You would work at a regular job in your community with ongoing support from a local disability agency.

The U.S. Department of Labor's (DOL) Employment and Training Administration (ETA) supports a wide variety of programs to ensure that all youth have the skills and training they need to successfully make the transition to adulthood and careers. These programs include:

- Job Corps—Job Corps is the nation's largest and most comprehensive residential education and job training program for at-risk youth, ages 16 through 24. Private companies, state agencies, federal agencies, and unions recruit young people to participate in Job Corps, where they can train for and be placed in jobs.

- Youth Discretionary Grants—Discretionary grants are aimed at specific populations of at-risk youth, such as young offenders, youth living in high-poverty areas, and foster youth.

- Youth Formula-Funded Grant Programs—These programs provide services to eligible youth, ages 14–21, in local communities. Funds are allocated to states based on the number of unemployed individuals in areas of substantial unemployment; the relative excess number of unemployed individuals in a state; and the relative number of disadvantaged youth in a state.

- Apprenticeship—Apprenticeship is a combination of on-the-job training and related classroom instruction in which workers learn the practical and theoretical aspects of a highly skilled occupation. Applicants for apprenticeship programs must be at least 16 years old and meet the program sponsor's qualifications.

(Source: "Youth Programs," U.S. Department of Labor (DOL).)

Choosing College or Vocational Training

If you would like to go on to college or vocational training:

- Find out which schools offer programs that interest you. You can look online or ask them to send you information.

- Ask schools to provide information on how to apply for financial aid.

- Contact schools' disability offices to make sure they can meet your needs. Examples of the things these offices can do for you include helping with note-taking if you have a learning disability or chronic fatigue syndrome, arranging to give you more time to take tests if you have attention deficit hyperactivity disorder (ADHD), and helping you find textbooks in Braille if you're blind.

- Find out what exams you have to take to get into college, study, and take them.

- Work with your guidance counselor and vocational rehabilitation counselor to choose which school to go to and how to pay for it.

Different Ways to Keep Learning

There are many different ways to keep learning:

- Choose a two-year college (or community college) or a four-year college.

- Take classes at a community college even if you do not plan to go for a full degree.

- Go to college close to home and live with your parents, or live at a college further away.

- Take college classes or get a full college degree online.

- Take part in vocational or technical training.

If You Would Like to Live on Your Own

If you decide to live on your own, you must be able to arrange for all of your healthcare needs. This may mean that you handle all your health needs on your own or have a nurse or family member come to help you. Or you may live in a home where health staff is there for you on site.

- **Talk to your parents, doctor, and other caregivers.** They will help you learn about the daily tasks that go along with living on your own. Together you can decide what the best living situation will be for you.

- **Take on some responsibilities from your parents.** For example, if your mom gives you your medicine in the evening, try doing this yourself to see how it feels. Or offer to get the mail, do the laundry, or cook dinner to build independence.

- **Find a place to live.** Some people live in their own apartments, some choose to live in group homes for extra support, and some choose to stay with their parents. These are all great options.

- **Learn how to manage money and budget household expenses.** Ask your parents to give you an idea of what it costs to run a household each month. A vocational rehabilitation counselor can also give you tips.

- **Understand leases and know about utilities (electricity, phone, water, heat).** A vocational rehabilitation counselor can give you information about the bills you'll need to pay if you live in your own place.

Things You Will Have to Do

No matter which path you take, you will need to:

- Check with the Social Security Administration (SSA) to see whether you will continue receiving supplemental security income if you have been receiving it before age 18. Ask what benefits you can qualify for on your own.

- Practice the social skills you will need to go about daily life, such as asking for help when you need it, getting around town, and feeling comfortable spending time with friends.

As you move into your future, you'll build more of the skills you need—and the confidence that comes with them. It takes time and effort to create your path in life. Give yourself the credit you deserve!

Chapter 13

Internships: Previewing a Profession

An ounce of experience can be worth a ton of research—especially when it comes to exploring careers. Internships are one of the best ways to get that experience and test a career choice. And later, when it's time to get a job, internships attract employers. Internships provide short-term, practical experience for students, recent graduates, and people changing careers. Most internships are designed for college students, but many are open to high schoolers; others welcome career changers seeking exposure to a new field. Internship positions are available in a number of disciplines. They can be arranged through your school or the organization for which you'll work. And they often provide either pay or academic credit—sometimes, both. Regardless of how it is coordinated, completing an internship increases your chances of getting

Nearly all young people—98.6 percent—hold at least one job between the ages of 18 and 25. The average young person holds 6.3 jobs between 18 and 25. Some work part-time or summers only, while others see full-time permanent employment as their path to economic independence. Employment can be beneficial for youth by teaching responsibility, organization, and time management and helping to establish good work habits, experience, and financial stability. There are many advantages to working during high school, especially for low-income youth, including higher employment rates and wages in later teen years and lower probabilities of dropping out of high school. Knowing how to find and keep a job is not only critical for admission to the adult world but also is an important survival skill for which there is little in the way of formal, structured preparation.

(Source: "Employment," (Youth.gov).)

About This Chapter: This chapter includes text excerpted from "Internships: Previewing a Profession," U.S. Bureau of Labor Statistics (BLS), U.S. Department of Labor (DOL), June 23, 2006.

a job that you'll enjoy. Not only do you discover your job likes and dislikes, but you enter the job market with experience that is related to your career goals. This chapter is geared toward college students. It discusses the who, where, which, and how of pursuing an internship.

Who Should Pursue an Internship?

Almost anyone—both students and nonstudents who have yet to settle into a career—can benefit from doing an internship, no matter what their motivations. A liberal arts major, for example, may have a less obvious career path than, say, a nursing student. But even well-directed students can benefit from the practical experience that an internship provides. After all, a hospital emergency room, a pediatrician's office, and a nursing home each provide different work environments for nurses.

College students often take part in a summer internship after their junior year. Other students might work as interns during the school year, receiving academic credit toward their degree. Some students participate in more than one internship over the course of their academic careers. Part of an internship's value comes from the opportunity for experiential learning. Whether students have some, little, or no idea about the kind of work that they want to do, they can get firsthand knowledge about a particular type of work or work environment.

Where Are Internships Located?

Internships may be located anywhere in the world. It's probably easier for students to arrange something closer to their homes or schools than to set up something halfway around the world. But with a little effort, an internship can be created just about any place.

There are several ways to locate available internship opportunities. Public libraries, career centers, and offices of school counselors usually have resources that contain hundreds, even thousands, of national listings. These internships include positions with fashion designers, publishing companies, biotechnology research firms, software developers, and federal and state government agencies, to name a few examples. Job fairs can also be a source of information about internship opportunities, as can the Internet. For example, the U.S. government has a list of available internships online.

In addition, colleges and universities usually maintain local listings of employers who hire interns. Career counselors and academic advisors may be aware of possibilities, and professors may know what types of internships students in a particular field of study have had in the past.

Programs that offer academic credit typically have an internship coordinator who oversees placement and monitors interns' progress. Some companies have formal internship programs. Others accept informal arrangements. Directly contacting companies, or visiting the career section of their websites, is usually the best way to learn whether they offer internships. Students might also be able to propose and set up their own internships.

Which Internships Are Best?

The best internships allow students to learn by doing, helping them to focus their career goals. Not surprisingly, most students choose an internship that is related to their major or to their career objectives. But many students aren't sure what they want to major in, let alone what they want to do for a career. And the differences between one internship and another can be hard to discern, particularly for students who are new to the working world. Making several important decisions can help students choose the best internship for them.

Perhaps most important, and most difficult, for some students is to decide which fields or occupations they are interested in. Career counselors, academic advisors, and vocational guidance publications, including the Occupational Outlook Handbook (OOH), can aid in the process. A related decision that students must make is which industry to work in. Occupations, and their related internships, differ from one industry to the next: An internship for a would-be management analyst would be much different in a bank, for example, than in a nonprofit organization. Internship duties often vary, but any position can be worthwhile. Whether interns do odd jobs around the office or do challenging work that is related to their fields of study, they get a feel for workplace culture and make contacts that may be valuable for career networking.

How Do I Apply for an Internship?

Start early when applying for internships. Deadlines for turning in application materials vary, but many summer internships require that applications be submitted by February or March. Career counselors often say that Thanksgiving break is a good time to start gathering materials and researching opportunities for a summer internship. Other experts suggest starting the process a few semesters before the desired internship period.

Applying for an internship might seem overwhelming, especially for those who have never written a résumé or cover letter. But preparing these documents when applying for an internship means not having to start from scratch when applying for a job.

In addition to requiring a résumé and cover letter, internship sponsors might request other items, such as a completed application, transcripts, coursework samples, and references. Applying for several internships increases the chances for success. Because high-profile employers are likely to get many applications, students who use personal or school contacts are most likely to stand out. Reviewing application materials for accuracy and completeness before submitting them is a must. The most careful students have someone else read over their application as well. Materials should be sent on time, with a follow-up telephone call confirming that the application was received.

Some internship sponsors might require candidates to appear for an interview. To prepare for such a meeting, students should read up on employment interviewing, participate in mock interviews, and attend interviewing workshops offered at their school. And students who follow up with a thank you note after the interview make a good impression.

Career counselors, books, and other resources can be helpful in the application and interviewing process.

Still Not Convinced?

Students who still aren't sure of an internship's value should consider this: Job seekers who have completed an internship have an edge in the job market. According to a survey by the National Association of Colleges and Employers (NACE), employers reported that, on average, more than three out of five college hires had internship experience. Moreover, many employers hire directly from their internship programs. The association's survey also reported that, on average, more than half of all students were offered a full-time job after completing their internship. Internships aren't the only path to postcollege success, of course. But the process of researching, finding (or creating), and applying for an internship may be as valuable as the benefits gained from the internship itself. The entire experience is likely to make your job search easier—after all, you'll have previewed the steps.

Chapter 14

Job Opportunities

Networking

Believe it or not, talking to people you know is one of the most common ways to land a job. And guess what? Talking to people you know is networking. Your network includes friends, family, teachers, neighbors, former coworkers, volunteer supervisors, and anyone else you know, and the people they know. Together, all these people create a big group who can help you find out about a job.

Start by making a list of who is in your network, and then make a plan to get in touch with some people on your list every day. When you ask for their help, you could also ask how you could be helpful to them. You are also part of their network.

How Can You Use Networking?

Call or email to ask for a time to talk. Introduce yourself, how you got their contact information if someone referred you to them, and the kind of work you are looking for, and what some of your skills are. Then ask for help or advice, such as:

- Do you have any suggestions for me?

- What can you tell me about this workplace/type of job?

- Do you know anyone who might be able to help me find work in this job or this company? May I use your name to contact them?

About This Chapter: This chapter includes text excerpted from "Find Job Openings," Employment and Training Administration (ETA), U.S. Department of Labor (DOL), March 31, 2017.

Social Media

Your social media accounts can help you connect with employers. And they can also let employers learn about you before they decide to hire you. This means you want to keep your social media professional—and keep inappropriate stuff off of it. Follow these tips to make the best impression on future employers:

- Begin by deleting inappropriate photos and posts that are about alcohol or drug use or have profanity or discriminatory comments. Also, delete any posts that badmouth a previous employer.

- Post your job goal and what kind of help you are looking for.

- Include posts about jobs, volunteer work, your creativity, or your communication skills.

- Include photos that present an image of someone an employer would want to hire.

- Use privacy settings to limit sharing, but keep in mind that anything on the Internet is potentially public.

- Use an appropriate, simple email address. No SuperHotGuy@hottie.com or other unprofessional terms.

- Google search your name to see what comes up on the Internet; clean it up if needed.

- Start here to create an account:

  - **LinkedIn** is used for careers. Create your profile, and connect with LinkedIn users to find job openings, share job information, join groups, and follow companies.

  - **Facebook** is usually used for personal posts. But many use it to connect with friends about job contacts.

  - **Twitter** gives you access to Twitter users and their Tweets for job openings. You can send a link to your résumé or website.

Job Banks

Job bank websites allow you to search and apply for job openings. You can also post your résumé so employers can match you to their job openings. Visit Job Finder to get started using a job bank. You can find many other online job banks but follow the tips below before you start using one.

66

Job bank tips:

- Expect to register with a username and password. Write these down so you can get back into your account to check on jobs!

- It should be free to use a job bank. Do not pay money to post your résumé or apply for a job.

- Do not provide your Social Security or national ID number, your bank account, or credit card information online. Some job postings are scams that ask you to pay or to perform illegal activities.

- Beware of scams for fake jobs or training opportunities. If you're not sure if a post is for real, try Googling the company to check for employee reviews. Also, visit the company website to read their "About Us" and learn more about them.

Ask an Employer

Know of a place you'd like to work? Applying in person can be the best way to find a job. Stop in with your résumé, ask if there are any job openings; if there aren't any, ask to leave your résumé for the hiring manager. If there are openings, ask how to apply!

Use the Business Finder to find businesses in your area (sort by ZIP code to find the closest ones.) Look up their contact information and call or stop in to ask about job openings, or to send a résumé. Follow links to their websites to research company facts.

When you visit the employer, treat it like an interview:

- Be polite and respectful to everyone you meet.

- Dress professionally.

- Learn some facts about the company before you go.

- Bring your résumé or a personal data sheet to fill out a job application. Some employers use a computer kiosk for applications (like at Target or Home Depot). These usually have a time limit so you'll need your information handy.

Job Fairs

At job fairs, employers host tables where you can stop to talk about your qualifications, the types of jobs they have, and their requirements. Bring copies of your résumé!

Fairs are held by different organizations: one company, a group of similar companies, youth jobs, school-sponsored, or other. Find out about job fairs at your school, neighborhood employment program, or your local American Job Center.

Job fair tips:

- Dress cleanly, neatly, and as professionally as you can.

- Give employers a firm handshake and make eye contact. Introduce yourself and your job goal.

- Offer a copy of your résumé, and let them know you are interested in their organization.

- Get employers' business cards. Note any calls or emails you want to send after the job fair.

- After the fair, send an email to employers you met. Thank them for their time and ask about next steps. You can also connect on LinkedIn with any employers you met; send them a LinkedIn invitation and tell them you met them at the job fair.

School and Community Career Services

High school and college career services help students find jobs and plan education and training. Ask about the training you'll need for your dream job, where to find internships, summer jobs, job shadowing, or part-time work. They will help you write a résumé and practice interviews, too.

Job search help is also available in every state at public job centers. Find your nearest location on the State Resource Finder. Select your location and look for the Job Search tab.

Chapter 15

Networking for Teens

"Networking" is a fancy term for getting to know people and for cultivating productive relationships. Networking is an important professional skill that can help people be successful in their field of work. It is never too early to start networking. As a teen, the earlier you learn the art of networking, the greater your career success rate will be.

Importance of Teen Networking

Networking can help teens to:

- Get to know fellow teens

- Develop social skills

- Get recommendations for college admissions and scholarships

- Connect with professionals

- Find opportunities to volunteer or work as an intern

- Find part-time jobs

- Find potential employers and clients

- Choose the right career path

- Earn extra bucks while studying

About This Chapter: "Networking for Teens," © 2019 Omnigraphics.

Tips for Teen Networking

Here are few tips and suggestions that can help teens build a strong network.

Get Guidance from Your Parents

Your parents may have years of experience in networking. So it is always a good idea to take their guidance. Also, you can ask your parents to provide contacts with their friends and peers.

Be Nice

Pleasant and positive personas are two key factors of networking.

- Smile.

- Be polite.

- Listen more than you talk.

- Make proper eye contact when someone is talking to you.

- Be helpful to others.

These behaviors help ensure that you are seen as a likable person and will help you build healthy relationships.

Be Open to New People

Some teens may feel a bit nervous when meeting new people. If you are such a person, start your initial networking with people with whom you are already acquainted, such as your peers, teachers, and neighbors. Gradually, you will gain the confidence needed to meet and connect with new people. At that point, try to get out of your comfort zone and widen your social circle.

Be Yourself

Networking is not an opportunity to sell yourself, but rather a platform to be yourself. Therefore, do not hide your personality, feelings, or interests while networking. Let the people with whom you meet know who you really are. Always try to be authentic and keep the relationship as casual and professional as possible.

Join Clubs and Organizations

Schools or colleges offer many clubs and organizations in which teens can participate. You can join any club or organization that suits your interest. This will provide an opportunity for you to mingle with like-minded peers. There may be chances for you to meet professionals in a particular field of work. You may also take part in various community activities outside the school or college, which can help you expand your network.

Use Social Media Efficiently

Social media is an invaluable tool to build your network. Numerous social media websites let you stay connected with anyone or anything—friends, family, neighbors, schools, colleges, classmates, teachers, mentors, companies, employers, and coworkers.

Although social media is beneficial in many ways, it has its downsides, too. Here are few tips for safe social networking.

- Do not reveal your login credentials (username and password) to anyone.

- Take care of your privacy. Review your privacy settings regularly.

- Connect only with people you know or trust.

- Think twice about what you write in an open forum. Avoid posting something that you would not want your teachers or employers to see.

References

1. Cairns, Hilary. "How to Network in High School and College," *College Raptor*, March 16, 2017.

2. "6 Networking Tips for Teens," Leading Learners, July 10, 2015.

3. "Learning How to Network in High School," eCampusTours, July 31, 2014.

4. Butts, Thalia. "Five Networking Tips for Teens," Vox, June 26, 2015.

5. "Social Networking Advice for Teenagers," Webwise, March 30, 2006.

Chapter 16

Creating a Résumé

A résumé is a summary, usually one to two typed pages, of your experiences and education. You can send your résumé to a job advertised in the newspaper or on the Internet, or you can bring it with you if you are applying somewhere in person (such as a restaurant or retail store). Often, you may also need to complete a job application, too, which is provided by the employer.

Tips for Building an Effective Résumé

It is important to address any specific information required and ensure your résumé includes sufficient information to validate that you meet all requirements of the job for which you are applying.

In addition, an effective résumé should include the following information:

Job Information

Information related to a job such as:

- Job announcement number
- Title and grade level(s) of the job for which you are applying
- Locations for which you are applying (if applicable)

About This Chapter: Text in this chapter begins with excerpts from "Get a Job," girlshealth.gov, Office on Women's Health (OWH), April 17, 2015; Text under the heading "Tips for Building an Effective Résumé" is excerpted from "Tips for Building an Effective Résumé," U.S. Department of the Treasury, July 24, 2018.

Personal Information

Information related to you such as:

- Full legal name

- Contact information (day/evening phone numbers, email/mailing address)

- Indicate if you are a U.S. citizen (required by most federal jobs)

Work Experience and National Service (Volunteer Experience)

Experience refers to paid and unpaid experience, including volunteer work done through National Service programs (e.g., Peace Corps, AmeriCorps) and other organizations (e.g., professional; philanthropic; religious; spiritual; community, student, social). Volunteer work helps build critical competencies, knowledge, and skills, and can provide valuable training and experience that translates directly to paid employment. You will receive credit for all qualifying experience, including volunteer experience.

- Job title (include pay plan, series, and grade if federal, nonmilitary position)

- Employer's name and address

- Supervisor's name and phone number

- Starting and ending dates (month, day, and year)

- Hours worked per week

- Salary

- Date of last promotion (if federal, nonmilitary position)

- Duties and accomplishments (job descriptions are not recommended)

Education

You should provide the following information regarding your education:

- Name of each school, college, or university attended and location

- Degree or certificate awarded (if no degree, show total credits earned and indicate whether semester or quarter hours)

- Date your degree was received or when it is expected

- Grade point average and scale (e.g., 3.6 of 4.0-grade scale)

Other Qualifications

You can also add other qualifications such as:

- Skills (e.g., other languages, computer software/hardware, tools, machinery, typing speed)

- Certificates and licenses (current only)

- Honors, awards, and special accomplishments (e.g., publications, memberships in professional or honor societies, leadership activities, public speaking, and performance awards)

- Training courses (title and year)

Additional Tips

- Search on the Internet or ask your guidance counselor for sample résumés.

- You can follow the formatting style from the sample résumé if you need ideas on how your résumé should look.

- A well-organized and well-written résumé will show an employer that you are a smart and careful person.

- Ask a teacher or parent to look over your résumé—they may be able to catch mistakes that you missed.

- Proofread your résumé. You don't want any mistakes on it because this is the first thing a potential employer will see from you.

(Source: "Get a Job," girlshealth.gov, Office on Women's Health (OWH).)

Chapter 17

What Is a Cover Letter?

What Is the Purpose of a Cover Letter?

Your cover letter is your opportunity to make a good first impression with the hiring manager. It provides you with the chance to convince the hiring manager to read your résumé and it lets you explain how your experiences tie into the job to which you are applying.

Make sure that you have carefully read the description of duties outlined in the job announcement. Highlight qualifications and duties that your résumé speaks to and make sure that, if there are any gaps in your résumé, you can fill them in via your cover letter.

Research the agency to which you are applying. Your cover letter is your first chance to express how your mindset matches up with that of the organization and make a personal connection with the hiring manager.

Formatted clearly and professionally. Use a simple, clean font. Ensure that your cover letter is professional and matches your résumés format (font, size, header etc.)

Specific rather than vague. Tell exactly what experiences you have had that make you a great candidate for the position, not merely that you have experience.

Length. Your cover letter should be less than a page in length. Be concise and clear.

Once your letter is ready, be sure to proofread it. Grammatical and spelling errors should be avoided at all costs. Delete colloquialisms and contractions.

About This Chapter: This chapter includes text excerpted from "What Should I Know before Writing a Cover Letter for the Federal Government?" Internal Revenue Service (IRS), March 31, 2018.

What Should the Content Include?

The first paragraph should identify the position to which you are applying. It should grab the hiring manager's attention and make it clear that you are a great candidate for the job.

In your main paragraph, you should focus on matching your qualifications to the needs of the position. Include elements about the organization to which you are applying. This will not only emphasize that you are serious about the job and not sending out a form letter, but it will also make it easier for you to show how you can help the organization to reach its goals.

The last paragraph should direct the reader to your enclosed résumé. Follow with your availability for an interview.

Tips

Personalize

Do your best research to find out who you should address your cover letter to if it is not listed in the position description. Utilize your networks or call HR to find out to whom your letter should be addressed. Try not to default to "To Whom it May Concern" or "Dear Sir/ Madam."

Proofread

A poorly written or error-laden letter will quickly get you eliminated from the employer's list of potential candidates. Take time to review your letter and have it read by a second set of eyes.

Avoid beginning every sentence or paragraph with the word "I."

Demonstrate enthusiasm for the role and show you have done research about the position and organization.

Email Etiquette

Most of the time, cover letters are emailed instead of sent in a hard copy version. When emailing a cover letter and a résumé, you have two options:

1. Write a brief but professional message basically stating to see your attached résumé and cover letter for their review.

2. Attach your résumé and copy your cover letter (in a basic font with formatting removed) into the body of the email. In this option, there is no need to keep the letter in business letter format and you can delete the address and date.

(Source: "Guide to Cover Letters," National Institutes of Health (NIH).)

Chapter 18

Finding a Job

Finding and getting a job can be a challenging process, but knowing more about job search methods and application techniques may increase your chances of success. CareerOneStop (www.careeronestop.org) from the U.S. Department of Labor (DOL) offers information that can help you:

- Plan your job search

- Search for a job

- Write résumés and cover letters and fill out applications

- Create a career network

- Interview for a job and negotiate your salary

The other resources are:

- State Job Banks—Search your state to locate job openings in your area.

- Occupational Outlook Handbook (www.bls.gov/ooh)—Find information on educational requirements, growth rates, median pay, and more for hundreds of career fields.

- State, Regional, and Local Resources—Locate U.S. Department of Labor (DOL) programs and services near you.

- Federal government employment—Learn how to get a job with the federal government using USAJOBS.

About This Chapter: This chapter includes text excerpted from "Find a Job," USA.gov, May 11, 2018.

Jobs for Teens and Young Adults

- Get help entering the job market. If you're 16- to 24-years old and need help finishing school, exploring career options, finding training, or searching and applying for jobs, GetMyFuture (www.careeronestop.org/GetMyFuture/default.aspx?frd=true) is for you. There's a special section on support for young people who struggle with addiction, have a criminal record, have children, need help with housing, or face other challenges.

- Learn about Job Corps (www.jobcorps.gov), a free educational and vocational training program that helps low-income people 16- to 24-years old learn a trade, earn a high school diploma or GED, and get help finding a job.

Apprenticeships

Apprenticeships combine on-the-job training and related instruction to give you skills to advance in your chosen field. Apprentice programs vary in length from one to six years. During that time, as an apprentice, you'll work and learn as an employee. When you complete a registered program, you will receive a nationally recognized certificate from the U.S. Department of Labor (DOL) as proof of your qualifications.

For more information:

- Visit the DOL's website on Registered Apprenticeships (www.dol.gov/apprenticeship)

- To locate an apprenticeship program near you, click on your state on the Search Apprenticeships Near You map of the United States (www.dol.gov/featured/apprenticeship/find-opportunities)

- If you're a woman looking for an apprenticeship in the field of construction, transportation, or protective services, check out the Women Build, Protect & Move America portal (www.dol.gov/wb/NTO). You'll find resources for local and nationwide apprenticeships as well as information about the different jobs in each field, professional trade organizations, and your rights on the job.

Self-Employment and Working from Home

You are self-employed if you operate a trade, business, or profession either by yourself or with a partner. Find out the basics of self-employment to help you succeed in the small business world:

- Starting and Financing a Small Business—Explore opportunities and get tips to help you succeed.

Developing a Network

Research helps jobseekers in another important way: developing a network. Organizations tend to hire people they know or who are referred to them by someone they trust. Career experts say that organizations fill many openings through this "hidden," or unadvertised, job market. In other words, employers often fill new positions before those openings are ever publicized. A network includes family, friends, past and present employers and coworkers, association members, teachers, classmates, and others. In short, a network is everyone the candidate can communicate with. These contacts need not be close friends; they can be acquaintances or even friends of friends. A professional network is built from these personal contacts, and the best time to start building is now. Experts suggest attending industry events, training classes, and seminars; joining a social, trade, or professional organization; and pursuing volunteer and internship positions. Even something as casual as a meeting over coffee can help a jobseeker develop connections. Focused networking gives jobseekers the opportunity to establish contacts among prospective employers to learn about work life in the organization.

(Source: "Focused Jobseeking: A Measured Approach to Looking for Work," U.S. Bureau of Labor Statistics (BLS), U.S. Department of Labor (DOL).)

- Tax Information (www.dol.gov/general/location)—Learn about filing requirements for the self-employed, reporting responsibilities, and more.

- Health Insurance—Explore coverage options for the self-employed.

- Social Security—Information for the self-employed covers how to report your earnings when you file your taxes.

Work from Home

Are you thinking about basing your business out of your home? The U.S. Small Business Administration (SBA) offers a guide for home-based businesses. This includes the licenses and permits you need to run a home-based business.

Home Office Deduction

If you use a portion of your home for business, you may be able to take a home office tax deduction.

Work-at-Home Scams

Learn what to watch out for to avoid work-at-home scams. In one common scam, you may be tricked into paying to start your own Internet business. These scammers will keep asking you to send money for more services related to this fake business opportunity. To file a complaint about a scam, contact the Federal Trade Commission (FTC).

Federal Government Telework Guidelines

If you're a federal employee looking for information on teleworking, visit www.telework.gov.

Note: The federal government never charges a fee for information about, or applications for, government jobs. You can search and apply for federal government jobs for free at USA-JOBS (www.usajobs.gov).

Federal Employment Assistance for People with Disabilities

If you have a disability and you're looking for work, these resources can help:

- The Ticket to Work (choosework.ssa.gov/about/index.html) program helps 18-to-64-year-old Social Security disability recipients develop job skills that can lead to a higher standard of living. The program is supportive, free, and voluntary.

- The AbilityOne.gov (www.abilityone.gov) program provides employment opportunities with nonprofit agencies and community rehabilitation programs across the country for people who are blind or who have other significant disabilities.

- Learn how to find and apply for federal jobs open to people with disabilities through standard methods and through the Schedule A program. Find out about special federal hiring opportunities for young people and veterans.

Chapter 19

Jobs for Disabled Teens

Work Ethic, Communication, and Problem-Solving
Soft Skills: The Competitive Edge

What do employers look for in new employees? According to the 2006 report Are They Really Ready to Work? Employers' Perspectives on the Basic Knowledge and Applied Skills of New Entrants to the 21st Century U.S. Workforce, it may not be what some young job seekers expect. This in-depth survey of 461 business leaders conducted by the Conference Board, Corporate Voices for Working Families, Partnership for 21st Century Skills, and Society for Human Resource Management reveals that while the three "R's" (reading, writing, and arithmetic) are still fundamental to every employee's ability to do the job, employers view "soft" skills as even more important to work readiness. The report also finds that younger workers frequently lack these skills, which include:

- Professionalism or work ethic

- Oral and written communication

- Teamwork and collaboration skills

- Critical thinking or problem-solving skills

In 2007, the U.S. Department of Labor's Office of Disability Employment Policy (ODEP) discussed the importance of such skills with the Circle of Champions, a distinguished group

About This Chapter: This chapter includes text excerpted from "Essential Skills to Getting a Job," Office of Disability Employment Policy (ODEP), U.S. Department of Labor (DOL), August 2009.

of U.S. businesses that have received the Secretary of Labor's New Freedom Initiative Award for innovative and proactive efforts to recruit, hire, and promote people with disabilities.

As part of this dialogue, the companies identified the following competencies as key to the success of young workers in the 21st Century workplace.

Networking

Simply put, networking involves talking with friends, family members, and acquaintances about your employment goals, interests, and desires. It also involves reaching out beyond people you already know in order to expand the opportunities that may be available to you. When it comes to finding a job, networking is essential. According to Cornell University's Career Center, 80 percent of available jobs are not advertised. Therefore, if you are not connecting with other people, you are likely to miss out on many job opportunities.

To start networking, make a list of everyone who may be able to help your job search. Next, talk to people on the list and tell them that you are looking for employment. Ask if they know of any openings and to introduce you if they do. But don't stop with the names on your list. Talk to cashiers, barbers, clergy, and anyone else you meet about their work and ask if they know of any jobs that match your interests. It is also essential to follow up with those with whom you have networked. Talking with a person once will only provide leads available at that point in time. But by establishing an ongoing relationship, you may learn of other opportunities as they arise.

Once you find a job, it is important to continue to network effectively. Through ongoing networking, you can develop relationships with colleagues and increase your ability to move up in the organization.

Enthusiasm

Enthusiasm is also essential to success. When interviewing, you are likely to stand out in an employer's mind if you show excitement about the job. Prior to the interview, check out the company's website to learn about the business. Think of questions you might want answered, because asking questions is one way to show interest. Other strategies include arriving a few minutes early to the interview, dressing professionally, and staying engaged in the conversation. You should also bring a pad and pen so you can take notes during the interview; just make sure to ask if it is okay to take notes first. This shows the interviewer that you are actively engaged and paying close attention to what they are saying. It may also make it easier for you to think of additional questions to ask prior to accepting a job offer.

Once employed, continue to demonstrate enthusiasm by taking initiative and seeking new and more challenging work. In some work settings, this may mean performing tasks needing to be done before being asked. In a restaurant, for instance, in between meal rushes, a server might show initiative by wiping off dirty menus or filling salt and pepper shakers. In other work settings, you can show initiative by volunteering to take on needed work or pitching a new project idea to your supervisor. If she or he likes the idea, offer to do more research and followup with him or her. This provides you with some ownership of the project and shows your commitment to the company.

Professionalism

Make sure your résumé is "dressed to impress." Having an organized résumé is essential to making a positive first impression. A good tip is to have a college professor or a career counselor read your résumé and recommend edits before you submit it to a potential employer.

Once you have been called for an interview, it is important to research the company and find out more about your potential job responsibilities. This will not only allow you to ask better questions during your interview but also ensure you are well-informed should the company make you an offer.

Business etiquette and work ethic go hand in hand for employers. Some tips when it comes to making a good impression once employed include:

- Dressing properly for the work setting
- Arriving on time and staying productive until you leave
- Turning cell phone ringers off while at work and returning phone calls and text messages while on breaks or after work hours
- Using computers, if you have access to them, only for work-related tasks
- Speaking in a respectful manner with supervisors, peers, and customers or clients

Also remember that even when you are technically "off-duty" in the lunchroom or at a reception, you are representing the organization and are expected to act professionally. Don't contribute to office gossip or banter around too much with your coworkers. Although you are allowed to have fun and enjoy your job, you are still there to work.

Communication Skills

Communicating ideas in the workplace are different than in an academic setting. In a classroom, the instructor usually leads group discussions or assigns written homework, and students respond or ask questions when directed to do so. In the workplace, however, the format for interaction varies. Sometimes your supervisors may specifically ask you for your opinion or ask you to express that opinion in writing. More often than not, however, they assume that if they need to know something, you will bring it to their attention. The challenge of communicating in the workplace is learning how and when to share your ideas or concerns.

If you need to tell your supervisor about something that is not going well, it is important to remember that both timing and your attitude are extremely important. For example, if you are a cashier at a carry-out restaurant and the long lines during the lunch rush "stress you out," causing you to give customers incorrect change, it is best to wait to talk to your supervisor about the problem during a slower period. At an appropriate time, you may want to ask if it would be possible to have someone assist you during busy periods. And if you are able to explain that this would not only allow you to make fewer mistakes, but also allow the business to provide better service by making the line move more quickly, she or he will be more likely to take your ideas seriously. Another proactive strategy would be to talk to your supervisor or another senior employee about how you could do your job more efficiently.

Listening is also an important communication skill. Employers report that the average entry-level candidate struggles with knowing how to listen carefully. They may not immediately process essential instructions or be able to understand how their tasks relate to the overall goals of the organization. One way to improve your listening comprehension skills is to ask questions. Other tactics include restating what you thought you heard to confirm you understood correctly and taking notes.

Teamwork

Successful businesses rely on team players. This skill is so important that an article in a Society for Human Resource Management magazine encourages employers to include teamwork as part of the performance appraisal process if collaboration is essential to the job. Understanding how to act as a member of a team may begin when you play sports or work on group projects in school. In the workplace, knowing how and when to lead and follow takes practice, as does knowing how to avoid unnecessary conflict. Working on a team also allows you to build closer relationships with your coworkers, which can make any job more fun and interesting. When working on a team, make sure that the workload is shared and that everyone is communicating. While some competition between team members is healthy and contributes to productivity, too much negative personal interaction can have the opposite effect.

Problem-solving and Critical Thinking

Problem-solving and critical thinking refers to the ability to use knowledge, facts, and data to effectively solve workplace problems. As a new employee, you may question why an organization follows certain steps to complete a task. It may seem to you that one of the steps could be eliminated saving time, effort, and money. But you may be hesitant to voice your opinion. Don't be; employers are usually appreciative when new employees are able to offer insight and fresh perspective into better and more efficient ways of doing things. It is important to remember, however, that as someone new to the organization, you may not always have the full picture, and thus there may be factors you are unaware of that dictate that things be done a particular way. Another important thing to remember is that when you are tasked with solving a problem, you don't always need to answer immediately. The ability to develop a well thought out solution within a reasonable time frame, however, is a skill employers value greatly.

Chapter 20

Workplace Skills

Twenty-five percent of the global workforce is comprised of young people. Transitioning from your studies to work can be a challenge, however, and teens have to make major decisions based on how they want to progress in their career. After they have decided to start their career with a particular organization, one of the first steps they need to take is to learn the skills required in the workplace. Developing these skills helps ensure a smooth transition and helps new employees to develop core and employable skills that lead to workplace success.

Many employers require specialized skills for a specific job. However, any job also needs a range of other professional workplace skills. This chapter focuses on the general employable skills needed for teens to compete in the work environment. Some of the basic skills include communication, self-management, planning and organizing, teamwork, interpersonal effectiveness, learning skills, strong work ethics, analytical and problem-solving skills, and technology skills.

> What are your current skills, abilities, and talents? If you struggle to answer this, as many people do, ask three significant people in your life what they think are your skills and talents. You may be surprised.
>
> *(Source: "Mastering Soft Skills for Workplace Success," U.S. Department of Labor (DOL).)*

Communication

Effective communication is necessary and vital for workplace success. On-the-job communication includes listening, speaking, and writing skills. Successful employees should be able

About This Chapter: "Workplace Skills," © 2019 Omnigraphics.

to understand and interpret what others say, and express their thoughts clearly to their fellow workers. Writing skills are equally important, as most jobs require correspondence. An effective communicator always has an advantage over others.

Self-Management

Self-management means completing work assignments without direct oversight every single time a task is assigned to you, meeting assigned deadlines, delegating work as necessary to complete deadlines, and resolving issues that could impede your progress. Employers expect responsible behavior from their employees and expect them to complete all tasks in a timely manner.

To improve your self-management skills:

- Complete an internship
- Join a volunteer organization
- Ask for new responsibilities

Planning and Organizing

The ability to effectively plan and organize your work is essential for success in your work career. As you transition from your studies to work, you will discover that you will need to forego certain activities and become disciplined about managing your work. Planning ahead for work is always beneficial; and employers always prefer someone who can plan well ahead of a deadline and execute the work in a diligent and timely manner. Planning and organizing involves knowing what is required to get a job done, how to do the job, and when to do the job.

To improve your planning and organizing skills:

- Create a timetable and stick to it
- Travel alone
- Manage time commitments around your studies, work, and family
- Help with family chores
- Organize an event

Teamwork

Teamwork is essential in any work environment, as most jobs require people to work together to accomplish a specific task. Many teens' teamwork skills are honed from being a part of team projects in college, playing team sports, or taking part in other extracurricular activities. The ability to work well with others is an important skill employers look for when recruiting.

Interpersonal Effectiveness

Interpersonal effectiveness is required for success in the workplace. Positive relationships with fellow workers ensure a smooth workflow within an organization. Skills such as effective communication and teamwork form the structure for displaying interpersonal effectiveness.

Learning Skills

Learning opportunities will present themselves to take place almost every day in a workplace setting, and you will be required to update your skills constantly. This means that work environments are natural environments in which you can improve your adaptability skills and ability to learn and grow.

To improve your learning skills:

- Start a new course or hobby

- Do some research on the required topics

Strong Work Ethics and Values

In this day and age, scams and dishonest methods of earning money are on the rise, and employers are looking for ethical people who can work honestly. Self-confidence, a positive attitude, dependability, and honesty are the qualities most valued by today's employers.

Analytical and Problem-Solving Skills

Solving problems is a skill every successful employee should possess. Teens should be able to apply their reasoning, creativity, and out-of-the-box thinking on the job. When a difficult situation arises, employees with analytical and problem-solving skills are able to deal with the situation more efficiently.

To improve your analytical and problem-solving skills:

- Take initiative when a crisis arises

- Learn from experienced people how they have dealt with problems

- Research about solutions for particular problems

Technology Skills

The ability to use technology is a must for today's workforce since most workplaces are computerized. The basic technology skills that workers need include being able to use a computer, send and receive e-mails, and create text documents and spreadsheets. Specific job-related technology skills may also include the ability to use programming languages, video-editing software, handle a cash register, or use social media.

While some skills, such as leadership and taking initiative, may be developed over several years on the job, the skills outlined above serve as a base for any job. Employers seek people who have already mastered these skills and can learn more as they move forward.

References

1. "8 Job Skills You Should Have," Youth Central, February 20, 2018.

2. Chinn, Diane. "The Definition of Workplace Skills," bizfluent, September 26, 2017.

3. "Youth Employability," Skills for Employment, October 17, 2013.

4. "Top 10 Employability Skills," Opportunity Job Network, May 30, 2010.

Chapter 21

Workplace Ethics

Workplace ethics are the moral principles that govern the behavior of individuals within the workplace. Every person has some inherited ethical behaviors that are learned from family, friends, and society. In addition, the organizations may specify a set of basic rules and guidelines for their employees based on their work culture. These rules and guidelines usually address topics such as the language of communication, work hours, dress codes, and so on, and may vary from organization to organization. Teens who are entering a professional work environment should possess these basic ethical behaviors in order to be successful in their work lives.

Fundamental Workplace Ethics

Some fundamental workplace ethics that every teen should learn and possess follow:

- **Punctuality.** Always arrive at work on time. Arriving late will not only affect your productivity but also leave the impression that you are not committed to your job.

- **Attire.** Wear a uniform if your job or organization demands it. Otherwise, wear a professional outfit. Your attire is an important factor that creates an impression about your character and professionalism.

- **Time management.** Prioritize your tasks properly and try to deliver projects before their deadlines. Never delay unless there is a justifiable reason. If you are unable to complete a task within the stipulated time, be honest in explaining the situation to your

About This Chapter: "Workplace Ethics," © 2019 Omnigraphics.

manager. Avoiding unnecessary distractions such as television, social media, phone calls, and so on during office hours can help you manage your time efficiently.

- **Adaptability.** Organizations always strive to improve their processes in order to achieve better results; therefore, employees should be ready to adapt to improvements and changes. When a change occurs, consider it an opportunity to improve yourself and move ahead.

- **Team player.** Developing a good rapport with your employer, supervisors, coworkers, customers, and clients is important to being a team player. Do not complain, gossip, or talk negatively about others in your workplace. Share your ideas and resources with your peers. Secrecy will result in counterproductivity. It is also essential that you don't share confidential information with anyone other than the people who are authorized to know it.

- **Positive attitude.** Be a self-motivated go-getter. Take initiatives and try to learn things by yourself. Improve your performance and productivity through continuous learning.

- **No blame games!** Do not blame others for your mistakes. Take responsibility for your own words and deeds.

A list of work ethics for an employee might include:

- To show up on time
- To tend to company business for the whole time while at work
- To treat the company's resources, equipment, and products with care
- To give respect to the company—that means honesty and integrity

(Source: "Mastering Soft Skills for Workplace Success," U.S. Department of Labor (DOL).)

How Parents Can Help

As the first teachers of their children, parents play a vital role in emphasizing and inculcating strong ethical behaviors in their teenagers. Here are a few things that parents should and should not do when their teenagers enter into the world of work.

- Help your children to manage their time by setting alarms and assisting them with transportation.

- Talk to your children regularly about their jobs and how well they are performing.

- Do not talk poorly about your children's employers or coworkers—and do not allow your children to do so.

- Do not encourage your children to bring home office supplies from their workplace.

- Do not visit your children's workplace often. It may sometimes embarrass them.

- Do not argue with your children's supervisors.

- Encourage your children when they encounter challenging tasks, but do not interfere with the dynamics of their work. Let them face and handle difficult situations on their own.

Benefits of Workplace Ethics

If employees in an organization have ethical behaviors, then:

- There will be a healthy relationship between employees and employer

- The work environment will be trouble-free and more productive

- Team coordination among the employees will improve

- The productivity and brand value of the organization will increase

- Decision-making and the implementation of advanced technologies will be easier

- Workplace harassment and legal issues will be minimized

References

1. Anastasia. "Work Ethic Definition and Elements of a Strong Work Ethic," Cleverism, March 19, 2016.

2. Amico, Sam. "Workplace Ethics and Behavior," Chron, June 30, 2018.

3. Loretto, Penny. "The Top 10 Work Values Employers Look For," TechnoSmarts, April 24, 2015.

4. Reddy, Chitra. "Ethics in the Workplace: Top 10 Benefits and Importance," Wise Step, May 8, 2017.

5. McQuerrey, Lisa. "Teen Summer Jobs," Chron, August 7, 2018.

Chapter 22

Workplace Stress

The last months of the year are when we all may feel a little more stress due to the demands of the holidays. Unfortunately, stress at work can be a year-round issue further exacerbated during these months.

Work organization and job stress are topics of growing concern in the occupational safety and health field and at National Institute for Occupational Safety and Health (NIOSH). The expressions "work organization" or "organization of work" refer to the nature of the work process (the way jobs are designed and performed) and to the organizational practices (e.g., management and production methods and accompanying human resource policies) that influence the design of jobs.

Job stress results when there is a poor match between job demands and the capabilities, resources, or needs of workers. Stress-related disorders encompass a broad array of conditions, including psychological disorders (e.g., depression, anxiety, posttraumatic stress disorder (PTSD)) and other types of emotional strain (e.g., dissatisfaction, fatigue, tension), maladaptive behaviors (e.g., aggression, substance abuse), and cognitive impairment (e.g., concentration and memory problems). In turn, these conditions may lead to poor work performance or even injury. Job stress is also associated with various biological reactions that may lead ultimately to compromised health, such as cardiovascular disease (CVD).

Stress is a prevalent and costly problem in today's workplace. About one-third of workers report high levels of stress, and high levels of stress are associated with substantial increases in

About This Chapter: Text in this chapter begins with excerpts from "Workplace Stress," Centers for Disease Control and Prevention (CDC), November 23, 2016; Text beginning with the heading "What's the Problem?" is excerpted from "Stress at Work," Centers for Disease Control and Prevention (CDC), September 15, 2017.

health service utilization (HSU). Additionally, periods of disability due to job stress tend to be much longer than disability periods for other occupational injuries and illnesses. Evidence also suggests that stress is the major cause of turnover in organizations.

Attention to stress at work has intensified in the wake of sweeping changes in the organization of work. Organizational downsizing and restructuring, dependence on temporary and contractor-supplied labor, and adoption of lean production practices are examples of trends that may adversely influence aspects of job design (e.g., work schedules, workload demands, job security) that are associated with the risk of job stress.

There is also growing appreciation that work organization can have broader implications for the safety and health of workers—not just for stress-related outcomes. For example, long hours of work may increase exposures to chemical and physical hazards in the workplace, or night shifts may expose workers to a heightened risk of violence.

The good news is that there are steps organizations can take to reduce job stress. As a general rule, actions to reduce job stress should give top priority to organizational change to improve working conditions. But even the most conscientious efforts to improve working conditions are unlikely to eliminate stress completely for all workers. For this reason, a combination of organizational change and stress management is often the most useful approach for preventing stress at work. The best design for a stress prevention program will be influenced by several factors—the size and complexity of the organization, available resources, and especially the unique types of stress problems faced by the organization.

Case Example

Theresa is a contract worker in the customer service department of a large company. She is always on the phone because the computer continuously routes calls to her; she never has a moment to herself. She even needs to schedule her bathroom breaks. All day long she listens to complaints from unhappy customers. She tries to be helpful but she can't promise anything without getting her boss's approval. She often feels caught between what the customer wants and company policy. To make matters worse, Theresa's mother's health is deteriorating and she can't even take time off to look after her. Theresa also has health problems of her own, and attributes migraine headaches and high blood pressure to stress at work. Because she is a contract worker, Theresa doesn't have benefits, and has to work a second stressful job to get health insurance. She finally sees her doctor, who recommends she take an extended leave because she is at risk for a possible heart attack, but Theresa doesn't have enough sick leave and can't afford to have her income reduced.

What's the Problem?

The ways that work processes are structured and managed, called "work organization," can directly heighten or alleviate workers' on-the-job stress. Studies suggest that work organization also may have a broad influence on worker safety and health, and may contribute to occupational injury, work-related musculoskeletal disorders (MSDs), cardiovascular disease, and even may intensify other occupational health concerns (such as complaints about indoor air quality (IAQ)).

Who's at Risk?

One-fourth to one-third of U.S. workers report high levels of stress at work. Americans spend eight percent more time on the job than they did 20 years ago (47 hours per week on average), and 13 percent also work a second job. Two-fifths (40%) of workers say that their jobs are very stressful, and more than one-fourth (26%) say they are "often burned out or stressed" by their work.

Not all stress is bad. But chronic (ongoing) stress can lead to health problems. Preventing and managing chronic stress can lower your risk for serious conditions like heart disease, obesity, high blood pressure, and depression.

You can prevent or reduce stress by:

- Planning ahead
- Deciding which tasks need to be done first
- Preparing for stressful events

Some stress is hard to avoid. You can find ways to manage stress by:

- Noticing when you feel stressed
- Taking time to relax
- Getting active and eating healthy
- Talking to friends and family

(Source: "Manage Stress," Office of Disease Prevention and Health Promotion (ODPHP), U.S. Department of Health and Human Services (HHS).)

Can It Be Prevented?

Yes. As widespread corporate and government restructuring continues to have an effect on workers in today's rapidly changing economy, it is important to recognize that stress does not have to be 'just part of the job.' Work stress can be prevented through changes in the work organization and the use of stress management, with an emphasis on work organization changes as a primary step.

The Bottom Line

Work-related stress is a real problem that can negatively impact health and safety. Identifying stressful aspects of work can help in devising strategies for reducing or eliminating workplace stress. Some strategies include:

- Clearly defining worker roles and responsibilities

- Improving communication

- Making sure workers participate in decisions about their jobs

Chapter 23

Work–Life Balance

Work–life balance is a familiar concept in the adult world, but is rarely associated with teens. Teens also experience tremendous pressure and must juggle various activities—such as sports, their studies, extracurricular activities, and part-time jobs—however. Although teens

How Do I Balance a Job and School?

For some students, working while in college is a necessity; for others, it is a way to build a résumé or earn extra money for luxuries. Whatever the reason, it's important to know the pros and cons of working while you're attending school.

If you have a job, determine how many hours a week you'll be able to work and still be able to stay on track with school demands. For example, if you want to earn more money and potentially reduce your need for student loans (or reduce the amount that you borrow), then you could consider working more hours. Managing a schedule with limited free time is an excellent way to prepare for your future. But remember, you may also need to take fewer classes to accommodate your work schedule. Keep in mind that part-time enrollment will delay your graduation, postpone your ability to earn a higher income, and possibly impact your eligibility for some federal aid. Tuition and fees may also be higher for part-time enrollment.

You may opt to work fewer hours and maximize the benefit of your student loans by taking a heavier class load instead of the minimum requirements. By taking extra classes, you may be able to graduate earlier. Alternatively, you may find that taking classes during the summer leaves you better able to balance work and school during the academic year and still stay on track to graduate on time. Keep in mind that the longer it takes to complete your program of study, the more you will pay in total.

(Source: "Budgeting," Federal Student Aid, U.S. Department of Education (ED).)

About This Chapter: "Work–Life Balance," © 2019 Omnigraphics.

spend the majority of their time studying, their part-time jobs can be quite demanding. And, since most teens are working for the first time, it may take them a while to gain a solid understanding of the world of work. Managing all of these activities at the same time can be overwhelming and stressful for teenagers, but establishing work–life balance can enable teens to socialize, focus on their studies, participate in a sport, pursue a hobby, and work a part-time job without getting overworked. This chapter explores the ways in which teens can have a good work–life balance.

Ways of Achieving Good Work–Life Balance
Realistic Goal Setting

Goal setting is important for anyone who wants to manage her or his resources wisely and be successful. When teens set goals early stages in life, they are better equipped to meet life's challenges and plan for their future. Goal setting enables them to gain insight into where they are headed. Some teens tend to overthink, however, and may plan too many things at the same time—a recipe for failure. This could result in activities becoming taxing and life feeling hectic, which in turn can make them lose interest in achieving some goals. Setting practical goals that can be achieved in a week, two weeks, and a month will help teens keep momentum while not making them too weary or overwhelmed.

Choosing the Right Career

Choosing our career is one of the most important decisions we make, and college-bound teenagers may find this decision particularly difficult when they are asked to decide before they even begin college. The courses available to teens, the scope of available subject matter, a

---

- **Learn something new:** Doing this will enhance your skill set or maybe ignite new creative thought. Whether that is reading a book or downloading an app that will help you be more efficient at something, broaden your horizon and go explore.

- **Give back to your community:** There's nothing quite like that feeling when you volunteer somewhere and give selflessly to others. Maybe organize a group to help at a local food shelter or you simply write a check to an organization doing work that you are passionate about. Remember, those that give get.

- **Make time for you:** Running on empty won't benefit anyone around you, including yourself. Be sure to regularly set time aside to recharge your battery. Maybe that is taking a yoga* class or going for a walk during lunch. Set time aside on your calendar to make sure it happens.

A mind and body practice with origins in ancient Indian philosophy. The various styles of yoga typically combine physical postures, breathing techniques, and meditation or relaxation.

- **Telework:** Take advantage of a telework policy if your organization has one or inquire about the possibility. The ability to work from home affords employees an opportunity to better manage the demands of work and family obligations in a flexible manner. GSA was one the federal government's telework pioneers and today about 80 percent are able to telework.

- **Update your workspace:** A happier workspace means happier employees which means an increased bottom line. If you don't have a permanent workspace, think about where you physically sit to work and what type of environment is going to allow you thrive that day.

- **Be considerate of others:** Many people share office space now so think about forgoing that fish or broccoli for lunch. Limit your personal grooming habits to your home. Nobody wants to hear you clip your nails. It's not fair to those around you to endure certain things so try to make 2015 great for all.

- **Don't take yourself too seriously:** Sometimes this is a tough one to tackle, especially when you are overworked. That exactly why you sometimes need to either laugh at yourself or flash those pearly whites and crack a joke now and then. Everyone benefits when the tension is brought down a notch, even for just a minute.

- **Set realistic goals:** With a lot of federal agencies feeling the budget crunch, striking a balance between what's expected and what's possible can be challenging. Assess your situation and be sure to keep the lines of communication open with your supervisor as to avoid any unwanted surprises or unnecessary stress. Learn to prioritize and delegate, it will help your cause to stay sane.

- **Give helpful feedback:** It takes time to provide thoughtful feedback. Help those around you grow and learn from your experience by making the time to give practical, concrete feedback. Who knows, maybe your actions will come full circle and you'll be the one on the receiving end.

- **Don't pass the buck:** Good customer service includes taking ownership for things that sometimes aren't a result of your actions. Be that person willing to listen and apologize. This is your opportunity to turn a negative situation into a positive one. What better way to develop a loyal relationship with someone than by identifying a solution and making it happen.

(Source: "10 Ways to Improve Your Work–Life Balance in the New Year," U.S. General Services Administration (GSA).)

teen's particular interests, available job opportunities, and many other factors help determine a teen's career choice. However, if a wrong field is chosen without taking into consideration their talents, the areas in which they are gifted, and their interests, then a lot of time and energy can be wasted in unproductive work and they may still struggle to find fulfillment in their career. Finding a career that genuinely interests a teen and suits her or him is tremendously beneficial, however, and will enable the teen to develop a life they can balance with engaging extracurricular activities.

Acknowledging Feelings

When teens are actively involved in many activities, their lives can feel really busy, and too much involvement can lead to stress and a sense of being overwhelmed. Acknowledging our feelings around such particular activities is a vital step in maintaining our work–life balance. If an activity feels overwhelming and no longer holds your interest, then dropping out of the activity would be beneficial, while continuing to pursue it could cause more harm than good.

Relaxation Time

Any learning activity requires lot of attention and focus, and it can drain our energy. Hence, teens who are involved in various learning activities should take the time to just relax and rest. During our teen years, we are generally very active and do not think that downtime is needed, but taking breaks and relaxing can do a world of good for a teen. When rest and relaxation become a part of our daily, weekly, and monthly routine, we achieve work–life balance.

Some relaxation activities include:

- Reading any interesting book
- Riding a bike
- Visiting a friend
- Taking a walk, etc.

Part-Time Jobs

Part-time jobs can take a toll on teenager, and employers may demand more hours of work. Statistics prove that teens who work part-time earn lower grades. A part-time job, however, teaches financial responsibility, provides experience and exposure, and enables teens to develop a deeper sense of self-worth. Balancing both work and studies is the challenge. Managing time and being resourceful is the key to work–life balance.

References

1. "Life Balance," Sutter Health Palo Alto Medical Foundation, February 5, 2005.

2. Marcus, Lilit. "Work-Life Balance Matters, Even (and Especially!) for Your First Job," April 30, 2014.

3. "The Great Teen Balancing Act: Sleep, Sport, Social Life, Study and, Part Time Jobs," Developing Minds, March 26, 2013.

4. "Work–Life Balance for Teens," Maine Teen Camp, January 23, 2011.

Chapter 24

Workplace Hazards

Young workers have high rates of job-related injury. These injuries are often the result of the many hazards present in the places they typically work, such as sharp knives and slippery floors in restaurants. Limited or no prior work experience and a lack of safety training also contribute to high injury rates. Middle- and high-school workers may be at increased risk of injury since they may not have the strength or cognitive ability needed to perform certain job duties.

Fast Stats on Injuries to Teen Workers

- In 2015, there were 24 deaths to workers under 18 years of age.
- In 2015, the incidence rate for nonfatal injuries for workers, ages 16–19, was 110.5 per 10,000 full-time employees (FTE).
- In 2014, the rate of work-related injuries treated in emergency departments for workers, ages 15–19, was 2.18 times greater than the rate for workers 25 years of age and older.

To help address this problem, the U.S. Public Health Service (PHS) developed a *Healthy People* objective to reduce rates of work-related injuries among workers 15–19 years of age by ten percent by the year 2020.

About This Chapter: Text in this chapter begins with excerpts from "Young Workers Safety and Health," Centers for Disease Control and Prevention (CDC), April 10, 2018; Text under the heading "Workplace Hazards That Teens Face" is excerpted from "Young Workers—Hazard," Occupational Safety and Health Administration (OSHA), May 10, 2012; Text under the heading "Safe Work for Young Workers" is excerpted from "Young Workers—You Have the Rights," Occupational Safety and Health Administration (OSHA), May 10, 2012.

Workplace Hazards That Teens Face

Young workers get injured or sick on the job for many reasons, including:

- Unsafe equipment

- Inadequate safety training

- Inadequate supervision

- Dangerous work that is illegal or inappropriate for youth under 18

- Pressure to work faster

- Stressful conditions

Workplace hazards associated with specific jobs are another major cause of injuries and illnesses. Employers must work to reduce or minimize hazards in the workplace and train employees how to work safely on the job.

Safe Work for Young Workers

Safe work is rewarding work. Your employer has the responsibility to provide a safe workplace. Employers must follow all Occupational Safety and Health Administration (OSHA) safety and health standards to prevent you from being injured or becoming ill on the job. If you are under age 18, there may be limits on the hours you work, the jobs you do and the equipment you use. Learn about the federal and state wage and hour child labor laws that apply to you.

You Have Rights at Work

You have the right to:

- Work in a safe place

- Receive safety and health training in a language that you understand

- Ask questions if you don't understand instructions or if something seems unsafe

- Use and be trained on required safety gear, such as hard hats, goggles, and ear plugs

- Exercise your workplace safety rights without retaliation or discrimination

- File a confidential complaint with OSHA if you believe there is a serious hazard or that your employer is not following OSHA standards

Your Employer Has Responsibilities

Your employer must:

- Provide a workplace free from serious recognized hazards and follow all OSHA safety and health standards

- Provide training about workplace hazards and required safety gear*

- Tell you where to get answers to your safety or health questions

- Tell you what to do if you get hurt on the job

Employers must pay for most types of safety gear.

Chapter 25

Workers' Rights and Safety

You're earning your own money. You're making new friends. You're learning new things and becoming independent. Work can be a fun, rewarding, and an exciting part of your life. But did you know that your job could harm you?

Every nine minutes, a U.S. teen gets hurt on the job. These teens are young people like Emily, who was working alone at a sandwich shop when a robber with a gun attacked her. And they're like Joe, a construction helper who was electrocuted on his job.

It doesn't have to be this way. You have a right to be safe and healthy at work.

Young workers get sick or hurt on the job for many reasons—dangerous equipment, an unsafe workplace, stress. Sometimes they're hurt from working too fast so they can keep up. As a young worker, you're more likely than an older person to be injured on the job. You may even be asked to do something that the law says you're not allowed to do!

This chapter gives you the facts you need to stay safe and healthy at work. It also shows you what jobs you can (and can't) do, and it teaches you about your rights and responsibilities as a young worker. (Farm jobs aren't covered here, because the laws for farm work are different.)

What Are My Rights at Work?

You have a right to:

- Work in a safe and healthy place

- Get safety and health training—where required—in words you can understand

About This Chapter: Text in this chapter begins with excerpts from "Are You a Teen Worker," Centers for Disease Control and Prevention (CDC), March 2012; Text under the heading "Workers' Safety" is excerpted from "Talking Safety," National Institute for Occupational Safety and Health (NIOSH), 2010.

- Earn at least the federal minimum wage. Find your state's minimum wage at www.dol. gov/whd/minwage/america.htm

- Get paid for medical care (for most jobs) if you are hurt or sick because of your job. You may also be paid for work you missed because you were hurt or made sick on the job.

- Work without being harassed or being treated poorly because of your race, skin color, religion, sex, pregnancy, national origin, disability or genetic information

- Ask for changes to your workspace because of your religious beliefs or a medical condition

- Help someone who is investigating or inspecting your workplace for possible violations of workplace safety, child labor, or wage laws, or laws that ban job discrimination and harassment. You can't be mistreated or fired for giving this kind of help

- Join or start a union. You can work in a group to try to improve working conditions, pay, and benefits

Remember:

You may have more workplace rights under other federal, state, or local laws or under your company's own rules.

By law, your employer must make the place where you work safe and healthy. Your employer must give you training about the hazards of your job when the law requires it. You must also be given protective gear (like safety glasses, earplugs, and gloves) at no cost to you if you need them.

But you also have responsibilities at work. Talk to someone—a parent, teacher, coworker, your boss—if you are asked to do dangerous work or tasks that make you uncomfortable in any way. Report hazards to a trusted adult, your supervisor, or to a federal or state agency.

The better you understand your employer's responsibilities—and your own—the better your chances of staying safe and healthy at work!

What Are My Employer's Responsibilities at Work?

Your employer must:

- Provide a safe and healthy place to work

- Choose and provide, at no cost to you, safety gear that can protect you as you work. This includes such things as ear plugs, gloves, safety glasses, or special clothing (if needed).

- Use words you can understand when you receive training about workplace hazards
- Tell you about hazards on your job site and, if required by law, how to deal with them. This includes training on how to handle chemicals safely and deal with other workplace hazards. You may also be required to get training on how to respond to emergencies.

What Are My Responsibilities at Work?

As a young worker, you should:

- Learn your rights and responsibilities that apply to safety and health where you work. Ask a coworker, school counselor, or your boss about this or read the employee bulletin board or handbook.

- Ask your boss about safety training and learn about the dangers before you start a job or a new task

- Report any health and safety hazards to your supervisor

- Find out what to do if you get hurt at work

- Know and follow all safety rules and instructions

- Use safety equipment and protective clothing when needed

- Stay alert and work safely

- Avoid taking shortcuts

- Look out for your fellow workers

- Find out what to do in an emergency from your supervisor or coworkers

- Respect the people you work with. Never harass or bully anyone

Workers' Safety

Millions of teens in the United States work. Surveys indicate that 80 percent of teens have worked by the time they finish high school. While work provides numerous benefits for young people, it can also be dangerous. Every year, approximately 53,000 youth are injured on the job seriously enough to seek emergency room treatment. In fact, teens are injured at a higher rate than adult workers.

As new workers, adolescents are likely to be inexperienced and unfamiliar with many of the tasks required of them. Yet despite teen workers' high job injury rates, safety at work is usually one of the last things they worry about. Many teens' most positive traits—energy, enthusiasm, and a need for increased challenge and responsibility—can result in their taking on tasks they are not prepared to do safely. They may also be reluctant to ask questions or make demands on their employers.

Health and safety education is an important component of injury prevention for working teens. While workplace-specific training is most critical, young people also need the opportunity to learn and practice general health and safety skills that they will carry with them from job to job. Teens should be able to recognize hazards in any workplace. They should understand how hazards can be controlled, what to do in an emergency, what rights they have on the job, and how to speak up effectively when problems arise at work.

School and community-based programs that place youth in jobs offer an important venue for teaching these skills. One national program that recognizes the importance of including these skills as part of the educational experience is the Career Cluster Initiative, developed by the U.S. Department of Education (ED), Office of Vocational and Adult Education (OVAE) and currently being implemented in a number of states. OVAE identified 16 career clusters that include the major job opportunities in today's workforce. Examples of clusters are finance, architecture and construction, and health science. Each cluster has a curriculum framework and a set of core knowledge and skills students should master, which includes workplace health and safety.

Finding Hazards

- **Safety hazards** can cause immediate accidents and injuries. Examples: hot surfaces or slippery floors.

- **Chemical hazards** are gases, vapors, liquids, or dust that can harm your body. Examples: cleaning products or pesticides.

- **Biological hazards** are living things that can cause diseases such as flu, AIDS, hepatitis, Lyme disease, and tuberculosis (TB). Examples: bacteria, viruses, or insects. In the workplace, you can be exposed to biological hazards through contact with used needles, sick children, animals, etc.

- **Other health hazards** are harmful things, not in the other categories, that can injure you or make you sick. These hazards are sometimes less obvious because they may not cause health problems right away. Examples: noise or repetitive movements.

Finding Ways to Make the Job Safer

1. **Remove the Hazard**

   The best control measures remove the hazard from the workplace altogether or keep it isolated (away from workers) so it can't hurt anyone. This way, the workplace itself is safer, and all the responsibility for safety doesn't fall on individual workers.

   Here are some examples:

   - Use safer chemicals, and get rid of hazardous ones
   - Store chemicals in locked cabinets away from work areas
   - Use machines instead of doing jobs by hand
   - Have guards around hot surfaces

2. **Improve Work Policies and Procedures**

   If you can't completely eliminate a hazard or keep it away from workers, good safety policies can reduce your exposure to hazards.

   Here are some examples:

   - Safety training on how to work around hazards
   - Regular breaks to avoid fatigue
   - Assigning enough people to do the job safely (lifting, etc.)

3. **Use Protective Clothing and Equipment**

   Personal protective equipment (often called "PPE") is the least effective way to control hazards. However, you should use it if it's all you have.

   Here are some examples:

   - Gloves, steel-toed shoes, hard hats
   - Respirators, safety glasses, hearing protectors
   - Lab coats or smocks

Emergencies at Work

When you start a new job, your employer should tell you what kinds of emergencies could happen in that workplace, and what procedures you should follow to make sure you are safe.

OSHA requires your employer to have an Emergency Action Plan that should include information on:

- What to do in different emergencies
- Where shelters and meeting places are
- Evacuation routes
- Emergency equipment and alert systems
- Procedures to follow when someone is injured or becomes ill
- Who is in charge during emergencies
- Your responsibilities
- Practice drills

You should receive training about these things and participate in the practice drills. More time will be spent talking about emergency preparedness, Emergency Action Plans, and what you should expect from your employer.

Chapter 26

Self-Employment

What's the best thing about being self-employed? Angella Luyk, owner of two businesses in Rochester, New York, doesn't hesitate to answer. "No one can tell me what to do, because I'm the boss," she says. "I'm in charge of my own future."

Luyk is one of nearly 15 million workers identified as self-employed in April 2014, according to the U.S. Bureau of Labor Statistics (BLS). These workers accounted for about 10 percent of the overall workforce.

But Luyk cautions that working for yourself isn't for everyone. "It can get tough and scary," she says, "because everything relies on you." Success takes preparation, determination, and time—and it's not guaranteed.

Is Self-Employment for You?

People choose to become self-employed for many reasons, including greater independence and flexibility. But they also consider the downsides, such as the long hours and lack of benefits.

As part of your decision-making process, you should weigh the pros and cons of starting a business, along with your own reasons for seeking self-employment. For example, hoping to make a lot of money quickly can lead you into trouble. But if you feel passionate about developing an idea, self-employment may be right for you.

About This Chapter: This chapter includes text excerpted from "Self-Employment: What to Know to Be Your Own Boss," U.S. Bureau of Labor Statistics (BLS), U.S. Department of Labor (DOL), June 2014.

Rewards

For many self-employed workers, autonomy is the biggest reward. They are able to make their own decisions, such as what kind of work they do, whom they do it for, where and when they do it—and even how much to pay themselves.

Self-employed workers usually take on many different tasks, learning to do each as the need arises. For example, a self-employed barber needs to find a suitable location for opening a shop, attract clients, and price services, in addition to cutting hair.

Many workers find that self-employment allows them not only to expand their professional skills, but also to enrich themselves personally. "I learned a lot more about business and life than I ever expected," says Megan Lebon, a physician who owns a practice in Atlanta, Georgia.

Self-employment can bring other rewards, too. Some workers enjoy creating a new business and watching it grow. They feel good about working for something they believe in.

Challenges

Self-employment is hard work, especially during the first few years. Workers may have difficulty finding clients, earning a steady income, securing business loans, and navigating laws. These challenges add up to financial risk and uncertainty.

And, with income frequently unpredictable, workers may try to handle all or most parts of the business themselves. "You end up working a lot more than you think, oftentimes way more than when you were working for someone else," says Vicki James, owner of a marketing business in Rochester, New York. This schedule can make balancing work and personal life difficult.

Another challenge with self-employment is lack of benefits. Public and private employers typically contribute to retirement, health, and other benefits, offering affordable options to their employees. But self-employed workers must find these benefits and pay for them entirely out of pocket. And there is no paid leave for vacation or illness: A day off work is a day without pay. These types of burdens may overstretch limited financial resources.

Get Started

Even after you choose an occupation for starting a business, becoming self-employed isn't as easy as deciding to work for yourself. You need certain skills and a lot of preparation before you can focus on setting up and growing a business.

But if getting started seems daunting, remember that you don't have to do everything at once and that help is available. Focus on taking one step at a time.

Skills and Knowledge

One of the most important requirements for self-employment, business experts say, is having the technical skills and knowledge you need to do the work you want to do. For example, a graphic design freelancer needs to know color theory and how to use design software. It's a bad idea to start a business in something you don't understand well.

Other technical skills, such as bookkeeping and marketing, are helpful for operating a business. You can learn these skills in a class, at school, with the help of a mentor, or on your own. Higher education, although not a prerequisite for success, is often useful.

Some occupations have specific entry requirements, regardless of whether workers are self-employed. Physicians, for example, must have a bachelor's degree and complete a medical degree program, residency, and licensure requirements. And real estate agents need to become licensed in their state.

Experts suggest that, in addition to having technical skills, you focus on improving "soft" skills, such as time management and people skills. And, regardless of what you do, having a passion for the work is key.

Time management. Self-employed workers often have multiple responsibilities and keep long hours. Being able to manage time efficiently—for example, through multitasking and scheduling—is crucial. These skills help you determine how much time you need to complete tasks and whether you can take on additional work.

People skills. Good people skills, such as communication and customer service, help you attract and retain both employees and clients—especially in the beginning. "Early on, you're the chief salesperson," says Dennis Wright, a small-business mentor in Santa Ana, California. "You have to sell people on your abilities and the value of your product or service."

Passion. Experts say that a passion for what you do can give you the belief, motivation, and commitment you need to overcome the challenges that self-employment may present. "You must like and be committed to what you're doing," Wright says, "or you're likely to give up when you hit bumps in the road."

Preparation

No matter how skilled and knowledgeable you are about the product or service you want to sell, you still need to prepare to ensure success in self-employment. Experts recommend that before you invest any money, you take some time to figure out what motivates you to become self-employed, do your research, and ask for help as you plan your business.

Understand why. Experts say that self-employed workers often feel discouraged, especially when just getting started. Understanding your motivations for becoming self-employed can help sustain you in times of struggle. "The reasons why are the catalyst that will push you forward," says James. "They will help you overcome the moments of doubt."

The reasons for becoming self-employed differ for everyone. Consider what your reasons are, and make note of them. Then, refer to them when you face challenges, to remind yourself of why you pursued self-employment.

Research. Researching your potential business is a way of evaluating whether your idea is marketable. Through research, you can also learn more about your potential customers, competitors, and collaborators. Experts suggest examining the prospective market for your product or service so that you can answer essential questions, such as the following:

- Who and where is the customer?

- How can your potential customers benefit from the product or service you are offering?

- Who are your competitors?

- What will set you apart from your competition?

Professional journals, focus groups, surveys, business clubs, seminars, and current business owners are among the sources that can provide answers to these questions. You may even find reports written by people who have done similar research.

But not every business idea is a winner. Experts suggest moving on when your research shows that an idea won't work. Your next idea might be the right one.

And be careful not to let research stop you from actually getting started. "I thought I first needed to know everything about running a business," James says. "Find the courage to make mistakes, and learn from them as you go."

Ask for help. Many of the principles of business are the same, so people who have already had success with self-employment are often good sources of information to those who are considering it. They may share tips and mistakes, experts say, or make valuable suggestions you hadn't considered. "Learn from people smarter and more experienced than you," says Luyk.

Another possible advantage in asking for help is finding a mentor: someone who offers guidance, encouragement, advice, and emotional support throughout the life of your business. You may meet a potential mentor informally or through a business organization.

Setting Up Shop

After you've determined that your business idea is viable, it's finally time to set up shop, right? Not quite; you still have work to do. For starters, you need to write a business plan, ensure that you meet all legal and tax requirements, and prepare to limit your legal and financial liability. These steps also apply if you decide to freelance, even if you get started quickly out of your own home.

Write Your Business Plan

A business plan is an essential roadmap for business success. This living document generally projects three to five years ahead and outlines the route a company intends to take to grow revenues.

For a more in-depth look at writing a business plan go to: www.sba.gov/starting-business/write-your-business-plan

The process of setting up a business can be confusing and difficult. You'll need to complete a lot of paperwork to ensure that you're complying with different laws and regulations, for example. Experts recommend consulting an accountant and a lawyer for help, and they say that this investment in your future business is money well spent. "Be upfront about what you want and what you can afford," says Luyk. "These professionals will save you money in the end."

Another difficulty is a lack of money early on. Experts suggest that, before you get started, you should save up enough money to last a couple of years so that you avoid financial pitfalls.

Write a business plan. A business plan describes what service you'll provide or product you'll make, along with how and when you'll do it. "If you don't set goals, you won't achieve them," says business mentor Jack Bernard. "You'll just chase your tail." Use your research to set goals for the business within specific timeframes. Your business plan should explain in detail every part of your business, including the following:

- Your business values and vision for the future

- Your business's strengths, weaknesses, opportunities, and threats

- Financial projections

- The experience and achievements of key staff

Business plans are important when you seek funding, which may include loans and grants. Most reputable creditors require applicants to have a business plan, a solid credit score, and a criminal background check before agreeing to lend or invest money in a business startup.

There are plenty of free resources available to help you write your plan. For example, you can find step-by-step guides and templates online or at your local library. And some business organizations offer individualized business counseling.

Meet legal requirements. To legally operate a business, you need a business license, as well as permits from the city and county, or both, in which the business is located. Local governments have many different requirements, but common ones include health and zoning permits.

You also need to meet Internal Revenue Service requirements. These include registering for an employer identification number, reporting wages and taxes withheld, and verifying employees' eligibility to work in the United States.

Other federal requirements may apply, depending on your business product or service. For example, a business that sells produce throughout the country needs a permit from the U.S. Department of Agriculture (USDA)to ensure that the food is safe.

Limit liability. The way you structure your business affects your legal and financial responsibilities. For example, a sole proprietor is someone who owns a business and is accountable for all of its assets, obligations, and so on. And sole proprietors take a great risk by assuming all responsibility for their business; lenders can take control of personal assets of a sole proprietor who fails to repay a business loan.

Some business structures are designed to limit personal liability. The most common are a limited liability company (LLC) and an S corporation. Both of these arrangements protect personal assets by risking only what is invested in the business. Generally speaking, an LLC is easier to set up and manage, but an S Corporation allows for the sale of business stock to investors.

Loans guaranteed by the U.S. Small Business Administration (SBA) range from small to large and can be used for most business purposes, including long-term fixed assets and operating capital. Some loan programs set restrictions on how you can use the funds, so check with an SBA-approved lender when requesting a loan. Your lender can match you with the right loan for your business needs.

(Source: "The SBA Helps Small Businesses Get Loans," U.S. Small Business Administration (SBA).)

Growing the Business

After you've completed the necessary steps for self-employment, you'll need to focus on growing the business. Networking, staying competitive, making adjustments, and working through challenges will increase your chances of success.

Network. Experts say that networking is one of the best ways for self-employed people to spend their time. Among other benefits it provides, networking offers opportunities for self-employed workers to reach potential clients, meet business mentors, and test ideas to gauge interest. "You have to make yourself visible to your market," Lebon says. "People can only do business with you if they can find you first."

People usually network at business events, clubs, and meetings. Volunteering with a professional organization or serving on a community board also can be useful. And networking doesn't have to be formal. "Sometimes I just have coffee with people and share ideas, without worrying about business," says Ryan Schwartz, a freelance communications specialist in Portland, Oregon.

Some self-employed workers also use traditional marketing tools, such as creating a website or advertising in a local paper, to attract clients. But experts caution against relying too heavily on marketing, which often is expensive and yields mixed results. "There is no better form of advertising than word of mouth," Wright says. "Give your customers a positive experience, and they'll come back with a friend."

Stay competitive. Competition is a part of being in business. To stay competitive with other businesses that are like yours, you have to stand out in areas such as price, quality, and service. "If you can't define what makes you better," says Bernard, "your customers certainly won't know, and they will take their business elsewhere."

Updating your research will help keep you informed about competition in your market. After starting her cleaning business, for example, Luyk asked potential clients what they liked and disliked about their existing cleaning service. She used their feedback to improve her business.

When trying to set yourself apart from other small businesses, don't compete on price, say experts. Large businesses often offer lower prices because they have some advantages, such as the ability to buy in bulk at reduced cost, that small businesses do not. Lowering prices also reduces profit, which makes it harder to stay in business. "There's always someone willing to undercut your prices," says James. "Be better in other ways."

Make adjustments. As your business evolves, it may outgrow your original vision. Keep up with developments by making adjustments as necessary. For example, you may have planned to run your business from home for several years, but brisk sales might allow you to rent office space sooner than expected.

Experts often recommend adding workers to your payroll as one of the first tweaks you make after your business is established. "Hire people to help you as soon as you can afford them," says Luyk. "Then you can spend your time working on your business—not in the business."

It's important to hire employees who have experience and skills that you don't have. For example, opening an eatery to showcase your culinary skills can be risky if you have never run a restaurant. Employing a manager will offset your lack of management experience and let you focus on your strengths, such as cooking or designing the menu.

Persevere. Working for yourself is not easy. The business might take longer than you expect to turn a profit, for example, or you might have trouble making rent or paying your employees.

As most self-employed workers will tell you, it takes lots of preparation, determination, and time to achieve success in a new business. "This is a marathon," Lebon says. "Temper your expectations, take things one step a time, and don't give up."

Remember, experts say, you don't have a chance for success unless you take the first step. "People are so afraid to fail that they become paralyzed," says Luyk. "But you can learn a lot from failure. And if you don't try, you'll always wonder what could have been."

Part Three
Creating and Living within a Budget

Chapter 27

Budgeting

Basics of Budget

A budget is a plan you write down to decide how you will spend your money each month.

A budget helps you make sure you will have enough money every month. Without a budget, you might run out of money before your next paycheck.

A budget shows you:

- How much money you make

- How you spend your money

Need for a Budget

A budget helps you decide:

- What you must spend your money on

- If you can spend less money on some things and more money on other things

For example, your budget might show that you spend $100 on clothes every month. You might decide you can spend $50 on clothes. You can use the rest of the money to pay bills or to save for something else.

About This Chapter: Text beginning with the heading "Basics of Budget" is excerpted from "Making a Budget," Consumer.gov, Federal Trade Commission (FTC), September 28, 2012; Text beginning with the heading "Differentiate between Needs and Wants" is excerpted from "Budgeting Tips," U.S. Department of Education (ED), April 10, 2014.

Necessity for Saving Money

You might need money for an emergency. You also might need to buy something more expensive, like a car. Saving money might help you buy a car, put a security deposit on an apartment, or pay for something else expensive.

How to Budget
Where to Start

Start a budget by gathering your bills and pay stubs. Think about how you spend money, besides paying your bills. For example, do you buy a cup of coffee every day? After a month, that coffee money could add up to an expense you might write down.

When you have your bills and pay stubs:

- Write down your expenses. An expense is the money you spend.
- Write down how much money you make. This is called income.
- Subtract your expenses from how much money you make

If the number is less than zero, you are spending more money than you make. Look for things in your budget you can change. Maybe something you do not need, or a way to spend less.

Have a budget sheet to keep track of your earnings.

What You Should Do If You Don't Get Paid Every Month

Some people do not get paid every month. If you expect things to be like they were last year, do this:

- Add all the money you earned last year
- Divide that number by 12. This is about how much money you will have for each month

For example,

Last year paychecks added up to $30,000.

$30,000 ÷ 12 = $2,500

had about $2,500 each month.

How You Can Use Your Budget

A budget is something you use every month. A written budget will help you:

- See where you spend money

- See where you can save

- Make a plan for how to spend and save your money

Your budget can help you save money for the future. You can make savings one of your expenses. You might find ways to spend less money. Then you can put money into savings every month—maybe into a bank or credit union.

Why You Should Save Money

It can be hard to save money. It is very hard when your expenses go up and your income does not. Here are some reasons to try to save money even when it is not easy.

- **Emergencies.** Saving small amounts of money now might help you later. Everyone has expenses they do not expect.

- **Expensive things.** Sometimes, we have to pay for expensive things—like a car, a trip, or a security deposit on an apartment. You will have more choices if you have money to pay for those expensive things.

- **Your goals.** You might want to pay for college classes. Maybe you need to visit family in another country. You can plan for these goals and save money. Then you might not have to use a credit card or borrow money to pay.

Other Ways to Save Your Money

You can try these ways to help save money:

- For one month, write down everything you spend. Small expenses, like a cup of coffee, can add up to a lot of money. When you know where you are spending your money, you can decide what you might not want to buy.

- Pay with your credit card only if you can pay the full amount when the bill comes. That way, you do not pay interest on what you owe.

- Pay your bills when they are due. That way, you will not owe late fees or other charges.

- Keep the money you are saving separate from the money you spend.

- Consider opening a savings account in a bank or credit union.

- If you keep cash at home, keep the money you are saving separate from your spending money. Keep all your cash someplace safe.

For example,

What you did not buy this month:

- Music downloads $5.00

- Shirt $30.00

- Movie ticket $10.00

- Top off gas tank $15.00

- Cups of coffee $12.00

- What I saved this month: $72.00

Making a Budget

A budget is a plan that shows you how you can spend your money every month. Making a budget can help you make sure you do not run out of money each month. A budget also will help you save money for your goals or for emergencies.

Write down your expenses. Expenses are what you spend money on. Expenses include:

Bills:

- Bills that are the same each month, like rent

- Bills that might change each month, like utilities

- Bills you pay once or twice a year, like car insurance

Other expenses, like:

- Food

- Gas

- Entertainment

- Clothes

- School supplies

- Money for family

- Unplanned expenses, like car repairs or medical bills

- Credit card bills

You might have bills that change every month. Look at what you paid for the same month last year. You might need $200 for your gas bill in January, but $30 in July.

Write down how much money you make. This includes your paycheck and any other money you get, like child support.

Subtract your expenses from how much money you make. This number should be more than zero. If it is less than zero, you are spending more money than you make. Look at your budget to see what you do not need or what you could spend less on.

How to Use Your Budget

You can use your budget every month:

- At the beginning of the month, plan for how you will spend your money that month. Write what you think you will earn and spend.

- Write down what you spend. Try to do this every day.

- At the end of the month, see if you spent what you planned.

- Use the information to help you plan the next month's budget.

Differentiate between Needs and Wants

One benefit of budgeting is that it helps you determine if you have the resources to spend on items that you want versus those you need.

- Start by making a list of things you'd like to save up for.

- Identify whether each item on the list is something you absolutely need or is really a want.

- If you decide you want something, ask yourself if you will still be happy you bought the item in a month.

- Next, prioritize each item on the list.

- Once you have set your priorities, you can then determine whether you should incorporate each item into your budget.

Pay Yourself First!

Include "Savings" as a recurring expense item in your monthly budget. Small amounts that you put away each month do add up.

Manage Your Budget

Keeping track of all of your spending may seem like a lot of work. But if you're organized, keep good records, and use some of the following tips, you'll find it's easier than you may think. And, don't be too hard on yourself if you slip up.

- **Record your actual expenses.** Have you noticed how fast your cash disappears? To get a handle on where your cash is going, carry a small notebook or use a phone app to record even the smallest expenditures such as coffee, movie tickets, snacks, and parking. Some expenses that are often ignored include music downloads, charges for extra cell phone usage, and entertainment expenses. Search for an online tool to assist you—many are free!

- **Organize your records.** Decide what system you're going to use to track and organize your financial information. There are mobile apps and computer-based programs that work well, but you can also track your spending using a pencil and paper. Be sure to be consistent and organized, and designate a space to store all your financial information. Good record-keeping saves money and time!

- **Create a routine.** Manage your money on a regular basis, and record your expenses and income regularly. If you find that you can't record your expenses every day, then record them weekly. If you wait longer than two weeks to record information, you may forget some transactions and be overwhelmed by the amount of information you need to enter.

- **Include a category in your budget called "Unusual."** There will be some expenses every month that won't fall neatly into one category or that you couldn't have planned for. An "Unusual" category will help you budget for these occasional expenses.

- **Review your spending for little items that add up to big monthly expenditures.** The daily cup of coffee and soda at a vending machine will add up. Consider packing your lunch rather than eating out every day. Spending $10 a day eating out during the week translates to $50 a week and $200 a month. A $5 packed lunch translates into a savings of $1,200 a year. Save even more by looking for ways to manage and reduce your transportation and entertainment expenses.

- **Make your financial aid credit balance refund last.** If your school applies your financial aid to your tuition and fees and there's money left over, the school will refund that money to you so you can use it for other education-related expenses (textbooks, transportation, food, etc.). Remember that your financial aid is supposed to help you cover your cost of attendance for the whole semester or term, so be sure to make that refund stretch over time rather than spending it all as soon as you get it.

- **Comparison shop.** Comparison shopping is simply using common sense to compare products in an attempt to get the best prices and best value. This means doing a little research before running out to buy something, especially when it comes to more expensive items. Make the most of tools like phone apps for comparing prices and value.

- **Use credit cards wisely.** Think very carefully before you decide to get your first credit card. Is a credit card really necessary, or would another payment options work just as well? If you receive a credit card offer in the mail, don't feel obligated to accept it. Limit the number of cards you get.

- **Don't spend more on your credit card than you can afford to pay in full on a monthly basis.** Responsible use of credit cards can be a shopping convenience and help you establish a solid credit rating and avoid financial problems. Consider signing up for electronic payment reminders, balance notices, and billing statement notifications from your credit card provider.

Expect the Unexpected

Your emergency fund should be used for expenses that fall outside the categories of annual and periodic bills. Unexpected expenses are the result of life events such as job loss, illness, or car repairs. Redefine your notion of "unexpected" bills to encompass these unforeseen events rather than more common but infrequent expenses. The good news is that if you do not use your emergency fund, you will have savings—which should always be a priority when managing your finances. And, if you have to use your emergency fund, you may avoid unnecessary borrowing.

Chapter 28

Avoiding Common Mistakes with Money

Common Mistakes Young Adults Make with Money and How to Avoid Them

Everybody makes mistakes with their money. The important thing is to keep them to a minimum. And one of the best ways to accomplish that is to learn from the mistakes of others. Here is the list of the top mistakes young people (and even many not-so-young people) make with their money, and what you can do to avoid these mistakes in the first place.

Buying items you don't need . . . and paying extra for them in interest. Every time you have an urge to do a little "impulse buying" and you use your credit card but you don't pay in full by the due date, you could be paying interest on that purchase for months or years to come. Spending the money on something you really don't need can be a big waste of your money. But you can make the matter worse, a lot worse, by putting the purchase on a credit card and paying monthly interest charges.

Research major purchases and comparison shop before you buy. Ask yourself if you really need the item. Even better, wait a day or two, or just a few hours, to think things over rather than making a quick and costly decision you may come to regret.

There are good reasons to pay for major purchases with a credit card, such as extra protection if you have problems with the items. But if you charge a purchase with a credit card

About This Chapter: This chapter includes text excerpted from "If at First You Don't Succeed: Common Mistakes Young Adults Make with Money and How to Avoid Them," Federal Deposit Insurance Corporation (FDIC), July 3, 2014.

instead of paying by cash, check or debit card (which automatically deducts the money from your bank account), be smart about how you repay. For example, take advantage of offers of "zero-percent interest" on credit card purchases for a certain number of months (but understand when and how interest charges could begin).

And, pay the entire balance on your credit card or as much as you can to avoid or minimize interest charges, which can add up significantly.

"If you pay only the minimum amount due on your credit card, you may end up paying more in interest charges than what the item cost you, to begin with," said Janet Kincaid, Federal Deposit Insurance Corporation (FDIC) Senior Consumer Affairs Officer. Example: If you pay only the minimum payment due on a $1,000 computer, let's say it's about $20 a month, your total cost at an annual percentage rate (APR) of more than 18 percent can be close to $3,000, and it will take you nearly 19 years to pay it off.

Getting too deeply in debt. Being able to borrow allows us to buy clothes or computers, take a vacation or purchase a home or a car. But taking on too much debt can be a problem, and each year millions of adults of all ages find themselves struggling to pay their loans, credit cards, and other bills.

Learn to be a good money manager by following the basic strategies outlined here. Also, recognize the warning signs of a serious debt problem. These may include borrowing money to make payments on loans you already have, deliberately paying bills late, and putting off doctor visits or other important activities because you think you don't have enough money.

If you believe you're experiencing debt overload, take corrective measures. For example, try to pay off your highest interest rate loans (usually your credit cards) as soon as possible, even if you have higher balances on other loans. For new purchases, instead of using your credit card, try paying with cash, a check or a debit card.

"There are also reliable credit counselors you can turn to for help at little or no cost," added Rita Wiles Ross, an FDIC attorney. "Unfortunately, you also need to be aware that there are scams masquerading as 'credit repair clinics' and other companies, such as 'debt consolidators,' that may charge big fees for unfulfilled promises or services you can perform on your own."

Paying bills late or otherwise tarnishing your reputation. Companies called credit bureaus to prepare credit reports for use by lenders, employers, insurance companies, landlords, and others who need to know someone's financial reliability, based largely on each person's track record paying bills and debts. Credit bureaus, lenders and other companies also produce "credit scores" that attempt to summarize and evaluate a person's credit record using a point system.

While one or two late payments on your loans or other regular commitments (such as rent or phone bills) over a long period may not seriously damage your credit record, making a habit of it will count against you. Over time you could be charged a higher interest rate on your credit card or a loan that you really want and need. You could be turned down for a job or an apartment. It could cost you extra when you apply for auto insurance. Your credit record will also be damaged by a bankruptcy filing or a court order to pay money as a result of a lawsuit.

So, pay your monthly bills on time. Also, periodically review your credit reports from the nation's three major credit bureaus—Equifax, Experian, and TransUnion—to make sure their information accurately reflects the accounts you have and your payment history, especially if you intend to apply for credit for something important in the near future.

Having too many credit cards. Two to four cards (including any from department stores, oil companies, and other retailers) is the right number for most adults. Why not more cards?

The more credit cards you carry, the more inclined you may be to use them for costly impulse buying. In addition, each card you own—even the ones you don't use—represents money that you could borrow up to the card's spending limit. If you apply for new credit you will be seen as someone who, in theory, could get much deeper in debt and you may only qualify for a smaller or costlier loan.

Also be aware that card companies aggressively market their products on college campuses, at concerts, ball games or other events often attended by young adults. Their offers may seem tempting and even harmless—perhaps a free T-shirt or Frisbee, or 10 percent off your first purchase if you just fill out an application for a new card—but you've got to consider the possible consequences we've just described. "Don't sign up for a credit card just to get a great-looking T-shirt," Kincaid added. "You may be better off buying that shirt at the store for $14.95 and saving yourself the potential costs and troubles from that extra card."

Not watching your expenses. It's very easy to overspend in some areas and take away from other priorities, including your long-term savings. Try any system—ranging from a computer-based budget program to handwritten notes—that will help you keep track of your spending each month and enable you to set and stick to limits you consider appropriate. "A budget doesn't have to be complicated, intimidating or painful—just something that works for you in getting a handle on your spending," said Kincaid.

Not saving for your future. We know it can be tough to scrape together enough money to pay for a place to live, a car and other expenses each month. But experts say it's also important for young people to save money for their long-term goals, too, including perhaps buying a home, owning a business or saving for your retirement (even though it may be 40 or 50 years away).

Start by "paying yourself first." That means even before you pay your bills each month you should put money into savings for your future. Often the simplest way is to arrange with your bank or employer to automatically transfer a certain amount each month to a savings account or to purchase a U.S. Savings Bond or an investment, such as a mutual fund that buys stocks and bonds.

Even if you start with just $25 or $50 a month you'll be significantly closer to your goal. "The important thing is to start saving as early as you can—even saving for your retirement when that seems light-years away—so you can benefit from the effect of compound interest," said Donna Gambrell, a Deputy Director of the FDIC's Division of Supervision and Consumer Protection. Compound interest refers to when an investment earns interest, and later that combined amount earns more interest, and on and on until a much larger sum of money is the result after many years.

Banking institutions pay interest on savings accounts that they offer. However, bank deposits aren't the only way to make your money grow. "Investments, which include stocks, bonds, and mutual funds, can be attractive alternatives to bank deposits because they often provide a higher rate of return over long periods, but remember that there is the potential for a temporary or permanent loss in value," said James Williams, an FDIC Consumer Affairs Specialist. "Young people especially should do their research and consider getting professional advice before putting money into investments."

Paying too much in fees. Whenever possible, use your own financial institution's automated teller machines or the ATMs owned by financial institutions that don't charge fees to noncustomers. You can pay $1 to $4 in fees if you get cash from an ATM that isn't owned by your financial institution or isn't part of an ATM "network" that your bank belongs to.

> Whenever possible, use your own financial institution's automated teller machines or the ATMs owned by institutions that don't charge fees to noncustomers.

Try not to "bounce" checks—that is, writing checks for more money than you have in your account, which can trigger fees from your financial institution (about $15 to $30 for each check) and from merchants. The best precaution is to keep your checkbook up to date and closely monitor your balance, which is easier to do with online and telephone banking. Remember to record your debit card transactions from ATMs and merchants so that you will be sure to have enough money in your account when those withdrawals are processed by your bank.

Financial institutions also offer "overdraft protection" services that can help you avoid the embarrassment and inconvenience of having a check returned to a merchant. But be careful before signing up because these programs come with their own costs.

Pay off your credit card balance each month, if possible, so you can avoid or minimize interest charges. Also send in your payment on time to avoid additional fees. If you don't expect to pay your credit card bill in full most months, consider using a card with a low-interest rate and a generous "grace period" (the number of days before the card company starts charging you interest on new purchases).

Not taking responsibility for your finances. Do a little comparison shopping to find accounts that match your needs at the right cost. Be sure to review your bills and bank statements as soon as possible after they arrive or monitor your accounts periodically online or by telephone. You want to make sure there are no errors, unauthorized charges or indications that a thief is using your identity to commit fraud.

Keep copies of any contracts or other documents that describe your bank accounts, so you can refer to them in a dispute. Also, remember that the quickest way to fix a problem usually is to work directly with your bank or other service providers.

"Many young people don't take the time to check their receipts or make the necessary phone calls or write letters to correct a problem," one banker told FDIC Consumer News. "Resolving these issues can be time-consuming and exhausting but doing so can add up to hundreds of dollars."

Final Thoughts

Even if you are fortunate enough to have parents or other loved ones you can turn to for help or advice as you start handling money on your own, it's really up to you to take charge of your finances. Doing so can be intimidating for anyone. It's easy to become overwhelmed or frustrated. And everyone makes mistakes. The important thing is to take action.

Start small if you need to. Stretch to pay an extra $50 a month on your credit card bill or other debts. Find two or three ways to cut your spending. Put an extra $50 a month into a savings account. Even little changes can add up to big savings over time.

Chapter 29

Basic Facts about Banks and Banking

The monetary system of the modern world is built around banks. They account for trillions of dollars in assets, making them a crucial driver of the global economy. And, closer to home, they provide a number of services that can help you manage your money wisely. But not everyone understands what banks are, what they do, and how they operate. Increasing your knowledge about banks can guide you to make better financial decisions and save you money in the long run.

The Origin of Banks

Although money-lending and the exchange of money for goods dates back to ancient times, the first institution most of us would recognize as a bank arose in fourteenth-century Italy. In the cities of Florence, Genoa, and Venice, prominent families established banks to loan money to merchants, finance military operations, and facilitate trade between city–states and regions.

Banks gradually sprang up throughout Europe from the fifteen to the seventeenth centuries. Most of them dealt in bullion (gold and silver bars or ingots) or coins made from gold, silver, copper, or other metals. But late in the seventeenth century, in Sweden, banks started issuing paper money, notes of credit that promised the holder could exchange the paper for a specified amount of precious metal. Banking continued to expand worldwide, and during the Industrial Revolution in the nineteenth-century banks became the key component in international trade that they remain today.

About This Chapter: "Basic Facts about Banks and Banking," © 2017 Omnigraphics.

Types of Banks

You're probably familiar with one kind of bank, the one near you with the drive-through ATM and where you may have a savings account. But there are actually a number of different types of banks, including:

- **Retail banks**: These are the ones you know. Also called consumer banks, they're usually local branches of larger banking systems that provide a variety of services to individual customers, including savings and checking accounts, loans, and credit and debit cards.

- **Savings and loans**: Less common than they once were, these institutions function similarly to a retail bank but usually offer more limited services. Their main purpose is to take in savings deposits and make loans, primarily home mortgages.

- **Commercial banks**: These banks cater to business customers with basic services like savings and checking accounts. But they can also accept payments for customers, extend lines of credit to help businesses manage cash flow, and facilitate cash transfers from overseas customers.

- **Investment banks**: Investment banks are set up to facilitate large transactions. Their services can include handling investors' funds, guaranteeing payments, helping institutional clients with mergers or corporate reorganizations, and acting as a broker or financial adviser.

- **Online banks**: These are retail banks that have no physical location, operating instead completely via the Internet. They provide most of the same services as a traditional bank but frequently offer better savings interest rates and more favorable terms on loans.

- **Central banks**: Central banks are national banks that provide services for their country's government. They also implement the government's monetary policy and issue the country's currency. In the United States, this function is served by the Federal Reserve Bank, which was founded in 1913.

Things to Consider When Choosing a Bank

- **Minimum deposit requirements**: Do you have to keep a minimum dollar amount in your account to earn interest or avoid account maintenance fees?

- **Limits on withdrawals**: Can you take money out whenever you want? Are there any penalties for doing so?

- **Interest**: Can you earn interest on your accounts? How much is it, and how frequently is it paid?
- **Online bill pay**: Can you pay your bills directly from your bank's website?
- **Deposit insurance**: Make sure that the bank is a member of the Federal Deposit Insurance Corporation (FDIC).
- **Mobile banking**: Can you access your accounts and make deposits from your mobile phone or tablet? Does the bank charge fees for this access?
- **Convenience**: Are there branches or ATMs close to where you to school, work, and live?

Retail Bank Services

Since it's unlikely that you'll need the services of other types of banks at the moment, it might be useful to concentrate on your interaction with retail banks, which can include online banks. Some of the services these banks provide include:

- **Savings accounts**: There pay a relatively small amount of interest on your deposits but allow you to withdraw your money at any time. Then there are other types of accounts that earn a higher rate of interest in exchange for leaving your money in the bank for longer periods, such as certificates of deposit (CDs).

- **Checking accounts**: When you open a checking account you deposit funds and receive a book of checks, slips of paper that are a promise to pay a specified amount of money from your account. Checking accounts also let you make deposits and withdrawals from an ATM using a debit card, pay bills online, and transfer money between accounts.

- **Loans**: One of the primary ways banks make money is by taking funds it receives from depositors and lending it to people who need it. The bank makes money by charging a higher fee for these loans than it pays out in interest.

- **Credit cards**: These are actually a kind of loan. The bank advances funds to a merchant or other payee with the understanding that the customer will pay the money back to the bank at the end of the month, usually with no fee, or overtime with a finance charge added.

- **Online and mobile banking**: Even physical banks now provide customers with access to their secure websites. This allows you to check your balances, transfer funds between accounts, and pay bills from any computer with an Internet connection. Most banks now also have mobile apps that allow you to perform these same functions from a phone or tablet.

> Most banks have savings and checking accounts designed specifically for students. You can find the details of these accounts, as well as tips and other useful information, on their websites.

Bank Regulation

Through the many centuries of banking, there have been numerous abuses that have sometimes led to personal bankruptcies, bank failures, and even the collapse of the monetary systems of entire countries. As a result, governments place restrictions on banks that regulate the way they handle money and interact with customers. In the United States, banking is regulated by the federal government, as well as by individual states. Many regulations were enacted after the bank failures of the Great Depression that began in 1929, and more were passed following the financial crisis that started in 2007. A few of the federal agencies responsible for overseeing the huge number of bank regulations include:

- **Federal Deposit Insurance Corporation (FDIC)**: Created in 1933, the FDIC insures the money in your savings and checking accounts. This agency guarantees that your funds will be there when you need them.

- **Federal Reserve Board**: Often called "The Fed," this is the governing body of the Federal Reserve System, which provides central control of the country's monetary system. This includes regulating banks, ensuring a stable economy, and providing services to individual banks.

- **Office of the Comptroller of the Currency (OCC)**: Established in 1863, the purpose of the OCC is to charter, supervise, and regulate banks to help ensure the stability and proper functioning of the entire banking system.

- **Office of Thrift Supervision (OTS)**: This agency was created in 1989 by the Financial Institutions Reform, Recovery and Enforcement Act (FIRREA) of that year. It primarily regulates savings and loans in the same way the OCC regulates other banks.

> The **Reserve Requirement** is the amount of funds, set by the Federal Reserve Board of Governors, that a bank must have on hand every night, either as cash in its vault or as a deposit at the local Federal Reserve bank. Large banks with more than $79.5 million on deposit must maintain a reserve of 10 percent of deposits.

Credit Unions

These financial institutions perform many of the functions of banks, providing customers with services like savings and checking accounts and loans. There are some differences, however, including:

- **Structure**: Most banks are corporations owned by shareholders who elect their governing boards. Credit unions are owned by their customers, called members. All members, regardless of the size of their deposits, get a vote when electing board members, and while banks pay their board members, credit unions are run by volunteers.

- **Profits**: Banks are in business to make money for their shareholders. Credit unions, on the other hand, are nonprofit organizations. When they make a profit from loans or other investments, they use it to increase interest rates on savings accounts or reduce the finance charges on loans to members.

- **Size**: Through the years, changes in regulations have resulted in the elimination of some restrictions on the way credit unions do business, bringing them more in line with banks. However, the fact remains that today even the biggest credit unions are tiny compared to most banks.

- **Regulations**: As we've seen, the many regulations on banks are overseen by a number of federal and state agencies. But national regulation of credit unions is handled by the National Credit Union Administration (NCUA), as well as individual state authorities. One of the responsibilities of the NCUA is to manage the National Credit Union Share Insurance Fund (NCUSIF), which is similar to the FDIC in that it insures depositor funds.

What's better, a bank or a credit union? Like a lot of questions, the answer depends on your individual circumstances. Credit unions have the reputation of providing better, more personal, customer service, which is an important factor for many people. They also generally pay higher interest rates on savings and charge lower fees for loans. But unlike banks, credit unions may offer limited access to ATMs. And you can't open an account at just any credit union; most of them have been created to serve specific organizations, employee groups, or geographic regions. But if you qualify for membership, a credit union may meet your needs. As with any financial decision, do your homework carefully before choosing an option.

References

1. Maxfield, John. "Credit Union vs. Bank: 4 Major Differences," Fool.com, June 7, 2015.

2. Roche, Cullen. "The Basics of Banking," Pragcap.com, n.d.

3. "The Role of Banks," ING.com, n.d.

4. Sylla, Richard. "The U.S. Banking System: Origin, Development, and Regulation," Gilderlehrman.org, n.d.

5. "Types of Banks and Federal Deposit Insurance Corporation (FDIC)," Teensguideto-money.com, n.d.

Chapter 30

How to Save and Invest

Getting Started in Saving and Investing

The thought of starting a savings or investment account can be overwhelming, but it doesn't have to be. No matter how much or how little money you have, you can get started planning your financial future today with just a few basic steps. The important thing is to begin by thinking about what you want to achieve and then learn about the opportunities that are available to you.

Step One: Make a Plan

Every successful investor or savings account holder started out with one thing in common—they made a financial plan and they were prepared to stick to it. Every savings plan is different because each person is different and has different goals in life. There is no wrong way to make a financial plan, and your plan doesn't have to stay the same forever. Your financial plan can change as your life changes, and there is no reason to wait for the perfect moment to begin. In fact, the sooner you make your financial plan, the better off you will be in the long run.

Here are some things to consider when thinking about your financial plan:

- What are your financial goals?

- How much money do you want to save, and why?

- Your savings goals can be anything that is important to you. For example: Are you saving to buy a car? Pay for college?

About This Chapter: "Savings and Investing," © 2017 Omnigraphics.

Make a list of your financial goals and then put them in order of importance. Include an estimate of the amount of money needed to reach each goal. Then think about how much time you will have to meet each specific goal. For example, in order to buy a car, how many months will you be able to save for that purchase? Knowing how much money you will need, and when you will need it, are the most important factors that will influence your savings and investment plan. Divide the amount of money you need by the number of weeks until the money is needed to determine how much money you will need to save each week in order to meet your goal. Online savings calculators can also help you figure how much money you will need to save each week or month in order to meet your goal. You can find a wealth of information about savings and investment, including savings calculators and links to other resources online at www.investor.gov.

Quick Tip

Getting started with saving and investing is as easy as 1-2-3!

1. Make a financial plan. What are your goals?
2. Understand your current financial status, including income, expenses, and debt.
3. Start saving and investing as soon as you've paid off your debts.

Step Two: Know Your Financial Status

The second step in getting started in saving and investing is understanding your current financial situation. To do this, you will need to know how much money you owe to others and how much money you currently have. There are worksheets and calculators available online to help you with this step.

Once you have listed all of your debts and all of the money you currently have, you can then move on to examining your current income and expenses. Begin by listing all of your expenses, either monthly or weekly. Then write down how much money you earn. If your income is greater than your expenses, you can begin saving immediately. If your expenses are greater than your income, you will have to do some additional calculations in order to be saving or investing.

When expenses are greater than income, you will need to find ways to reduce your expenses. You can begin this process by writing down how you spend your money. What kinds of things do you buy each day, each week, or each month? Take note of where your money is going. Once you start paying close attention to your spending habits, you might be surprised to see how quickly small everyday purchases add up over time. The next step is to identify where you might be able to cut back on expenses. For example, instead of buying coffee from a coffee shop every day, you could save money by making coffee at home. If you find that you buy lunch fairly often, you might be able to reduce that expense by bringing your own lunch from home instead. There are many ways to cut back on unnecessary expenses, and each person will find different ways to save according to their own priorities.

Once you have found some ways to reduce your expenses, your first priority should be to pay off any existing debts. This is especially important for high-interest debts such as credit card balances. After you have paid those debts, you can start using that money for savings and investments.

Step Three: Start Saving and Investing

When you are ready to begin saving and investing your money, you will need to learn about the different opportunities that are available to you. Saving and investing are two different ways to manage your money. The basic difference between saving and investing is the amount of risk involved.

A savings account is usually considered the safest place to keep your money. With savings accounts, you can generally access your money at any time, for any reason, whenever you need it. Savings account products include bank savings accounts, checking accounts, and credit union accounts. After you have paid off credit cards or other high-interest debts, some financial advisors recommend building a savings account containing the equivalent of up to six months of regular expenses. This amount is recommended because it can be used in case of an emergency, period of unemployment, or other financial need.

An investment is a way to manage money over a longer period of time. Unlike savings accounts, investments may not be as easy to access and there may be fees associated with withdrawing money. The longer-term commitment of an investment, such as in stocks, securities, and mutual funds, also comes with benefits and risks. When you make an investment, you give your money to a company or other enterprise such as a bank, hoping that the organization will be successful and pay you back with more money than you initially invested. The main benefit is that investments generally provide the opportunity to earn greater interest on the money you invest. Interest is the dividend that is paid when, for example, a stock that you purchased increases in value during the time that you own that stock. The main risk of certain investments is that there is a greater chance of losing some of the money you invested, for example, when a stock that you purchased decreases in value during the time that you own it. You will need to understand the relative benefits and risks associated with savings accounts and investments that you consider. You will also need to decide how much risk you are comfortable with in order to make the best investment decisions to meet your overall goals.

A recent study in which 8,000 teens were surveyed showed that 38 percent reported that they're actively saving money and 22 percent said they are saving more than they did the previous year. Fifty-seven percent of teens said they are saving money for new clothes while 36 percent are socking away cash to buy a car.

References

1. "Saving and Investing: A Roadmap to Your Financial Security through Saving and Investing," Office of Investor Education and Advocacy (OIEA), U.S. Securities and Exchange Commission (SEC), June 2011.

2. "Saving and Investing," The Money Advice Service, n.d.

3. "The Facts on Saving and Investing," Office of Investor Education and Assistance, U.S. Securities and Exchange Commission (SEC), n.d.

Chapter 31

Essential Money Management

You may decide that a checking or savings account is the right product for you. If you do, opening an account at a bank or credit union is quite simple.

Opening an Account at a Bank or Credit Union

First, you may want to get a recommendation from a trusted friend or family member for a bank or credit union. Find out about:

- The fees they charge

- The services they offer, like online bill payment

- The interest they pay for savings accounts

You will usually need between $25 and $100 to open a savings or checking account. You will deposit this money into your account.

> Find out how much you must keep in the account at all times to avoid or reduce fees. This is called the "minimum balance requirement." This may not be the same amount of money you need to open the account.

About This Chapter: Text in this chapter begins with the excerpts from "Checklist for Opening a Bank or Credit Union Account," Consumer Financial Protection Bureau (CFPB), June 7, 2015; Text beginning with the heading "Ways to Pay Your Bills" is excerpted from "Ways to Pay Your Bills," Consumer Financial Protection Bureau (CFPB), June 7, 2015; Text beginning with the heading "Ways to Receive Your Money" is excerpted from "Ways to Receive Your Money," Consumer Financial Protection Bureau (Cfpb), June 7, 2015.

You will also need two forms of identification to open an account. Some banks or credit unions will take one form of identification and a bill with your name and address on it. You will usually be required to present:

- A U.S. or state government-issued identification with your photo on it, such as a driver's license, U.S. Passport, or military identification

- If you do not have a U.S. government-issued form of identification, some banks and credit unions accept foreign passports and Consular IDs, such as the Matricula Consular card.

Additionally, you'll need one of the following:

- Your Social Security card

- A bill with name and address on it

- Your birth certificate

A Matricula Consular is an official Mexican Government identification document. Other countries, such as Guatemala and Argentina, offer similar IDs. Consulates in the United States offer them. If you come from another country and don't have a U.S. or state government issued ID, visit your country's consulate for more information about how to get an ID card, and check with the banks and credit unions about whether they accept it.

ITIN and Interest-Bearing Accounts

Interest on your savings or checking accounts is considered income. If you earn interest, you must pay taxes on it. That's why you must have a Social Security number or an Individual Taxpayer Identification Number (ITIN) to open an account that pays interest.

Checklists for Opening a Checking Account

Use the checklists below to ensure you have what you need to open an account at a bank or credit union.

Checking Account Checklists
Items Needed to Open a Checking Account

- The U.S. or foreign government-issued form of identification with your picture on it. Note that each bank or credit union has its own policy on which foreign IDs it accepts.

- The second form of identification: Your Social Security card, a bill with your name and address on it, or your birth certificate.

- A Social Security number or ITIN; if you do not have one, you may only be able to open a no-interest account.

- Money to open the account

Questions to Ask Your Representative

- Minimum balance required to avoid monthly service fees

- Monthly service fees

- Direct deposit and whether it eliminates the monthly fee

- Per-check or transaction fees

- Fees associated with the use of automated teller machines (ATMs)

- Internet banking access and any costs

- Online bill pay access and any costs

- How to avoid overdraft fees

- Low balance alert notifications

Ways to Pay Your Bills

When you move to a new place, it doesn't take long for bills to start coming. You may pay some bills like rent, utilities, and other payments each month. You may also have one-time bills, like a security deposit when you rent an apartment.

In many cases, you will have one or more options you can choose from to make these payments. The list below helps you understand different bill payment options and their potential advantages and disadvantages. Knowing how they work could help you avoid some fees, including fees from late or missed payments.

Table 31.1. Check

Definition	Benefits	Risks
Checks are forms that you fill out to pay for something from a checking account. You write the amount and the name of the person or company that you wish to pay on the check. The amount comes out of your bank checking account when the person or company who receives the check deposits it or cashes it. You can also get a similar account from a credit union.	• Convenient once you apply for and the account is set up at a bank or credit union. • Can be mailed. • Easy to prove payment if there is a dispute. • Funds are held in the checking account until you write out the check and the check is deposited. • Unlike cash, if a check is lost or stolen or someone forges your signature, you have protection for the money in your account. But, it can be hard to stop a check if the person who receives it deposits it quickly.	• If you pay bills by check without enough money in your account, the bank or company you send the check to may charge you fees. • You have to remember to pay a bill using a check each time it is due (not automated). • Postage costs of mailing the payment. • If you pay bills by automatic debit without enough money in your account, the bank or company you are paying to may charge you fees.
You provide the merchant or service provider (for example, your cell phone provider or utility company) with your checking account information and they take the funds from your account each time the bill is due (for example, every month).	• Convenient, saves time and free. • You may pay a lower interest rate for loans if you make your payments via automatic debit. • Makes it easy to pay for bills that are frequent and consistent. • Reduces chance of being late— once you set it up, it is automatic. • You have the right to end automatic payments. • Easier to prove payment should a dispute arise. • If the amount of the bill changes each month you may get a notice before the transfer is made to pay the bill.	**Warning:** When money is automatically taken from your account, you could accidentally spend more than you have. If you do not have enough money in your account to cover an automatic payment or other charges you've made, you may have to pay costly fees. To stop automatic withdrawals, contact both the merchant and your bank.

Table 31.2. Automatic Or Direct Debit

Definition	Benefits	Risks
You give your bank the merchant or service provider's information, and your bank makes the payment according to the amount and schedule you set up.	• Convenient and saves time. • Makes it easy to pay for bills that are frequent and consistent. • You can choose between making one-time payments each billing cycle or setting up recurring (automatic) payments using your bank or credit union's online web services. • Reduces the chance of being late—once you set it up, it is automatic. • Easier to prove payment should a dispute arise. • Easier to stop an unintended or erroneous payment.	• Takes time to set up and learn. • If you pay bills by online bill payment without enough money in your account, the bank or service provider may charge you fees. • If you have set up recurring payments and the amount changes, you may pay the wrong amount. If you pay less than the full amount of the bill, you may have to pay fees.

Table 31.3. Money Order

Definition	Benefits	Risks
A money order can be used instead of a check. You can buy a money order to pay a business or other party.	• Easy to understand. • Can be mailed. • No personal banking information appears on the money order.	• Maybe inconvenient because you have to buy a money order. • The cost to buy a money order and to mail the payment. • Maybe hard to prove payment unless you have the money order receipt and a receipt for payment. • Funds are difficult or impossible to recover if lost or stolen. • You have to remember to pay the bill each time it's due (not automated).

Table 31.4. Credit Card

Definition	Benefits	Risks
A credit card allows you to borrow money up to an approved credit limit. You will pay interest if you carry a balance, and you can be charged other fees based on the terms of the contract. You can expect to make a minimum monthly payment and you may want to pay more than the minimum to pay it off sooner.	• Can use a credit card to pay bills over the phone or online. • Easy to prove payment should a dispute arise. • Protects you from having to pay for some or all the charges if your card or information is stolen or lost and you report the theft. • Can be set up to automatically pay recurring bills. • Can help build your credit history if you make payments on time and don't get close to your credit limit.	• Costs more than paying for the purchase with cash or a check if you can't pay the credit card balance in full every month. If you carry a balance, you have to pay interest on the balance. • Creates another bill you have to pay. • Creates debt—you are borrowing money to pay for bills and other items.

Table 31.5. Cash

Definition	Benefits	Risks
Cash is money that you have in hand.	• Often no fees associated with paying cash directly to the company if paying the full amount owed. Buying or using a special product such as a money order or prepaid cards may cost money. • When you use cash, you're not incurring debt. • No risk of overdrawing your account.	• Not all bill payments can be made in cash. • Can be inconvenient and costly to travel to the company to pay the bill in person. • Maybe hard to prove payment unless you have a receipt. • Cash is difficult or impossible to recover if lost, stolen or destroyed. • You have to remember to pay the bill each time it's due (not automated).

- Make a list of your bills and their due dates, and put them on a calendar so you can easily see when payments are due.
- Some creditors let you pick the day of the month that your bill is due.
- However, you choose to pay your bills, keep track of your money coming in and going out. It will help you avoid fees.

Ways to Receive Your Money

You can receive your wages in different ways, for example, you can be paid in cash, paper paychecks, direct deposit, or with a payroll card.

Each of these ways to receive money has some potential benefits and risks, especially when it comes to fees, security, and convenience. Knowing how these products work, how much it costs to use them, and when you'll be charged extra fees can help you make the most of your money.

Table 31.6. Cash

Definition	Benefits	Risks
Cash is money that you have in hand. **Tip:** Avoid carrying around or leaving in your home large amounts of cash. If cash is lost or stolen, it is difficult or impossible to get it back.	• Accepted almost everywhere.	• Difficult or impossible to recover if lost or stolen. • Can be tempting to spend cash on hand. • Can be hard to track spending for personal budgeting purposes.

Table 31.7. Paper Paychecks

Definition	Benefits	Risks
Paycheck is a check for your salary or wages made out to you.	• You can deposit into a checking or a savings account. A bank or credit union where you have an account will also cash your paycheck for free. • Safer than carrying cash. If lost or stolen, your employer may cancel and reissue the check if you report it quickly enough.	• If you do not have a bank account, you may have to pay to cash your paychecks. • If you deposit a paycheck in a bank or credit union account, you may not be able to access all the funds immediately

Table 31.8. Direct Deposit: Checking or Savings Account

Definition	Benefits	Risks
Your salary or wages are sent straight to your bank or credit union account electronically without the use of a paper check. May not be offered by all employers. **Tip:** Ask your employer how to arrange for direct deposit. Generally, if you receive your pay through direct deposit, your funds will be available to withdraw at least as soon as if you had deposited a paper check, and often sooner. In many cases, your money is available on your payday. Be aware of ATM fees you may be charged. Generally, you can avoid ATM fees by using your own bank or credit union's ATMs.	• Reduces your risk of loss or theft, compared to carrying cash or getting a check. • The account has consumer protections for funds taken by electronic error or theft. • Funds are usually available to you immediately. • Funds can be accessed via a debit card, ATM card, or personal checks. • Many employers allow you to split your deposit between a checking and savings account. This can help you build savings. • There are no fees to deposit your check. Many banks and credit unions also offer checking and savings accounts with no monthly fees when you set up direct deposit.	• Keeping your money in a bank account requires you to go to an ATM or storefront location to withdraw cash when cash is needed.

Table 31.9. Payroll Cards

Definition	Benefits	Risks
Prepaid debit cards arranged by an employer. Your salary or wages are automatically sent to your payroll card electronically, without the use of a paper check. **Tip:** Your employer can't require you to receive your wages on a payroll card. They have to give you at least one other option (which might include check, cash, or direct deposit to your bank or credit union account).	• Reduces your risk of loss or theft, compared to carrying cash or checks. • The payroll card has consumer protections for funds taken by electronic error or theft.	• Many cards charge fees for inactivity, purchases, ATM use, monthly fees, etc. • Potential overdraft fees if an employee uses a card without enough funds. • You have to go to an ATM or storefront to withdraw cash when cash is needed. • There may also be fees if you don't use ATMs from the bank or credit union that issued the card. • You may not be able to deposit other funds in the account.

Table 31.10. Prepaid Cards

Definition	Benefits	Risks
Your salary or wages are electronically sent to your prepaid card without the use of a paper check.	• Maybe safer and more secure than carrying cash or checks.	• The card does not have the same consumer protections as a checking account or payroll card for funds taken by electronic error or theft. • You might be limited in the types of transactions you can use the card for. For example, you might not be able to use your prepaid card to pay bills. • Many cards charge fees for inactivity, purchases, ATM use, monthly fees, etc. • You have to go to an ATM or storefront to withdraw cash when cash is needed.

Chapter 32

Fine-Tuning Your Money Management

Any time of year, but particularly the start of a new year, is a good time to reflect on how you are managing your finances and to consider whether you would benefit from some changes. Here's a checklist of questions and suggestions that can help you better evaluate and meet your goals.

Saving

What Are My Current Short- and Long-Term Financial Goals?

Write them down. They may include paying off a debt, buying a home or a car, or financing a child's college education. "With goals and target dollar amounts in mind, you may be more motivated to save money and achieve your objectives," said Luke W. Reynolds, Chief of the Federal Deposit Insurance Corporation's (FDIC) Outreach and Program Development Section.

Can I Do Better Making Automatic Transfers into Savings?

"Arranging for your bank or employer to automatically transfer funds into savings or retirement accounts is a great way to build savings, but don't just set it and forget it," said Keith Ernst, Associate Director of the FDIC's Division of Depositor and Consumer Protection in charge of consumer research. "Ask yourself whether you should increase the amount you are automatically saving."

About This Chapter: This chapter includes text excerpted from "Is It Time for Your Financial Checkup?" Federal Deposit Insurance Corporation (FDIC), October 15, 2014.

Do I Have Enough Money in an Emergency Savings Fund?

The idea is to cover major unexpected expenses or a temporary reduction in income without borrowing money. Figure out how much you would need to pay for, say, three to six months of essential expenses (housing, transportation, medical costs, and so on). If you don't have that much money in a savings account, start setting aside what you would need. For anyone struggling to build a "rainy day fund" or reach any major savings target, setting up automatic transfers is a steady way to work toward that goal.

Do My Checking and Savings Account Choices Meet My Needs at a Reasonable Cost?

Start by talking to a representative at your current bank and/or visiting your bank's website. That's because some banks only offer certain deals in their branches but not online, or vice versa. "If you paid checking account overdraft fees recently, look into ways to avoid them, starting with keeping a closer eye on your balance," said Luke W. Reynolds, Chief of the FDIC's Outreach and Program Development Section. "And for money, you don't need in the near future, remember that nondeposit investment products may have the potential for a higher return, but you can also lose some or all of the money you invest." He added that if you have multiple accounts, consider whether consolidating them may save you money and time in monitoring transactions.

Taking Precautions
Am I Adequately Insured?

Having enough life, health, disability, property, and other insurance is essential to protect your finances from a sudden shock. You may find savings on your existing policies by getting updated quotes from your current insurer and comparing them to quotes from at least two other companies.

Am I Prepared Financially in Case of a Fire, Flood, or Other Emergency?

In addition to having your most important possessions insured, ask yourself how your most important documents would be saved from ruin.

Is the Personal Information on My Computer and/or Smartphone Properly Protected?

Use and automatically update anti-virus software and a firewall to secure your computer. Arrange for your computer or phones to regularly download and install any "patches" (system updates) the manufacturers produce to address security weaknesses. For unlocking your computer and mobile devices and for logging into websites and apps, create "strong" IDs and passwords with combinations of upper- and lowercase letters, numbers and symbols that are hard to guess, and then change the passwords regularly. "Try not to use the same password at more than one site," advised Michael Benardo, manager of the FDIC's Financial Crimes Section. "And if you feel a need to keep a written list of passwords, which is not recommended, try instead to use word and number combinations that vary slightly between sites, which may be easier for you to remember."

Am I Taking Precautions with My Personal Information When I Go to Social Networking Sites?

Scammers try to collect even minor details about an individual, such as a pet's name or a high school mascot, in hopes that they can use this information to reset the passwords on a bank or investment account and commit fraud. Social media sites are places where criminals can often find this information.

Am I Keeping the Right Financial Records?

When it comes to paper versions of records like old bank statements, credit card bills, and receipts, consider keeping only those you may need to protect yourself in the event of, say, a tax audit or a dispute with a merchant or manufacturer. Documents you don't need can be discarded, but shred or otherwise securely destroy records that contain personal information. It's also good to keep a list of your financial accounts and personal documents in one secure place, so that a loved one responsible for your affairs could easily find it.

Spending
Do I Have a Good Plan for How I Spend My Money?

Start by listing how much money you take in over a typical four-week period, what expenses you need to pay, and how much goes to savings. Include any large expenses you pay annually or semiannually, such as taxes or insurance premiums. Also pay attention to small expenses, from entertainment to snack food, which can take a toll on your finances. Then jot down ways you can control your spending. Online tools also can help you develop a more comprehensive budget.

Are All the Expenses I'm Paying for Automatically Each Month Really Worth It?

Some expenses you've put on auto-pilot may look small but can add up over the course of a year. Start by reviewing your credit card and checking account statements for expenses that get charged on a recurring basis. Consider whether you still get value from each product or service. Also, find out if you may already be receiving the same benefits elsewhere or if you can negotiate a better deal with the company.

"Examples of spending you might be able to reduce could include memberships, extras on your cable TV subscription, or certain options on a cellphone package," said Reynolds. "And, if you are paying for identity theft or credit protection plans [products that would postpone or make your loan payments if you die or become ill or unemployed] ask yourself whether you get the value you pay for them. Keep in mind that federal law affords you considerable protections in the event of fraudulent activity involving your bank accounts or credit cards."

Borrowing
Am I Reviewing My Credit Reports for Accuracy?

Correcting errors may help you improve your credit history and credit score, which can save you money when you need to borrow money. And reviewing your credit reports can help you detect identity theft or errors that could cause you other hassles, such as higher insurance premiums.

Federal law gives you the right to one free copy of your credit report every 12 months. There are three major nationwide consumer reporting agencies (also called "credit bureaus")—Equifax, Experian and TransUnion—and each one issues its own report. Go to www.AnnualCreditReport. com, or call toll-free 877-322-8228, to order your free credit reports from each agency. There also are "specialty" credit bureaus that, for example, track a person's history of handling a checking account or prepare risk profiles that insurers may use when determining your insurance premium.

Is There More That I Can Do to Cut the Costs of a Mortgage Loan?

For example, if you have an adjustable-rate mortgage with an interest rate about to go up, find out if there are lower rates for which you might qualify. Also inquire about your options for refinancing into a different, better loan. You also can research the pros and cons of making additional payments to principal (to pay off the loan sooner) or even paying off the mortgage outright.

Can I Do More to Reduce the Interest I'm Paying on Other Debts?

Any reduction of outstanding debts, particularly those that charge you the highest interest rate, will bring you savings in interest expenses. For example, look into paying all—or at least more—of your credit card balance.

Am I Truly Benefiting from My Credit Card Rewards Programs?

These features can be beneficial, but you have to know what to do to earn extra cash or keep "points" or miles. A rewards program also may have changed since you last looked at it. Also, don't let the allure of rewards be the only factor in choosing a card. "It's not just cash back or points that can make a card appealing. Features like a low interest rate and minimal or no fees can also be beneficial," said Elizabeth Khalil, a Senior Policy Analyst at the FDIC.

If you're considering closing a credit card account that you've managed well for a long time, instead consider the alternative of keeping the card but not using it. That's because closing the account could adversely affect your credit score, which lenders often use to determine your interest rate. According to Jonathan Miller, Deputy Director for Policy and Research in the FDIC Division of Depositor and Consumer Protection, "If you do keep the account open and continue to use the card occasionally, be careful to keep it in a secure place and periodically monitor the account to make sure a fraudster isn't using it instead."

Your Rights to Financial Privacy: How to Stay Informed

You're probably used to receiving privacy notices from your financial institutions explaining how they handle and share your personal information. Federal law requires that you receive a notification about your privacy rights when you open an account, then at least annually, and again if the institution changes its privacy policy. And, in some cases, these privacy statements are available for review anytime online. Unfortunately, many consumers don't review these disclosures, which describe how your information will be used, whether you can choose to "opt out" or say "no" to some sharing of your personal financial information, and how you can do so.

"The privacy notices include important descriptions of rights you may have to limit information sharing with other parts of the same company as well as with unaffiliated companies," said

Beverly Shuck, Acting Chief of the FDIC's Consumer Response Center. "If you want to control information sharing, you should take these mailings seriously.

The privacy notices also will explain what you can't prevent from being shared. This is likely to include customer information provided to outside firms that market your financial company's own products, handle data processing services or mail out monthly statements to customers. Banks that limit their sharing to these circumstances will provide a privacy notice stating that, as well as the fact that the customers don't have the right to opt out of any data sharing.

In October 2014, the Consumer Financial Protection Bureau (CFPB) adopted a rule that allows financial institutions that do not engage in certain types of information-sharing to post their annual privacy notices online rather than delivering them individually. In these circumstances, consumers also must be able to call a toll-free number to request a paper copy of the privacy disclosure. Contact your financial institution if you have questions or concerns about its privacy policy. If you're not satisfied with the answers, you may wish to contact the institution's primary federal or state regulator.

"Remember that privacy practices differ at various financial institutions," said Ed Nygard, a Senior Consumer Affairs Specialist at the FDIC. "If you are uncomfortable with the way your information will be treated at one institution, you may wish to shop around for a different one." You also have the right to prohibit credit bureaus from providing information about you to lenders and insurers that want to send you unsolicited offers of credit or insurance.

(Source: "Your Rights to Financial Privacy: How to Stay Informed," Federal Deposit Insurance Corporation (FDIC).)

Chapter 33

Financial Empowerment

Borrowing Money
Higher Education Loans

If you need to borrow for higher education, do your homework and have a repayment plan. College or graduate degrees can provide career options and higher income, but they also can be expensive. If you need to borrow for school, carefully consider your options, keep the loan amount as low as possible, and have a clear repayment plan. Here are strategies to keep in mind.

Obtaining a Student Loan

- **First look into your eligibility for grants and scholarships.** Many students qualify for some aid, so start by filling out the *Free Application for Federal Student Aid (FAFSA®)* on the U.S. Department of Education's (ED) website at www.studentaid.gov.

- **Know how much you need to borrow and that you can make the monthly payments.** Your anticipated costs (tuition, textbooks, housing, food, transportation) minus your education savings, family contributions, income from work-study or a job, scholarships and/or grants will help determine how much you may need to borrow. Again, your goal should be to limit the amount you borrow, even if you are approved for a larger loan, because the more you borrow, the more money you will owe.

Also consider the minimum you will owe each month to pay off your loans, including interest, after you graduate and how it compares to your projected earnings. To help you project your future salary in the lines of work you're considering, look at the U.S. Department of

About This Chapter: This chapter includes text excerpted from "For Young Adults and Teens: Quick Tips for Managing Your Money," Federal Deposit Insurance Corporation (FDIC), 2012.

Labor's (DOL) statistics on wages in more than 800 occupations (www.bls.gov/oes). Your monthly repayment amount also will generally depend on your interest rate and the term of your loan, which can vary from 10 years to more than 20 years.

"Even though most student loans won't require you to begin monthly payments until after you graduate—generally six to nine months later—a student loan is a serious commitment," said Matt Homer, a Federal Deposit Insurance Corporation (FDIC) policy analyst. He noted, for example, that many adults who borrowed more than they could afford to repay have faced serious debt problems for many years following their graduation. Unlike some other loans, federal and private student loans generally cannot be discharged through bankruptcy. Borrowers who fail to pay their student loans could be referred to debt collection agencies, experience a drop in their credit score (which will make credit more expensive and perhaps make it harder to find a job), and have a portion of their wages withheld.

If you need help deciding how much to borrow, consider speaking with a specialist at your school (perhaps a school counselor at your high school or admission or financial aid officer at your college). A college budget calculator also can be helpful, and you can use one from the U.S. Department of Education (ED) by going to www.studentloans.gov/myDirectLoan/financialAwarenessCounseling.action?execution=e1s1 and clicking on "Manage Your Spending."

- **Consider federal loans first if you need to borrow.** Experts say that, in general, federal loans are better than private student loans, and that you should only consider private loans if you've reached your borrowing limit with federal loans. Why? The interest rates on federal loans are fixed, meaning they won't change over time. But the interest rates on private loans, which are often significantly higher, could be either fixed or variable (they can fluctuate). Federal student loans also offer more flexible repayment plans and options to postpone your loan payments if you are having financial problems.

When You Are in School

Set up direct deposit for your student aid money. Although some schools or financial institutions may encourage you to select a certain debit card or prepaid card for receiving part of your student loan or other aid (the part left after your school has subtracted tuition and fees), carefully weigh all of your options. School-preferred products may come with high fees and inconvenient ATM locations. Remember that you can always deposit federal loan proceeds anywhere you choose.

Keep track of the total amount you have borrowed and consider reducing it, if possible. For example, if your loan accrues interest while you're in school, you may be able to make interest payments while still in school, and this can reduce the amount owed later on. You could also repay some of the principal (the amount borrowed) before the repayment period officially begins.

Paying Off Your Loan

- **Select your repayment plan.** Federal loans offer a variety of repayment options and you can generally change to a different repayment plan at any time. For example, one type of loan starts off with low payment amounts that increase over time. Another is the "Pay as You Earn" program that the ED will soon make available, in which your monthly payment amount will be 10 percent of your "discretionary" income (defined by the Department's regulations but generally what you have left over after paying key expenses). In addition, it may be possible to have any remaining balance forgiven after 20 years of payments. In contrast, private loans generally require fixed monthly payments over a period of time.

  With federal loans, you also may qualify for special loan forgiveness benefits if you pursue certain careers in public service. Remember, though, that the longer you take to repay any loan, the more you pay in interest (although in some cases you may receive a tax benefit for the interest you pay).

- **Make your loan payments on time.** "Student loans are typically reported to credit bureaus, so paying on time can help build a good credit history, and paying late can harm your credit history," said Elizabeth Khalil, a Senior Policy Analyst in the FDIC's Division of Depositor and Consumer Protection (DCP). To help you stay on schedule, consider having your payments automatically deducted from your bank account or arranging for e-mail or text message reminders.

  Also, make sure your loan servicer—the company that collects your payments and administers your loan—has your current contact information so you don't miss important correspondence, such as a change in a due date.

- **Consider making extra payments to pay off your loan faster.** If you are able to, start by paying the student loans with the highest interest rates. If you have more than one student loan with a particular servicer, make it clear that you want to apply any extra payments to reduce the balance of the higher-rate loans.

- **Look into refinancing opportunities.** You may be able to obtain a lower interest rate and even consolidate multiple loans of the same type into one loan. However, be aware that if you consolidate or refinance a federal loan into a private loan, you may lose important benefits associated with the federal loan (such as loan forgiveness for entering public service). In some cases, even consolidating one type of federal loan into a different kind of federal loan can result in loss benefits.

- **Contact your loan servicer immediately if you're having difficulty repaying.** Repaying student loans can be challenging, especially during tough economic times. "Remember that if you have a federal student loan that you're having trouble paying, you have options that could help. Private loan borrowers may be able to get some assistance as well," noted Jonathan Miller, Deputy Director In the FDIC's DCP.

Auto Loans: How to Get a Good Deal

Many young people look forward to getting their own car but overlooks what they may need to do to comfortably afford it, especially if they'll be borrowing money. Here are strategies to consider well before you go to the dealership.

- **Start saving early.** "The more money you put down, the less you have to borrow—and that means the less money you'll pay in interest on a loan, if you need to borrow at all," said Phyllis Pratt, an FDIC community affairs specialist.

- **Decide how much you can afford to spend each month on a car.** In addition to car payments, consider how much you'll need for insurance, taxes, registration fees, routine maintenance, and unexpected repairs. Online calculators can help you figure out what you can afford.

- **Remember that there are alternatives to buying a car.** Lease payments may sometimes appear lower than loan payments, but at the end of the lease you will not own the car and you may have to pay more money for excess mileage or body repairs. If you need a car only once in a while, consider using a service that rents cars for periods as short as an hour.

- **Shop for a loan at your bank as well as several other lenders.** Compare the offers based on the annual percentage rate (APR) you're quoted by each lender. The APR reflects the total cost of the loan, including interest and certain fees, as a yearly rate. Then consider getting "prequalified" by the lender offering the best deal. That's not the same as a loan approval, but it will expedite the process once you find a car you like. Before you start shopping for a loan, review your credit report to correct wrong information, which can help you qualify for a lower interest rate In addition, a dealer's special financing (such as zero-percent interest) may not be the best value if it means foregoing an extra discount on the car. In that situation, you may come out ahead if you borrow from a financial institution, even at a higher interest rate, and save on the purchase price. Also, don't purchase a more expensive car than you feel you can comfortably afford, even if you qualify for a larger loan.

- **Whether you are buying or leasing, negotiate with the dealer based on the total cost of the car, not the monthly payment.** Why? "By extending the length of the loan, a dealer can offer a more expensive vehicle with the same monthly loan payment you were quoted for a less expensive car, but you will pay more in interest costs," said Luke W. Reynolds, Acting Associate Director of the FDIC's Division of DCP.

Build a Good Credit Record: It's Important for Loan and Job Applications

As you become responsible for paying your own debts—for credit card purchases, rent, car or student loans, and other obligations—you are building a credit history. In general, the better your credit history and the resulting credit score (a number summarizing your credit record prepared by companies called credit bureaus), the better your chances of getting a loan with a good interest rate. A strong credit score also can help when you apply for a job, an insurance policy, or an apartment. How can you build and maintain a good credit history?

- **Pay your loans, bills, and other debts on time.** This will show you are responsible with your finances.

- **If you have a credit card, try to charge only what you can afford to pay off immediately or very soon.** If you can't pay your credit card bill in full, try to pay more than the minimum balance due so that you can minimize the interest payments. Also be aware that your credit score will likely fall if you owe a significant amount on your credit card compared to the card's credit limit. Applying for multiple cards also can lower your credit score.

- **Review your credit reports for errors.** Correcting wrong information in your credit history may improve your credit report and score. To obtain a free copy of your credit report from each of the three major credit bureaus, visit www.annualcreditreport.com or call toll-free 877-322-8228. If you are unable to resolve a dispute with a credit bureau over wrong information in your file, you can submit a complaint online at www.consumerfinance.gov/complaint.

Saving Money
Simple Ways to Rev Up Your Savings

You can meet your goals with automated deposits and investments. Many people starting out in their careers find themselves burdened with lots of debt (perhaps from student loans, credit cards, and car loans) and very little savings for future needs. But there are simple strategies for gradually building small savings or investments into large sums, even during your school years, and often with the help of automated services that make it easy. Here are key examples.

- **Save for specific goals.** You should have a savings plan for large future expenses that you anticipate—perhaps education costs, a home or car purchase, starting a small business, or preparing for retirement (even though that may be many years away). And, young adults just starting to be responsible for their own expenses should build up an "emergency" fund that would cover at least six months of living expenses to help get through a difficult time, such as a job loss, major car repairs, or unexpected medical expenses not covered by insurance.

- **Commit to saving money regularly.** This is important for everyone, but especially if you are supporting yourself financially. "Even if you don't make a big salary or have a steady source of income, the combination of consistently adding to savings and the compounding of interest can bring dramatic results over time," said Luke W. Reynolds, Acting Associate Director of the FDIC Division of Depositor and Consumer Protection (DCP).

Aim to save a minimum of 10 percent of any money you earn or otherwise receive. Putting aside a designated amount is known as "paying yourself first," because you are saving before you're tempted to spend.

- **Put your savings on autopilot.** Make saving money quick and easy by having your employer direct-deposit part of your paycheck into a federally insured savings account. Your employer and your financial institution may be able to set this up for you. If you don't yet have a steady job, you can still set up regular transfers into a savings account.

- **Make use of tax-advantaged retirement accounts and matching funds.** Look into all your retirement savings options at work, which may come with matching contributions from your employer. "Chances are your retirement savings will hardly reduce your take-home pay because of what you'll save in income taxes, and the sooner you start in your career, the more you can take advantage of compound growth," Reynolds said.

If you've contributed the maximum at work or if your employer doesn't have a retirement savings program, consider establishing your own individual retirement account (IRA) with a financial institution or investment firm and make regular transfers into it. Remember that you can set up an automatic transfer from a checking account into savings or investments for retirement or any purpose.

- **Decide where to keep the money intended for certain purposes.** For example:

  - Consider keeping emergency savings in a separate federally insured savings account instead of a checking account so that you can better resist the urge to raid the funds for everyday expenses. Be sure to develop a plan to replenish any withdrawals from your emergency fund.

  - For large purchases you hope to make years from now, consider certificates of deposit and U.S. savings bonds, which generally earn more interest than a basic savings account because you agree to keep the funds untouched for a minimum period of time.

  - For other long-term savings, including retirement savings, young adults may want to consider supplementing their insured deposits with low-fee, diversified mutual funds (a professionally managed mix of stocks, bonds, and so on) or similar investments that are not deposits and are not insured against loss by the FDIC. With nondeposit investments, you assume the risk of loss for the opportunity to have a higher rate of return over many years.

  - For future college expenses, look into 529 plans, which provide an easy way to save for college expenses and may offer tax benefits.

  - For healthcare, find out whether you are eligible for a "health savings account," a tax-advantaged way for people enrolled in high-deductible health insurance plans to save for medical expenses.

  - Think about ways to cut your expenses and add more to savings. For your financial services, research lower-cost checking accounts at your bank and some competitors. And if you are paying interest on credit cards fee for spending more money than you have available in your checking account, develop a plan to stop. More broadly, look at your monthly expenses for everything from food to phones and think about ways to save.

Your Bank Accounts
For Everyday Banking: Choosing the Best Account for You

Whether you're a 20-something just starting a career or you're still in school, a checking or other transaction account will be essential to making payments and managing your income and budget. These tips can save you time and money.

- Look for a bank account that offers the services you want and low fees. Contact multiple institutions and determine which accounts are considered best for young adults or students. Look at services you are most likely to use and the related fees, including any penalties if the balance drops below a minimum. One service you should expect to use is direct deposit of your paycheck. "With direct deposit, you don't have to worry about getting to the bank to deposit the funds because it will be done automatically for you," said Nancy Tillman, an FDIC Consumer Affairs Specialist. Direct deposits will arrive at your bank fast, and it may save you money on your bank account.

For guidance on what an affordable transaction account or savings account for a young consumer could look like, aspects of some low-cost accounts suggested by the FDIC may be helpful.

- Consider a low-cost banking account before settling for a prepaid card. Reloadable prepaid cards that can be used at merchants and ATMs are sometimes marketed as alternatives to traditional bank transaction accounts. While prepaid cards may be useful in some situations, they generally cannot match a well-managed, properly selected, low-cost, insured deposit account when it comes to federally-guaranteed consumer protections, the safety of deposit insurance, monthly charges and transaction fees, and the flexibility to save money and conduct a wide range of everyday banking transactions.

"Before you get a prepaid card, you should carefully read the cardholder agreement, which should be readily available on the card's website, to make sure you understand the terms and fee schedule," suggested Susan Welsh, FDIC Consumer Affairs Specialist.

Also be aware that the funds you place on a prepaid card may or may not be protected by FDIC insurance if the bank that holds the money (for you and other customers) were to fail. If you have questions, call the FDIC toll-free at 877-ASK-FDIC (877-275-3342).

- Debit cards provide a great service, but understand the pros, cons, and costs. Debit cards, which deduct funds directly from your checking or savings account, offer a convenient way to pay for purchases and to access cash at stores or ATMs. "Debit cards can help you stay within budget as long as you don't overdraw your account. Then you are spending money, not money you have borrowed," said Alberto Navarrete, an FDIC Consumer Affairs Specialist.

But debit cards can be costly if you're not careful. For example, expect fees if you drop below a minimum required account balance or you use the card at another bank's ATM. Also, you should report a lost or stolen card immediately to minimize your liability for unauthorized transactions. Welsh added that consumers who lose a debit card they rely on for all their transactions can ask for speedy delivery of a replacement card.

- Avoid overdraft costs. Ask your bank if it can link your checking account to your savings account and automatically transfer money between accounts if you empty your checking account. The transfer fee will probably be considerably less than a regular overdraft fee. Also review your account frequently, if not daily, online. "Many banks have online banking services that send text or e-mail alerts when your balance reaches below a certain dollar amount that you can set," advised Joni Creamean, Chief of the FDIC Consumer Response Center.

Also, think carefully before you "opt-in" (agree) to an overdraft program, which can be costly. In general, opting in means that if you swipe your debit card and don't have enough funds to cover the transaction, the bank will charge you an overdraft fee to let the transaction go through. That could result in a $5 purchase, such as a cup of coffee and a muffin, costing you an extra $35.

"Remember that your decision whether or not to opt in only applies to everyday debit card transactions. The bank could still charge a significant fee if, for instance, you write a check when you don't have enough money in your account to cover it," cautioned Jonathan Miller, Deputy Director in the FDIC's Division of Depositor and Consumer Protection.

You can also avoid unexpected fees by keeping a close watch on your balance before spending money from your checking account.

Finally, if you are billed an overdraft fee that you believe is incorrect, contact your bank immediately. If the institution will not refund the fee, contact its federal regulator for assistance. "If you are not sure who regulates the bank, you may always file your complaint with the FDIC and we will make sure it gets forwarded to the correct agency for investigation," said Creamean. You can submit your complaint online at www2.fdic.gov/StarsMail/index.asp.

- If you're a college student receiving financial aid, do your homework before choosing an account and a debit card. "Before your financial aid is disbursed, checkout the program offered through your school. You need to understand the terms of that product before you are committed to use it to access your financial aid," Tillmon said. "If you have an existing bank account with a debit card that you will be using on campus, you may be better off having the financial aid money deposited there."

Where to Begin: Saving and Managing Your Own Money

As a teen, you start taking more responsibility for handling money and choosing how you want to save or use it. Here are a few ideas to help make your decisions easier ... and better.

- Consider a part-time or summer job. A job can provide you with additional money as well as new skills and connections to people who may be helpful after you graduate.

  If you are filling out a job application for a company with a local office, experts say it's generally safe to provide information such as your date of birth and Social Security number (which may be needed for a background check). If you are applying in person, hand the application to the manager (not just any employee), and if you are applying online, make sure you are using the company's legitimate website.

  "But be very suspicious of online job applications for part-time, work-from-home jobs offered by unfamiliar companies without a local office," warned Michael Bernardo, Manager of the FDIC's and Financial Crimes Section. "They may only want to commit identity theft, not hire you."

- Open a savings account and put money in it for specific goals. "Some goals will be for the next few weeks or months, while others are for several years away, such as college," said Irma Matias, an FDIC Community Affairs Specialist. Get in the habit of putting at least 10 percent of any gifts or earnings in a savings account right away. Saving a certain percentage of your income before you're tempted to spend it is what financial advisors call "paying yourself first."

  Also, think about where you can add to savings by cutting back on spending. "Money you spend today is money you won't have for future wants or needs," added Matias.

- If you're ready for a checking account, choose one carefully. Many banks offer accounts geared to teens or other students that require less money to open and charge lower fees than their other accounts. "Even if the account appears to be attractive, think about how you're going to use it—for example, if you mostly want to bank online or with your smartphone—and look into how much that account is likely to cost monthly," said Luke W. Reynolds, acting associate director of the FDIC's Division of Depositor and

Consumer Protection. "The shop around and compare this account to what is offered by several other institutions."

When you open an account that comes with a debit card, you will decide how you want the bank to handle an everyday debit card transaction for more than what you have in the account. If you "opt in" (agree) to a bank overdraft program, it will cover these transactions but will charge you fee of as much as $40 each time. "One overdraft can easily lead to another and become very costly," Reynolds explained. "If you don't opt in, your transactions will be declined, but you won't have to face these penalty fees."

You may also be able to arrange with your bank to automatically transfer money from a savings account to cover the purchase. You'll probably pay a fee, but it will likely be much less than an overdraft fee.

- If you're thinking about using a prepaid card instead of a bank account, understand the potential drawbacks. Prepaid cards often do not offer you the same federal consumer protections as credit or debit cards if, for example, the prepaid card is lost or stolen and used by someone else. And, while prepaid cards may advertise no monthly fee, they may charge for making withdrawals, adding money to the card or checking the balance. "It's hard for a prepaid card to beat a well-selected, well-managed checking account for every-day transactions and allowing easy transfers into a savings account," Reynolds concluded.

- Once you have a bank account, keep a close eye on it. Watch your balance the best way you can. For example, keep receipts and record expenses so you don't spend more money than you have in your account and run the risk of overdraft costs.

- Take precautions against identity theft. Even if you don't have a credit card, you can be targeted by a criminal wanting to use your name to get money or buy goods. So, be very suspicious of requests for your name, Social Security Number, passwords, or bank or credit card information.

"Don't fall for an e-mail, call, or text message asking you for financial information," Benardo cautioned. "Never give out any personal information unless you have contacted the company first and you are sure it is legitimate."

- Understand that borrowing money comes with costs and responsibilities. When you borrow money, you generally will repay the money monthly and pay interest. Always compare offers to borrow money based on the annual percentage rate (APR). The lower the APR, the less you will pay in interest. And, the longer you take to repay a debt, the more you will pay in interest. If you miss loan payments, you can expect to pay fees and have a hard time borrowing money at affordable rates for some time into the future.

Chapter 34

Taxes and Tax Benefits for Education

What Tax Benefits Are Available to Help Pay for Your Education?

There are various tax benefits available to help pay for college or graduate school:

Credits

An education credit helps by reducing the amount of tax owed on your tax return. If the credit reduces your tax to less than zero, you may get a refund.

There are two education credits available:

1. **American opportunity tax credit (AOTC).** This is a credit for qualified education expenses paid for an eligible student for the first four years of higher education. You can get a maximum annual credit of $2,500 per eligible student.

2. **Lifetime learning credit (LLC).** This credit is for qualified tuition and related expenses paid for eligible students enrolled in an eligible educational institution. It can help pay for undergraduate, graduate, and professional degree courses, including courses to acquire or improve job skills. There is no limit on the number of years you can claim the credit.

About This Chapter: This chapter includes text excerpted from "Tax Credits and Deductions," USA.gov, October 29, 2018.

What Is the Lifetime Learning Credit Worth?

The amount of the credit is 20 percent of the first $10,000 of qualified education expenses or a maximum of $2,000 per return. The LLC is not refundable. So, you can use the credit to pay any tax you owe but you won't receive any of the credit back as a refund.

(Source: "Lifetime Learning Credit," Internal Revenue Service (IRS).)

Deductions

A deduction reduces the amount of your income that is subject to tax, which means it reduces the amount of tax you may have to pay.

There are several types of deductions for education:

- Tuition and fees deduction
- Student loan interest deduction
- Qualified student loan
- Qualified education expenses

Savings Plans

Some savings plans allow the accumulated earnings to grow tax-free until money is taken out or allow the distribution to be tax-free. Other savings plans allow both tax-free accumulated earnings and distribution.

There are two types of savings plans available:

1. 529 Plans. States, colleges, and groups of colleges sponsor these qualified tuition programs—authorized under section 529 of the Internal Revenue Code (IRC)—to either prepay or contribute to an account for paying a student's qualified higher education expenses.

2. Coverdell education savings account (ESA). This account was created as an incentive to help parents and students save for education expenses. Unlike a 529 plan, a Coverdell ESA can be used to pay a student's eligible K-12 expenses as well as postsecondary expenses.

Scholarships and Fellowships

A scholarship generally represents an amount paid for the benefit of a student at an educational institution to aid in the pursuit of studies. The student may be either an undergraduate or a graduate. A fellowship is generally an amount paid for the benefit of an individual to aid in the pursuit of study or research.

Whether the scholarship or fellowship is tax-free or taxable depends on the expense paid with the scholarship or fellowship amount and whether you are a degree candidate.

Exclusions from Income

You may exclude certain educational assistance benefits from your income. That means that you won't have to pay any tax on them. However, it also means that you can't use any of the tax-free education expenses as the basis for any other deduction or credit including the lifetime learning credit.

Help with Tax Benefits for Education

The IRS has information and services covering education tax credits, deductions, and savings plans:

Use the Interactive Tax Assistant (www.irs.gov/help/ita) to help determine if you're eligible for educational credits or deductions including the American opportunity credit, the lifetime learning credit, and the tuition and fees deduction.

Chapter 35

Working with Financial Professionals

Personal Financial Advisors

Personal financial advisors are professionals who help people decide how to manage their money in the best way. There are many different types of financial advisors, including investment managers, stockbrokers, bankers, insurance brokers, tax preparers, tax attorneys, and so on.

Some common services provided by personal financial advisors include:

- Helping people identify and prioritize financial goals

- Helping people learn about various types of financial services that can help them meet their goals

- Advising people on the best approaches to meeting their financial goals

- Answering questions about various investment choices

- Offering seminars or workshops to educate people about financial matters

- Researching investment opportunities

- Identifying potential investment risks

- Recommending specific investments

- Selecting investments on behalf of their clients

- Managing investment portfolios on behalf of their clients

About This Chapter: "Working with Financial Professionals," © 2017 Omnigraphics.

- Monitoring client accounts to identify opportunities for investment performance improvement

---

Consider This

An investment adviser is a "fiduciary" to the advisory clients. This means that they have a fundamental obligation to act in the best interests of their clients and to provide investment advice in their clients' best interests. They owe their clients a duty of undivided loyalty and utmost good faith. They should not engage in any activity in conflict with the interest of any client, and they should take steps reasonably necessary to fulfill their obligations. They must employ reasonable care to avoid misleading clients and must provide full and fair disclosure of all material facts to their clients and prospective clients. Generally, facts are "material" if a reasonable investor would consider them to be important. They must eliminate, or at least disclose, all conflicts of interest that might incline the client—consciously or unconsciously—to render advice that is not disinterested. If they do not avoid a conflict of interest that could impact the impartiality of their advice, they must make full and frank disclosure of the conflict. They cannot use their clients' assets for their own benefit or the benefit of other clients, at least without client consent. Departure from this fiduciary standard may constitute "fraud" upon the clients.

Financial Planners

Financial planners are financial advisors who specialize in certain areas of money management. Some financial planners focus on one or two areas of finance, and others offer a wider range of services depending on the needs of their clients. Because financial planning services cover so many different aspects of money management, it is important to identify the kind of financial planning services you need before hiring a financial planner.

Examples of common financial planning services include:

- Comprehensive planning that covers all aspects of finance and money management, such as saving and investments for both short-term and long-term goals like retirement, tax planning, estate management, insurance needs, and so on

- Planning specific aspects of financial planning, such as saving for retirement or a large future expense like paying for college tuition or buying a home

- Preparation of detailed financial plans and strategies for meeting lifetime financial goals

- Recommending specific investment products such as stocks, bonds, mutual funds, or securities

- Management of existing investment portfolios

Before hiring a financial planner, make sure you understand exactly which services they can provide, how much these services will cost, and how the financial planner is paid. Financial planners sometimes charge a flat fee for certain services and an hourly rate for other services. Some are paid a commission on each financial transaction they perform for you or collect a percentage of the total money you have invested through their services. Depending on the financial planning services you need, these fees can add up quickly.

Once you have an idea of the financial planning services you need, it is equally important to learn about the professional background of any financial planner you are thinking of hiring. Find out where they went to school, what kind of professional experience they have, how long they have been working in financial planning, and if they have any professional credentials such certification as a Certified Financial Professional or Chartered Financial Analyst. These credentials can be verified by the organization that issued the certification, usually via the organization's website or by phoning the organization's main office. You can learn more about professional credentials for financial planners on the Financial Industry Regulatory Authority's website (www.finra.org/investors/professional-designations). Depending on the size of their business, professional financial planners who provide advice on investments must be registered with the U.S. Securities and Exchange Commission (SEC) and/or the securities regulatory authority in their state. Information about verifying state registrations is provided by the North American Securities Administrations Association at www.nasaa.org/about-us/contact-us/contact-your-regulator. The SEC provides assistance with verifying registrations online at www.sec.gov/investor/brokers.htm.

How to Pick a Financial Professional

Because financial advisors and financial planners offer such a wide variety of services and collect their fees in different ways, it is important to evaluate more than one potential financial service provider before choosing one. Depending on your individual financial goals and money management needs, you may be able to get financial advice from a banker or a Certified Public Accountant (CPA). Or you may benefit more from working with an investment advisor, broker, or a financial planner who provides comprehensive money-management services.

In any case, it is critical to evaluate the professional reputation of any potential financial advisor that you are considering. Before you hire any financial professional, ask for a copy of their registration Form ADV. Carefully read both parts of this form. The first part of Form ADV provides information about the advisor's business and whether they have had any complaints or other problems with clients or regulatory authorities. The second part of the form explains the advisor's services, fees, and commonly used money-management strategies. You can also get a copy of an advisor's Form ADV from the SEC's Investment Advisor Public Disclosure website (https://adviserinfo.sec.gov).

Money-management strategies are one of the most important life decisions that most people will ever make. When choosing a financial professional, remember that you are looking for someone trustworthy to provide advice and services related to your hard-earned dollars. Make sure that you ask questions and that you completely understand the answers. Some questions to consider asking during your initial meeting with a potential advisor include:

- What is the advisor's educational background, including school, training, and other experience?

- Does the advisor hold any professional certifications or credentials? If so, which ones?

- How long has the advisor been in business?

- How many clients does the advisor have?

- Can the advisor provide any client references?

- What is the advisor's investment philosophy? Do they prefer risky short-term gains or long-term growth investments?

- What is the advisor's fee structure and how do they collect their fees? For example, by stockbroker commission, flat rate, hourly rate, percentage, etc.

- What is the total cost of doing business with the advisor? Are there up-front costs, ongoing costs, or both?

Quick Tip

If a financial advisor collects fees or charges based on a percentage of the money they will manage for you, be sure to ask for the equivalent of that percentage in dollars. This will help you better understand the amount of money you will be charged for their services.

References

1. "Fast Answers: Financial Planners," U.S. Securities and Exchange Commission (SEC), August 20, 2008.

2. "Personal Financial Advisors," U.S. Bureau of Labor Statistics (BLS), U.S. Department of Labor (DOL), Occupational Outlook Handbook, 2016-17 Ed.

3. "Investment Advisors: What You Need to Know Before Choosing One," U.S. Securities and Exchange Commission (SEC), August 7, 2012.

4. "How to Pick a Financial Professional," U.S. Securities and Exchange Commission (SEC), February 1, 2007.

Part Four
Living on Your Own

Chapter 36

Renting an Apartment or House

What Is Renting?

You rent an apartment or house when you pay the owner money every month to live there. The money you pay is called "rent."

What Is a Lease?

A lease is a contract that you sign to rent an apartment or house. A lease says:

- How much rent you will pay and when you will pay
- How long you will rent the apartment or house
- What happens if you do not pay on time
- The rules you must follow
- Other costs you have to pay

A lease will say whether the costs of utilities are included in your rent. If utilities like heating and water are included, your landlord pays those bills. If utilities are not included in your rent, you must pay those bills yourself. Utilities can be expensive.

How Long Does a Lease Last?

Leases might last a year or longer. If you do not plan to stay in the apartment or house for a year, look for a short-term or month-to-month lease.

About This Chapter: This chapter includes text excerpted from "Renting an Apartment or House," Consumer. gov, Federal Trade Commission (FTC), December 17, 2014.

Moving out before the end date in your lease it is called "breaking your lease." You might have to pay extra money. Read your lease to see how much money you will have to pay if you move out before the lease period ends.

What Is a Security Deposit?

A security deposit is extra money you pay one time when you rent an apartment or house. A security deposit is not part of the rent you pay every month. The security deposit might be the same amount of money as one month of rent.

The owner of the apartment or house is called a landlord. The landlord keeps your security deposit until you move out. Most of the time, you get your deposit back when you move out. But you might not get your security deposit back if you:

- Damage the apartment or house

- Leave before your lease period ends

Most states have laws about how much money a landlord can charge you for a security deposit. Most states also have laws saying when a landlord may keep your security deposit. For example, you might get part or all of your security deposit back if a landlord finds someone else to take your place when you leave.

What Do I Need to Rent an Apartment or House?

When you apply to rent an apartment or house, you will need:

- Information about your employer and your income

- Identification, like a driver's license, for a credit or background check

- Information about where you lived before

You also might need money to pay for:

- Your first month's rent

- A security deposit

- Extra rent if you have bad credit

- Utility deposits for electricity, heat, water, or other utilities

- A credit check or a background check

Do I Need Good Credit to Rent an Apartment?

Landlords usually check your credit to see if you pay your bills when they are due. Some landlords might not rent to you or might ask you to pay more rent in advance if your credit history isn't good, or if you don't pay your bills when they are due.

What Does My Landlord Have to Do?

There are laws that landlords must follow. For example, almost every state or city has a law that a landlord must provide hot water and make certain repairs. Agencies and organizations in your state can tell you what the laws are where you live.

What If I Cannot Afford an Apartment or House?

Some apartment owners offer lower rents to people who do not have a lot of money. To apply for a subsidized apartment, contact the management office at an apartment building. You can search for subsidized apartments at the U.S. Department of Housing and Urban Development (HUD) website (hud.gov).

Public housing and housing choice vouchers, also called Section 8 vouchers, are available to:

- Families without a lot of money

- Older people

- People with disabilities

There might be a long waiting list for these programs. Talk to your local Public Housing Agency.

HUD Rental Assistance Programs

- Privately owned subsidized housing – HUD helps apartment owners offer reduced rents to low-income tenants.
- Public Housing – affordable apartments for low-income families, the elderly and persons with disabilities.
- Housing Choice Voucher Program (Section 8) – find your own place and use the voucher to pay for all or part of the rent.

(Source: "Rental Assistance," U.S. Department of Housing and Urban Development (HUD).)

What If a Landlord Wants Me to Wire My Security Deposit?

Do not wire the money. Dishonest people lie about being landlords and pretend they have apartments or houses to rent. These dishonest people try to trick others into sending them money. Wiring money is the same as sending cash. After you send the money, you cannot get it back.

Should I "Rent-To-Own"?

Renting-to-own means your landlord agrees that you can buy the apartment or house later. The landlord agrees to the price, then you pay the landlord extra money every month.

But after you have paid a lot of money, you might find out your credit is not good enough to buy the house. Dishonest landlords also might make it too hard for you to buy the house. You might lose all of the money you have paid. Renting-to-own is not a good idea.

Instead of renting-to-own, consider saving your extra money. Then use your savings to buy a house later.

Lease Obligations

A lease is a contract that you sign to rent an apartment or house. When you sign a lease, you agree to follow the rules written in the lease.

The landlord who owns the apartment or house also must do what the lease says and must obey the law. If you think your landlord is breaking the law or breaking the lease, there are people who can help you.

Read the lease before you sign it. When you sign a lease, you agree to do what it says. You might not understand everything in the lease. Find someone you trust to help you read the lease.

The landlord might make promises. Check that they are written in the lease. After you sign the lease, get a copy and keep it.

What If a Landlord Won't Rent to Me Because of My Credit or a Background Check?

If you have bad credit, you need to show the landlord that you can pay your rent. The landlord might ask you to:

- Show pay stubs or bank statements

- Pay more money in your security deposit

- Pay your first and last month's rent before you move in

Landlords must tell you if they will not rent to you because of information in your credit report or background report. Landlords also must tell you if they will charge you more money because of information in your report. This is called an adverse action notice.

The adverse action notice must tell you how to contact the organization that created the credit report or background report. That agency must give you a free copy of your credit report if you ask for it within 60 days. You have a right to question wrong information in your report with that agency and try to correct it.

What Should I Do If I Think My Landlord Is Breaking the Law?

You might think a landlord is breaking the law or that a landlord is breaking your lease. Here is what you can do:

- Find out about your rights as a tenant. Go to hud.gov and click on Find Rental Assistance.

- Find low-cost or free legal help. Go to lsc.gov and look up your state under Find Legal Aid.

- Talk to your local housing counseling agency. Go to hud.gov and click on Find Rental Assistance.

A landlord cannot change the rental deal or refuse to rent to you because of your race, color, national origin, religion, gender, disability, or family status. That would be discrimination.

You can file a complaint about housing discrimination with the U.S. Department of Housing and Urban Development (HUD). Call 1-800-669-9777 or go to hud.gov/fairhousing.

Chapter 37

Renter's Guide: Ten Tips for Tenants

Tip 1: Bring your paperwork.

The best way to win over a prospective landlord is to be prepared. To get a competitive edge over other applicants, bring the following when you meet the landlord: a completed rental application; written references from landlords, employers, and colleagues; and a current copy of your credit report.

To get a copy of your credit report

You can order your credit report by mail, phone, or online at www.annualcreditreport.com or directly from the websites of the three major national credit bureaus:

- Equifax

- Experian

- TransUnion

Tip 2: Review the lease.

Carefully review all of the conditions of the tenancy before you sign on the dotted line. Your lease or rental agreement may contain a provision that you find unacceptable for example, restrictions on guests, pets, design alterations, or running a home business. Ask questions; make sure you fully understand the lease.

About This Chapter: This chapter includes text excerpted from "Renter's Guide: Ten Tips for Tenants," U.S. Department of Housing and Urban Development (HUD), September 23, 2017.

Tip 3: Get everything in writing.

To avoid disputes or misunderstandings with your landlord, get everything in writing. Keep copies of any correspondence and follow up an oral agreement with a letter, setting out your understandings. For example, if you ask your landlord to make repairs, put your request in writing and keep a copy for yourself. If the landlord agrees orally, send a letter confirming this.

Tip 4: Protect your privacy rights.

Next to disputes over rent or security deposits, one of the most common and emotion-filled misunderstandings arises over the tension between a landlord's right to enter a rental unit and a tenant's right to be left alone. If you understand your privacy rights, for example, the amount of notice your landlord must provide before entering, it will be easier to protect them.

Tip 5: Demand repairs.

Know your rights to live in a habitable rental unit—and don't give them up. The vast majority of landlords are required to offer their tenants livable premises, including adequate weatherproofing; heat, water, and electricity; and clean, sanitary, and structurally safe premises. If your rental unit is not kept in good repair, you have a number of options, ranging from withholding a portion of the rent, to paying for repairs and deducting the cost from your rent, to calling the building inspector (who may order the landlord to make repairs), to moving out without liability for your future rent.

Tip 6: Talk to your landlord.

Keep communication open with your landlord. If there's a problem – for example, if the landlord is slow to make repairs – talk it over to see if the issue can be resolved short of a nasty legal battle.

Keep in mind, your first line of contact is the on-site manager. If an issue cannot be resolved at this level, it should be directed to the on-site manager's supervisor. Legal action should be the last course of action.

Tip 7: Purchase renter's insurance.

Your landlord's insurance policy will not cover your losses due to theft or damage. Renters' insurance also covers you if you're sued by someone who claims to have been injured in your rental due to your carelessness. Renters' insurance typically costs $350 a year for a $50,000 policy that covers loss due to theft or damage caused by other people or natural disasters; if you don't need that much coverage, there are cheaper policies.

Tip 8: Protect your security deposit.

To protect yourself and avoid any misunderstandings, make sure your lease or rental agreement is clear on the use and refund of security deposits, including allowable deductions. When you move in, do a walk-through with the landlord to record existing damage to the premises on a move-in statement or checklist.

Tip 9: Protect your safety.

Learn whether your building and neighborhood are safe, and what you can expect your landlord to do about it if they aren't. Get copies of any state or local laws that require safety devices such as deadbolts and window locks, check out the property's vulnerability to intrusion by a criminal, and learn whether criminal incidents have already occurred on the property or nearby. If a crime is highly likely, your landlord may be obligated to take some steps to protect you.

Tip 10: Deal with an eviction properly.

Know when to fight an eviction notice—and when to move. If you feel the landlord is clearly in the wrong (for example, you haven't received proper notice, the premises are uninhabitable), you may want to fight the eviction. But unless you have the law and provable facts on your side, fighting an eviction notice can be shortsighted. If you lose an eviction lawsuit, you may end up hundreds (even thousands) of dollars in debt, which will damage your credit rating and your ability to easily rent from future landlords.

Federal Law Protects Renters during Foreclosure

A new federal law helps protect the rights of tenants in properties facing foreclosure, say experts at the Office of the Comptroller of the Currency (OCC). The Protecting Tenants at Foreclosure Act of 2009 establishes national standards to provide renters sufficient notice when foreclosure happens.

The new national standard provides uniform protection to renters who are vulnerable to sudden eviction.

The new law states:

- In all cases, renters will get at least a 90-day notice prior to eviction.
- Renters can stay until their lease runs out except when the new owner will occupy the home as a primary residence, when renters have no lease or when renters have only a month-to-month lease. Even for these three exceptions, the 90-day notice still applies.

(Source: "Know Your Rights," U.S. Department of Treasury (USDT).)

Chapter 38

Sharing Rooms and Related Agreements

Some teens are able to line up friends or relatives to share a living space with them when they move out on their own. For others, finding a roommate who is compatible with their lifestyle can feel like an overwhelming experience. But online forums and shifts in landlord preferences make it far easier today for young adults to identify suitable roommates while decreasing the likelihood that a teen may have to vouch for a stranger's financial responsibility.

Today's landlords, particularly in urban areas, prefer to enter into separate lease agreements with each tenant who shares common housing. For instance, if a landlord wants to rent a three-bedroom apartment to you and two roommates, then that landlord will likely search for suitable roommates for you and then enter into separate lease agreements with each of them. This arrangement shifts the onus of finding roommates to the landlord and appears to work well for both parties. since the landlord is assured of a steady cash flow and the tenants benefit from living in a fancier place at a lower overall cost.

Roommates in these kinds of living arrangements benefit from agreeing to and abiding by a roommate agreement.

A Residential Sublease Agreement

Another way that a tenant may legally share common living space with a roommate or continue to lease property while traveling is to enter into a residential sublease agreement. A residential sublease agreement is a legally binding contract made between a tenant and a subtenant. In this arrangement, a tenant who has signed a lease agrees to sublet a part of the property under lease, such as a room, or the entire space under lease to another tenant for a determined amount of time. Residential sublease agreements require the consent of the landlord.

About This Chapter: "Sharing Rooms and Related Agreements," © 2019 Omnigraphics.

A legally binding sublease agreement allows the main tenant, to share an already-rented property with a subtenant or to vacate the premises temporarily—to study abroad for a semester, for example—and then return to living at the same property once such travels are complete. In the first scenario, the main tenant agrees to share common rented space with a subtenant. The main tenant and subtenant enter into a sublease agreement that outlines each tenant's responsibility for shared expenses associated with the property. A roommate agreement is recommended in such cases. In cases in which the main tenant vacates a rented space for a predetermined amount of time, the subtenant agrees to make payments associated with the subleased property—the rent and utility payments, for example—and to fulfill other tenant obligations during the main tenant's absence.

While the sublease agreement is legally binding, it does not eliminate or replace the master lease entered into between the landlord and the original tenant. The main tenant remains liable for any and all lease violations, even though the subtenant is responsible for the contravention of the terms of the original lease agreement. The conditions for terminating occupation/tenancy of the roommate are usually described in the residential sublease agreement.

What Is a Roommate Agreement?

A roommate contract, also known as a housemate agreement, is a document that outlines the rights and responsibilities of two or more tenants occupying a shared space. A roommate agreement should always be a documented—or written, rather than verbal—agreement. This agreement outlines the mutual expectations and obligations of roommates and establishes how tenants will handle conflicts when they arise.

A roommate agreement:

- Underscores the importance of maintaining the safety, cleanliness, comfort, and well-being of the shared property

- Outlines the agreed-upon expectations that roommates have regarding how they will respect each other's property, privacy, rest schedules, well-being, and common safety

- Sets expectations for how roommates will share and maintain common and private spaces

- Establishes specific expectations regarding the cleanliness, safety, maintenance, and well-being of the shared dwelling

- Establishes and ensures shared accountability

Roommates who enter into a roommate agreement together agree to:

- Abide by the agreements outlined in the document

- Behave in accordance with the established ground rules when conflicts arise

- Comply with specific reasonable requests regarding the agreements whenever possible

The roommate agreement outlines how each person living in the shared dwelling will participate in and take responsibility for ensuring that common and private areas are cleaned and maintained in a manner that ensures the ongoing enjoyment and safety of each person living in the space. Abiding by these agreements increases the likelihood that your rental deposit will be returned in full when your lease expires and helps to ensure the comfort, safety, and well-being of everyone. Detailed roommate agreements also reduce the likelihood of conflicts.

Some important legal items to include in the roommate agreement include:

- Landlord and roommate information

- Terms of the agreement

- How rent payments will be split among roommates

- How utilities (heat, electricity, and Internet, etc.) payments will be split among roommates

- If a security deposit is required, how this payment will be shared

- Rules for terminating a roommate's tenancy

All important quality-of-life and maintenance considerations should be outlined and agreed upon in the roommate agreement.

The following sections outline common agreements that are made in roommate agreements. Typically, roommates either rotate household weekly and monthly chores or agree beforehand on which specific chores each will complete within a certain time period.

Global Agreements

- Turn off lights when you leave a room.

- Pick up after yourself.

- Wipe up your spills when they happen and throw away the paper towels.

- Return all shoes, clothing, remote controls, gaming equipment, personal items, etc. to their designated locations when you leave a room.

- Recycle, compost, or throw away any used items such as cups or cans, etc. that you bring into space when you leave the room.

- Let roommates know in advance before you bring a visitor into your shared space.

- Wipe your feet (or, in some cases, remove your shoes) before entering the dwelling.

- Establish and maintain a monthly process for checking fire extinguishers and smoke-detector batteries.

- Follow established agreements regarding the use of designated spaces.

Pet Expectations

Landlords typically require a deposit for each pet that dwells at a rental property. This deposit is the sole responsibility of the owner of the pet. The roommate agreement further outlines acceptable behavior, clean-up, and care of the pet. Examples include:

- Pet owner is responsible for walking, feeding, watering, brushing, cleaning up after, and otherwise caring for the pet.

- Pet owner is responsible for cleaning up pet waste in the yard at the time that it occurs.

- Pet owner is responsible for quieting noisy pet promptly.

- Pet owner is solely responsible for reimbursing the landlord for any and all damage the pet makes to the landlord's property.

- Pet owner is solely responsible for reimbursing roommates for any and all damage the pet makes to the personal property of a roommate.

Visitor Expectations

Roommate agreements typically outline when and how a roommate may bring a visitor into the shared dwelling and for how long. Two common examples are:

- Roommate agrees to notify roommates before entering the dwelling with a visitor.

- Roommate agrees that a visitor may not stay overnight for more than one consecutive night without establishing a special household agreement beforehand.

Food Expectations

How roommates manage the sharing and storage of food is the source of many conflicts; therefore, it is important to establish how your household will manage food. Many roommates designate specific refrigerator and cabinet shelves for each roommate and agree to not eat or otherwise use another roommate's personal food items. Other households decide to share common meals that they purchase communally and rotate cooking responsibilities. It is important that roommates of all shared households establish in the roommate agreement how they will handle food expectations.

The following section provides examples of common expectations shared by roommates in regards to the cleanliness, safety, and maintenance of their shared dwelling.

Cleanliness Expectations
Kitchen Agreement

Roommates will ensure that the kitchen remains clean and tidy each day by committing to the following with each use:

- Wipe up your spills when they happen and throw away the paper towels. This includes spills

- On the stovetop, countertops, shelves, or floor, etc.

- Around the trash can or coffeepot, etc.

- In the microwave, oven, refrigerator, or cabinets, etc.

- Recycle, compost, throw away or return all packaging, containers, cans, bags, boxes, seals, food scraps, empty bottles or jars, or other items that you open or use.

- Empty the trash can and replace the trash bag if you fill up the bag.

- Wash or place into the dishwasher every dish, cup, glass, pot, pan, knife, cutting board, or other kitchen items that you use before you leave the kitchen or as soon as you finish eating your meal.

- Clean items in the dishwasher if you fill the dishwasher up.

- Return clean dishwasher contents to their designated locations if the dishwasher contains clean items and you need to add dirty ones.

- Return all dish drain contents to their proper place if the dish drain contains dry items and you need to add newly washed ones.

- Empty the food screen in your sink if you leave food in it while cleaning up after yourself.

- Run the in-sink food disposer if you discarded any food into it.

- Wipe, clean, and return all kitchen items that you use (cutting boards, oil, oven mitts, whisks, blenders, mixers, food processors, juicers, woks, rice pots, crockpots, corkscrews, herbs, spices, and so on) to their cabinets or other designated locations when you finish using them.

- Wipe the backsplash and stove clean, including knobs and handles—and, if needed, the hood and nearby appliances—each time you cook or spill on it and throw away the paper towels.

- Wipe up spills in the oven if you make them and throw away the paper towels.

- Remove tinfoil from the oven each time you place it there (leaving tinfoil in an oven can short out the oven's heating element).

- Wipe the tabletop clean each time you use it and put away all items (such as napkins, placemats, special sauces or spices, etc.) that you placed on it.

- Put away or store all leftovers, labeling and dating the storage container.

- Replace a kitchen towel that you soiled with a clean towel and place the soiled towel in the dirty laundry area.

- Replace the paper towel roll if you empty it and throw away the empty roll.

- Replace the butter in the butter dish with a new stick of butter if you use the last of it.

- Refill the sugar in the sugar bowl with more sugar if you use the last of it.

- Refill the salt or pepper grinders or shakers if you use the last of them.

- Throw out or recycle containers that you empty and make a note to replace these items if your household maintains a household shopping list.

- Sweep or mop the floor and throw away any waste you spilled on it, returning the mop or broom to their designated storage location when you are done.

Weekly Kitchen Chores

- Clean and disinfect sink, faucets and the space behind them.

- Sweep or vacuum the floor,

- Dust surfaces.

- Check refrigerator for expired items and discard or compost them (washing all expired food item containers).

Bathroom Agreement

Roommates will ensure that bathrooms remain clean and tidy each day by committing to the following with each use:

- Hang up towels and washcloths.

- Wipe up spills and throw away paper towel.

- Remove and discard hair from shower drain after each use.

- Wrap and safely dispose of all sanitary products.

- Wipe mirror clean if you leave toothpaste on it.

- Wrap counter clean if you spill makeup, powder, or anything else on it.

- Replace toilet paper when the roll is empty and discard the empty roll.

- Return all personal items (razors, toothbrushes, hairbrushes, makeup, and so) to their designated locations.

- Empty the trash if you fill it up and replace the bag.

Weekly Bathroom Chores

- Clean and disinfect the toilet bowl, seat, and base.

- Clean and disinfect the sink, faucets, and base.

- Sweep or vacuum the floor as needed.

- Dust surfaces (such as the back of the toilet).

- Clean the mirror with a glass cleaner as needed.

- Wash and dry shower mat and towels.

- Wash shower curtain as needed to avoid mold.

Laundry Area Agreement

Roommates will ensure that the laundry area remains clean and tidy each day by committing to the following with each use:

- Wipe up your spills and throw away paper towels.

- Move washed clothes from the washer to the dryer promptly or hang them on the clothesline so that everyone has access to the facilities.

- Fold and remove dried clothes promptly so that everyone has access to the facilities.
- Return supplies to their cabinet, shelf, or other designated location.
- Throw away or recycle dryer clothes and containers that you empty, and add the item to the household shopping list.
- Remove and throw away lint that accumulated in the dryer during your drying cycle.

Weekly Laundry Chores

- Sweep, vacuum, wipe, and dust area.

Monthly Laundry Chores

- Clean dryer lint trap and hose.
- Check washer hoses for wear and replace soft or cracked ones promptly (or ask the landlord or maintenance staff to do this).

Common Living Area Agreement

Roommates will ensure that the common living areas of their dwelling remain clean and tidy each day by committing to the following with each use:

- Wipe up all spills when they happen and throw away the paper towels.
- Return any moved furniture or electronic accessories to their designated locations.
- Remove all personal items from the room when you leave it.

Weekly Common Area Chores

- Sweep, vacuum, and dust area.

Bedroom Agreement

Roommates will ensure that the dwelling remains clean and tidy and free of rodents and pests by committing to the following:

- Wipe up all crumbs and spills when they occur and throw away the paper towels.
- Remove all dirty dishes, silverware, and cups from your room as soon as you are done using them (see kitchen agreements)—or, better yet, confine your eating to the kitchen or dining areas of the dwelling.
- Never leave open food in your room. If you are saving a food item to eat later, then place it in a sealed storage container that cannot be accessed by rodents or pests.

- Recycle or remove all bottles or cans as soon as you are done with them.

- Do not store flammable products or explosives in your room.

- Leave sufficient walking space on your floor in case you have to make a fast escape in an emergency.

- Replace chirping batteries in your smoke alarm as soon as you become aware of the chirping.

Weekly Bedroom Chores

- Sweep, vacuum, and dust area.

- Put away clothes.

Landscape Expectations

In some cases, a landlord expects rental tenants to maintain the yard and landscaping of the property. In these cases, the roommate agreement should state how each person living in the shared dwelling will participate in and take responsibility for ensuring that common outdoor areas are clean and maintained in a manner that ensures the ongoing enjoyment and safety of each person leasing space in the dwelling. Many roommates rotate yard-maintenance responsibilities. It is important for roommates of all shared households establish how you will handle landscaping responsibilities in yo roommate agreement.

Even if your landlord maintains the dwelling's landscaping, it is important that the roommate agreement outlines how common outdoor space will be used. Some sample agreements include:

- Wipe up any spills on the deck or patio when they occur and throw away the paper towels.

- Clean up after yourself (for example, no drink cans left by the fire pit or on the patio table).

- If you move the outdoor furniture, return it to its designated location before going indoors.

- If you leave a wet blanket, pet carrier, bathing suit, towel, surfboard, or other items outside to dry, return it to its proper location as soon as it dries.

- If you hang clothes on the laundry line, remove the clothes as soon as they are dry so that others can use the line.

- If you use a tool from the storage closet or garage, return the tool as soon as you finish using it. Do not leave it outside to rust.

- Wipe and brush clean the outdoor grill after each use.

- Place the cover back on the outdoor grill as soon as the grill is cool enough for you do so.

As mentioned earlier, abiding by these agreements will also increase the likelihood that your full rental deposit will be returned to you when your lease expires.

Living together can become difficult when values and habits differ, and conflicts sometimes occur even between people who have known each other for some time. Roommate agreements that contain agreements such as the ones cited above set the ground rules for living together in harmony and establish the importance of acceptable behaviors and actions. These important factors ensure the quiet and respectful enjoyment of each person who shares the space. And, when the need arises for negotiation, all roommates have already agreed to negotiate in good faith in an effort to resolve the conflict, whether it is perceived or real.

Is a Roommate Agreement Legally Binding?

While a lease agreement is a legal document, the same is not the case with roommate agreements, which are essentially agreements made between cotenants in an effort to maintain a peaceful coexistence. A roommate agreement primarily averts misunderstandings and disputes on a number of contentious issues, such as the division of labor regarding household chores, allocation of parking spaces, pets or visitors on the premises, or use of common areas. The most important part of the agreement, however, is the manner in which the individual financial obligations of the tenants toward rent, utility payments, and other expenses are defined. Once the roommate agreement has been vetted and approved by all parties, it should be printed and signed by all tenants, each of whom should retain a copy for reference.

References

1. "Supporting People in Developing their Roommate Agreements," North Carolina Department of Health and Human Services (NCDHHS), October 30, 2015.

2. "Landlord and Tenant," State of Colorado, September 2, 2009.

Chapter 39

Landlord Requirements

You're about to rent an apartment. You've saved for your security deposit and lined up a moving truck. But have you checked your credit report? Landlords may, so you should too. If a landlord does a background check, here are some things to know about your rights.

Landlords can check your credit, criminal history, and even your rental history. They may ask your permission, but they're not required to. So, if you know you'll be looking for a new place to live—or if you're about to renew your lease–then here are a few things you can do:

- Go to annualcreditreport.com to check your credit. That way, you can fix any errors before a landlord sees them.

- Give the landlord your correct full name—first, middle, and last—and date of birth. This helps make sure the landlord gets information on the right person.

- If you have a criminal history or previous housing court actions, gather any paperwork showing how the action was resolved in case you need to fix errors.

Some landlords might say not to apply if you have a criminal record. That could be discrimination. If that happens to you or if you think that a landlord illegally discriminated against you for another reason, such as your race or gender, contact the U.S. Department of Housing and Urban Development (HUD).

About This Chapter: Text in this chapter begins with excerpts from "Renting an Apartment? Be Prepared for a Background Check," Federal Trade Commission (FTC), November 28, 2016; Text under the heading "What Is a Consumer Report?" is excerpted from "Using Consumer Reports: What Landlords Need to Know," Federal Trade Commission (FTC), October 19, 2016.

What if a landlord refuses to rent to you or charges you more because of something in a background check? Then you have rights:

- The landlord must give you notice of the action—orally, in writing, or electronically.

- The notice must give you contact information for the company that supplied the report.

- The notice must tell you about your rights to correct inaccurate information and to get a free copy of the report if you ask for it within 60 days of the landlord's decision.

You should obtain your free report, fix any errors, and have the company that supplied the report gives the corrected report to the landlord. Tell the landlord about the mistake, too.

If you think a landlord or property manager violated your rights—or anyone else's—when using a background check, report it to the Federal Trade Commission (FTC).

What Is a Consumer Report?

A consumer report may contain information about a person's credit characteristics, rental history, or criminal history. Consumer reports are prepared by a consumer reporting agency—a business that assembles such reports for other businesses—and are covered by the Fair Credit Reporting Act (FCRA).

Examples of these reports include:

- A credit report from a credit bureau, such as Trans Union, Experian, and Equifax, or an affiliate company;

- A report from a tenant screening service that describes the applicant's rental history based on reports from previous landlords or housing court records;

- A report from a tenant screening service that describes the applicant's rental history, and includes a credit report the service got from a credit bureau;

- A report from a reference checking service that contacts previous landlords or other parties listed on the rental application on behalf of the rental property owner; and

- A report from a background check company about an applicant or tenant's criminal history.

Before Obtaining a Consumer Report

A consumer report requires a permissible purpose. Landlords may obtain consumer reports on applicants and tenants who apply to rent housing or renew a lease. They also need to obtain written permission from applicants or tenants to show that they have a permissible purpose. They must certify to the company from which they are getting the consumer report that they will only use the report for housing purposes.

What Is an Adverse Action?

An adverse action is any action by a landlord that is unfavorable to the interests of a rental applicant or tenant. Examples of common adverse actions by landlords include:

- Denying the application;
- Requiring a cosigner on the lease;
- Requiring a deposit that would not be required for another applicant;
- Requiring a larger deposit that might be required for another applicant; and
- Raising the rent to a higher amount than for another applicant.

After a Landlord Takes an Adverse Action

If a landlord rejects an applicant, increases the rent or deposit, requires a cosigner, or takes any other adverse action based partly or completely on information in a consumer report, the landlord must give the applicant or tenant a notice of that fact—orally, in writing, or electronically.

An adverse action notice tells people about their rights to see information being reported about them and to correct inaccurate information. The notice must include:

- The name, address, and phone number of the consumer reporting company that supplied the report;
- A statement that the company that supplied the report did not make the decision to take the unfavorable action and can't give specific reasons for it; and
- A notice of the person's right to dispute the accuracy or completeness of any information the consumer reporting company furnished, and to get a free report from the company if the person asks for it within 60 days.

The adverse action notice is required even if the information in the consumer report wasn't the primary reason for the decision. Even if the information in the report played only a small part in the overall decision, the applicant or tenant must be notified.

While oral adverse action notices are allowed, written notices provide proof of FCRA compliance.

Chapter 40

Landlord–Tenant Responsibilities

Landlord Responsibilities

The responsibilities of a landlord are listed below:

A. Security Deposits and Other Prepayments

A landlord can take a security deposit from a tenant at the beginning of a new rental term but it cannot exceed the limit set by the state housing laws. The deposit must be returned within twenty days after the tenant gives proper notice, moves out, returns the key, and provides a forwarding address. When returning the deposit, the landlord must send the tenant an itemized notice listing any legal deductions withheld from the money being returned. Such deductions can only be for unpaid rent (not future rent that might be legally owed), and physical damages other than ordinary wear and tear. If the landlord fails to comply with the law concerning the return of a security deposit, the court may require a damage payment to the tenant of twice the amount illegally withheld, plus attorney fees. When a rental property is sold, security money should be transferred to the new owner, since it is this individual who will be held legally responsible for the return of funds when the tenant moves.

B. Disclosure

At or before the time a tenant moves into a new unit, the landlord must provide the name, address, and phone number of the person owning or legally responsible for managing the

About This Chapter: This chapter includes text excerpted from "Landlord–Tenant Handbook," Office of Housing and Community Development (OHCD), 2007.

rental premises and to whom legal notices and court orders should be sent. This information must be kept current or the person failing to do so automatically becomes responsible for receiving/sending all notices and demands. In such a case, this person would also be responsible for all other landlord obligations and agreements to the tenant as well.

C. Delivering Possession

At the beginning of a rental term, the landlord must make the dwelling unit available to the tenant as per the rental agreement (if a rent payment has been made). If a former tenant, or occupant in that tenant's household, has not vacated the unit but been given legal notice to do so, it is the landlord's responsibility to bring a court action to gain possession.

D. Maintaining Premises

Landlords must comply with state building-code requirements concerning all new construction, additions, or repairs that are done or are needed. It is also extremely important that rental units be kept in a continually fit and habitable condition. When a unit is initially rented and during any period of occupancy, state law requires that a unit meet the housing standards of the state Housing Maintenance and Occupancy Code, as well as local related ordinances. If a unit is substandard and repairs are not made in a prompt and satisfactory manner, there are certain options available to the tenant under the Residential Landlord and Tenant Act as well as under the aforementioned housing code laws.

The landlord is responsible for maintaining all common areas both inside and outside the dwelling unless the rental agreement specifies otherwise. It is also the landlord's responsibility to make sure all electrical, plumbing, sanitary, heating, and other facilities (and appliances provided as part of the rental agreement) are kept in operable condition and meet housing code standards. The landlord must provide rubbish containers (or other storage facilities) for occupants if there are four or more rental units in the dwelling. She or he is also obligated to provide hot and cold running water at all times, except when heat or hot water are generated by an installation controlled solely by the tenant and supplied directly by a public utility connection.

Generally, minor repairs of a structural nature are the responsibility of the landlord (if needed as a result of normal wear and tear) as well as all major repairs. As will be mentioned elsewhere, certain minor repairs, as well as cleanliness, and repairs needed as a result of the tenant's (or guest's) negligence or purposeful destruction are usually the tenant's responsibility. There can be a written agreement made between a landlord and a tenant which allows the tenant to do specified repairs, maintenance, alterations, and remodeling, but such an agreement must be made in good faith, in writing, signed by both parties, and supported by adequate compensation. The agreement cannot be made so the landlord can avoid his or her responsibility under an applicable building and housing codes, nor does it in any way diminish or affect the landlord's obligation to other tenants on the premises.

E. Duty to Notify Tenant of Violation

Within 30 days of getting a housing-code violation notice from the state or municipality, a landlord must send copies to affected tenants, unless violations have been corrected to the satisfaction of the housing-code inspector. By law, a landlord must inform a prospective tenant of any outstanding housing-code violations which exist in the building where the rental is going to be.

F. Limitation of Liability

An owner will be relieved of legal responsibility for a rental unit as of the date it is sold if proper written notice has been given to the tenants. This notice must include the name, address, and telephone number of the person or persons purchasing the property. Likewise, a manager is relieved of liability upon termination of employment if tenants have been informed of the effective date and have been told who will be assuming responsibility at that time. If applicable, an owner must also include in the notice that housing-code violations have been eliminated or that the buyer or lessee has been provided with copies of all outstanding violations and that the local housing-code enforcement office has been notified of the sale and name of the buyer or lessee.

Tenant Responsibilities

The responsibilities of a tenant are listed below:

A. Maintaining Premises

A tenant must comply with required State and local health and safety code standards. The rental unit and shared interior/exterior areas must be kept clean and safe from hazards. The garbage, rubbish, and other wastes must be removed from the unit (as necessary) and disposed of in a proper manner. The plumbing fixtures and facilities must be kept in a clean and satisfactory condition. All electrical, plumbing, sanitary, heating, and other facilities and appliances on the premises must be used in a reasonable manner. There must be no deliberate or negligent destruction, defacing, impairment or removal of anything that is attached to or otherwise part of the premises. Also, the tenant is responsible for the conduct of family members and visitors in regard to the previously mentioned situations.

The tenant should: avoid causing noisy or unruly disturbances which may bother other people; bring regular maintenance and major repair situations to the landlord's attention on an "as needed" basis, and notify the landlord promptly of any conditions that may cause deterioration of the premises.

B. Rules and Regulations

The tenant has a legal obligation to abide by lawful rules and regulations concerning the use and occupancy of the premises if properly informed of them at the time the initial rental agreement was made, or upon proper notice thereafter. After entering into a rental agreement, substantial changes in rules or regulations that will have a material effect on the rental cannot be made unless agreed to in writing by the tenant. Rules and regulations must promote the convenience, safety, and welfare of all tenants; preservation of the property from damage or abuse; and a fair distribution of services and facilities among tenants.

C. Access

A landlord must give a minimum two-day verbal or written notice when needing to enter a tenant's rental unit. The entry should be during reasonable hours and only for such legitimate business reasons as inspections, repairs, alterations, improvements, supplying necessary services, or showing the unit to potential buyers or renters. Only under extreme circumstances, emergencies, or as provided for under Residential Landlord and Tenant Acts can the landlord enter without notice or a court order. The right of entry must not be abused or used to harass the tenant. If such actions take place, or the landlord enters without notice (note aforementioned exceptions), the tenant may go to the local district court to seek injunctive relief to prevent reoccurrences or terminate the rental agreement. If a request for access has been properly made, the tenant must allow reasonable entry or negotiate an alternative time. If the tenant refuses lawful access, the landlord can seek an injunction to compel access or terminate the rental agreement. Actual damages incurred plus court costs and attorney's fees may be sought if either party has to take court action over the aforementioned access problems.

D. Other Obligations

Unless otherwise agreed, the tenant must use the rental unit only as a place to live. The tenant may be required (if stipulated in the rental agreement) to notify the landlord of any intended absence from the unit which exceeds ten days; notification (in such a case) is to be given no later than the first day of the extended absence.

Chapter 41

Cosigning Requirements for Young Renters

Most laws across the country set the legal age for signing a lease agreement at eighteen. But turning eighteen may not be enough. You may need to be emancipated before you are legally considered an adult. Some exceptions under which you can be under the age of eighteen and still enter into a legal contract (such as a rental lease) include serving in the military or being married. Some states also bestow adult status if you have a child or have been emancipated through a court. For court approval, you may be required to prove that you have your own income, barring welfare payments and that you are capable of making appropriate decisions without the assistance of parents or legal guardians.

What Is Cosigning?

If you are of legal age, then you can enter into a lease agreement with your landlord with or without parental consent. In some states, minors may also be allowed to enter into a lease agreement, but the landlord may insist on a cosigner/guarantor before leasing to you. A cosigner commits to legally guarantee another person's lease, and most states hold the cosigner "jointly and severally" liable to the same extent as the tenant. This is because a minor is not legally bound by such contracts and, as such, cannot be held accountable in court for failing to honor the contract. This puts the landlord in a risky position, as the minor can renege on the contract and leave the landlord with little recourse. A cosigner guarantees that the tenant minor or major will honor the contract. In the event of the tenant failing to do so, the cosigner is legally bound to fulfill the contractual obligations between the tenant and landlord.

About This Chapter: "Cosigning Requirements for Young Renters," © 2019 Omnigraphics.

Why Do You Need a Cosigner?

Although federal law protects most people from housing discrimination, landlords safeguard their interests by setting strict limits on the income requirements of prospective tenants. They do this by running a check on the credit history, pay stubs, and bank statements of their prospective tenants. This becomes a deterrent for young people who are looking to lease, as their credit history is often nonexistent or slim at best. To make matters worse, their credit scores may be low from overspending and accruing a few late payments while they were learning how to handle their first credit cards. Also, most of them are probably employed on a part-time basis and earn entry-level pay—which does little to increase their creditworthiness.

Identifying a Cosigner

- **A credit-worthy family member or friend.** Parents would be the most logical choice when it comes to cosigning your lease. A close relative, mentor, or friend with credit-worthiness would equally fit the bill.

- **A credit-worthy roommate.** A high-income, credit-worthy roommate could be the cosigner for the entire lease, including your half of it. Or you could avoid the cosigner requirement altogether if your roommate elects to sublet a room or even the entire space to you. This agreement would be subject to the discretion of the landlord and the existing laws in the state.

- **Apartment cosigner service.** A cosigning company stands guarantee for you and undertakes with the landlord to honor your rental-payment obligations in the event of a default. This allows you to rent your own apartment despite falling short of the rental industry's expectations in terms of rental history or credit history. In return for their guarantee, you will be required to pay a service fee, which could typically add anywhere from 7 to 15 percent of your monthly rent to your monthly expenses. This fee is either a flat payment in full, as in the case of high-risk applicants, or is spread out over the term of the lease as monthly payments. Some companies also charge an upfront application fee, that is sometimes refundable, for running your credit and background checks and processing your papers.

If You Are a Cosigner

As a cosigner, you would be legally bound to the contract and liable to pay any outstanding debt on behalf of the tenant. This would include rent, utility bills, and any expenses incurred for damages beyond reasonable wear and tear. An important point to keep in mind when cosigning for a relative or friend is the presence of other tenants or roommates. As a cosigner, you would be obliged to honor the lease obligations of all the tenants. So, if the tenant you want to stand guarantee for leaves the contract midway, you may find yourself in a precarious position—and especially so if you are not certain about the creditworthiness of the remaining renters. One possible workaround is to have a roommate agreement in place before deciding to become a cosigner.

What Should I Do before I Rent an Apartment or House?

- Read the lease before you sign it. When you sign a lease, you agree to do what it says. You might not understand everything in the lease. Find someone you trust to help you read the lease.

- The landlord might make promises. Check that they are written in the lease. After you sign the lease, get a copy and keep it.

(Source: "Renting an Apartment or House," Federal Trade Commission (FTC).)

References

1. "Landlord and Tenant Guidelines," Idaho Department of Health and Welfare (IDHW), 2011.

2. "Colorado Renters Guide," State of Colorado, 2010.

Chapter 42

Managing Renters' Insurance

A renters' insurance protects your home and personal property against damage or loss and insures you in case someone gets hurt while on your property. Renters' insurance, or tenant insurance, offers renters' coverage similar to homeowners insurance. If you are a renter, do not assume your landlord carries insurance on your personal belongings; you may wish to purchase a separate policy.

What Can Renters' Insurance Cover?

Renters' insurance may pay claims for:

- Damage to your home, garage, and other outbuildings

- Loss of furniture and other personal property due to damage or theft, both at home and away

- Additional living expenses if you rent temporary quarters while your home is being repaired

Renters' insurance may also:

- Include liability for bodily injury and property damage that you cause to others through negligence

- Include liability for accidents happening in and around your home, as well as away from home, for which you are responsible

About This Chapter: Text in this chapter begins with excerpts from "Yes, Renters Can Buy Flood Insurance," U.S. Department of Homeland Security (DHS), May 4, 2018; Text under the heading "How to Apply for Flood Insurance" is excerpted from "Property Insurance," USA.gov, August 13, 2018.

- Pay for injuries occurring in and around your home to anyone other than you or your family

- Provide limited coverage for money, gold, jewelry, and stamp and coin collections

- Cover personal property in storage

Ask about the special coverage you might need. You may have to pay extra for computers, cameras, jewelry, art, antiques, musical instruments, stamp collections, etc.

Flood and earthquake damage are not covered by a standard homeowners policy. The cost of a separate earthquake policy will depend on the likelihood of earthquakes in your area.

For help in deciding how much insurance coverage to buy, contact your state insurance regulator.

Flood Insurance

Flood insurance isn't just for homeowners and businesses. If you are a renter, you can buy a policy from the National Flood Insurance Program (NFIP) to cover contents up to $100,000.

The difference between an NFIP renters' policy and a traditional renters' insurance policy is that the NFIP policy covers your personal property and contents during a flood event. The cost of the policy is based on several factors, including the flood risk of the building in which you live.

If you are a renter in low-to-moderate risk areas, you may be eligible for a Preferred Risk Policy. These policy premiums are the lowest premiums available through NFIP. Nearly 26 percent of all NFIP flood claims occur in the low-to-moderate risk areas.

If you live in an area that has a high risk of floods, a standard rated policy is the only option for you.

Renters' flood insurance premiums are calculated based on factors such as:

- Year of building construction

- Building occupancy

- Number of floors

- The location of your contents

- The flood risk (i.e., flood zone)

- The location of the lowest floor in relation to the elevation requirement on the flood map (in newer buildings only)

- The deductible you choose and the amount of coverage

How to Apply for Flood Insurance

- Find out if your community participates in the program. You can only purchase a flood insurance policy if you're a renter, homeowner, or business owner, and your property is located in an NFIP participating community.

- Contact an insurance agent in your area. You can only buy flood insurance through an insurance agent; you cannot buy it directly from the federal government. If your local insurance agent is unfamiliar with the NFIP, you can find an agent serving your area by calling the NFIP Help Center at 1-800-427-4661.

Do I Need Flood Insurance?

Here are some important facts to keep in mind:

- **FACT:** Homeowners' and renters' insurance does not typically cover flood damage.
- **FACT:** More than 20 percent of flood claims come from properties outside high-risk flood zones.
- **FACT:** Flood insurance can pay regardless of whether or not there is a Presidential Disaster Declaration.
- **FACT:** Disaster assistance comes in two forms: a U.S. Small Business Administration loan, which must be paid back with interest, or a FEMA disaster grant, which is about $5,000 on average per household. By comparison, the average flood insurance claim is nearly $30,000 and does not have to be repaid.

(Source: "Why Buy Flood Insurance," U.S. Department of Homeland Security (DHS).)

What Flood Insurance Covers and Other Things You Should Know

- There are two types of flood insurance coverage: building property and personal property (contents). Flood insurance only covers physical damage to your building or personal property directly caused by a flood.

- Rates are set nationally and do not differ from company to company or agent to agent. These rates depend on many factors, such as the date and type of construction of your home and your building's level of risk.

- Typically, there's a 30-day waiting period from the date of purchase before your policy goes into effect.

- All National Flood Insurance policies include a congressionally-mandated surcharge. If your community participates in the Community Rating System, you may qualify for an insurance premium discount.

File a Complaint

If you have a problem with an insurance company or agent regarding flood insurance, contact the company first. If you cannot find a solution, contact your state insurance regulator.

Chapter 43

Transportation Needs

Every day, teens need to travel to many places, such as schools, colleges, workplaces, etc. When they reside in the parental nest, their parents may take care of their daily transportation needs; however, once they move out, it becomes their own responsibility to plan and arrange their transportation. Hence, an understanding of transportation options is essential for teens to survive independently and avoid late arrivals.

Modes of Transportation

For daily commuters, the different transportation options available are:

- Public transportation
  - Bus
  - Subway/train
- Private transportation
  - Walking
  - Bicycle
  - Motorcycle
  - Scooter
  - Car

About This Chapter: "Transportation Needs," © 2019 Omnigraphics.

- Taxi
- Ride-share service

It is important to consider various factors when deciding which mode of transportation is right for you. These factors include:

- Traveling time
- Distance
- Cost
- Convenience

How to Prepare Yourself

Before heading out on the road, a teen should possess basic knowledge and skills related to transportation.

- You should have an idea about the different kinds of transportation options available in your city or town.

- You should be aware of the fares that will be charged by various public transportation systems.

- You should know how to read the schedules and timetables of the public transportation systems and learn how to make reservations and book tickets on buses, trains, or flights.

- You should be able to read maps and identify the symbols given on them. This skill will be helpful for determining directions and navigating properly when you go to a new place. Though the modern technology and Global Positioning System (GPS) have made navigation easier, this option may not be available or helpful all of the time.

- When you take a cab, you should be able to provide the driver with proper information, such as the address, direction, time, etc. You should also be able to estimate the approximate cost of the trip.

- You should learn how to ride a bicycle/motorcycle. Also important is learning how to drive a car and obtain a driver's license.

- You should have a working knowledge of all traffic signage and road terminology.

Tips for Teen Drivers

Driving is an important life skill that can help a teen be self-dependant. But it's not enough to learn how to drive.

Here are a few things that a teen driver should also know or observe.

- Know how to obtain a driver's license.

- Know how to register and insure your vehicle.

- Remember to carry important vehicle documents, such as your driver's license, vehicle registration, and insurance policy, and emergency contact information each time you drive.

- Obey the traffic rules.

- Always wear the seat belt when traveling in a car.

- Always wear a helmet when riding a motorcycle.

- Strictly follow the posted speed limit. Speeding may lead to traffic tickets or a fatal accident.

- Do not drink and drive.

- Avoid distractions when driving. Place your cell phone aside as soon as you start driving a car.

- Limit the number of passengers in the vehicle. Overloading a vehicle or noisy conversations may increase the risk of an accident.

- Keep the car in good condition.

- Be aware of the state safety inspection requirements and annual vehicle registration requirements.

How to Cut Down on Transportation Costs

Transportation costs can take a big bite out of your budget, but there are a number of ways to minimize them.

- Try to rent a home close to your school, college, or workplace so that you can save on daily transportation costs.

- When the distance is not too far, always opt for walking instead of driving. This habit not only cuts down on transportation costs but also help you stay fit.

- Public transportation is the most cost-effective way to get around; therefore, use public transportation whenever possible. It can also help you save on fuel and parking charges.

- Be aware of discounts that are offered by the public transportation system and avail yourself of them whenever possible.

- Renew your driver's license, car insurance, and vehicle registration on time to avoid paying additional charges.

- Maintain your car properly. Check the tire pressure, fluid levels, lights, etc. regularly. Proper maintenance can help you save on fuel charges and avoid expensive repair costs.

References

1. "Module 4: Housing, Transportation and Community Resources," Washington State Department of Social and Health Services, July 20, 2005.

2. Gongala, Sagari. "21 Essential Life Skills for Teens to Learn," Mom Junction, January 9, 2017.

3. Kochrekar, Manjiri. "8 Important and Safe Driving Tips for Teenage Drivers," Mom Junction, April 6, 2017.

4. "Teaching Transportation Skills," Middle Earth, March 13, 2012.

Chapter 44

Managing Expenses

Once teens decide to move out of their parental nests, they start fantasizing about this joyful part of their independent life. Yes, it is amazing to be independent. But, at the same time, teens should get ready to plan and manage their expenses.

Things to Do before You Move Out
Savings

Moving out is a major life decision. So before you plan to leave, start saving some money. It is always a good rule of thumb to have sufficient funds to meet your basic needs for a period of three to six months.

Debt

Before you move out, pay off the loans and bills that you may have already accumulated. Try to start your new and independent life with a clean slate. This can help you avoid new debt if you run into unexpected financial trouble.

Budget

It is important to estimate the cost of living on your own and prepare a budget accordingly. There are often hidden expenses that you failed to consider, though. Therefore, while creating your budget, request the help of your parents, siblings, and friends who live independently.

About This Chapter: "Managing Expenses," © 2019 Omnigraphics.

List of Essentials

Make a list of household essentials that are required at your new home. This list may include items such as a refrigerator, washer and dryer, furniture, bed, pillows, sheets, towels, utensils, toiletries, trash cans, a lawn mower, and so on. Try to purchase the items that you do not yet own before you leave.

Movers

You may require the assistance of a moving service to move your personal items to your new location. Moving companies usually charge on an hourly basis and their prices may vary depending on the list of items that you wish to move. If you do not have too many items, though, you may be able to avoid this fee by enlisting the help of friends and family.

List of Expenses

Here is a list of the most common expenses that a teen needs to prioritize when living alone.

- Rent
- Furnishings
- Utility bills (gas, water, electricity, and so on)
- Home maintenance
- Groceries/meals
- Clothing
- Toiletries
- Laundry
- Mobile phone
- Transportation
  - Automobile (monthly payment, maintenance costs, and gas)
  - Public transportation
- Insurance (automobile and rental)
- Healthcare—medical check-ups, treatment, medication, and so on

- Books and tuition fees if you are a student

- Entertainment (movies, eating out, games, clubs, vacations, and so on)

- Subscriptions and memberships (gym, spa, magazines, and so on)

Expect the Unexpected

You can expect to encounter unexpected expenses, such as a major car or house repair or a medical emergency. This makes it important to set aside money each month as an emergency savings fund. Avoid using this fund for general expenses. Your emergency savings fund can help you handle unexpected expenses without ruining your budget. It will also help you avoid worrying about where to borrow money in the event of a crisis. Your emergency savings fund can give you peace of mind and confidence that you can handle unexpected expenses when you encounter them.

How to Cut Down on Expenses

Here are a few useful tips that teens can use to cut down on their expenses.

- Strictly stick to your monthly budget to avoid overspending. You can also set spending limits for each week and carry only that amount of money with you when you go shopping.

- Cook your own food. Homemade food is not only a cheaper option but also a healthier one. If you are not well-versed in cooking, start by making basic meals such as tacos, sandwiches, avocado toast, fried eggs, and so on.

- Remember to turn off your lights, fans, and other electrical appliances when they are not being used. This will help you keep your electricity bills low.

- Take public transport instead of driving your car. This can help you save on transportation and parking charges and will extend the life of your vehicle. You can also take advantage of the share-ride services offered by some transportation services in order to reduce your transportation costs.

- Don't use a credit card very often. Save it for emergencies.

- Pay all of your bills on or before the due date to avoid paying additional penalty charges. If you tend to forget these dates, then set reminders on your mobile phone or calendar.

Spending Smart

Pay yourself first. Many people get into the habit of saving or investing by following this advice: "Pay yourself first." Many people find it easier to pay themselves first if they allow their bank to automatically remove money from their paycheck and deposit it into a savings or investment account. Other people pay themselves first by having money automatically deposited into an employer-sponsored retirement savings account, such as a 401(k).

(Source: "Spending Smart," U.S. Securities and Exchange Commission (SEC).)

Chapter 45

Electronic Banking

For many people, electronic banking means 24-hour access to cash through an automated teller machine (ATM) or direct deposit of paychecks into checking or savings accounts. However, electronic banking involves many different types of transactions, rights, responsibilities—and sometimes, fees. Do your research. You may find some electronic banking services more practical for your lifestyle than others.

Electronic Fund Transfers

Electronic banking, also known as electronic fund transfer (EFT), uses a computer and electronic technology in place of checks and other paper transactions. EFTs are initiated through devices like cards or codes that let you, or those you authorize, access your account. Many financial institutions use ATM or debit cards and personal identification numbers (PINs) for this purpose. Some use other types of debit cards that require your signature or a scan. For example, some use radio frequency identification (RFID) or other forms of "contactless" technology that scan your information without direct contact with you. The federal Electronic Fund Transfer Act (EFT Act) covers some electronic consumer transactions.

Here are some common EFT services:

ATMs are electronic terminals that let you bank almost virtually any time. To withdraw cash, make deposits, or transfer funds between accounts, you generally insert an ATM card and enter your PIN. Some financial institutions and ATM owners charge a fee, particularly if you don't have accounts with them or if your transactions take place at remote locations.

About This Chapter: This chapter includes text excerpted from "Electronic Banking," Federal Trade Commission (FTC), August 2012.

Generally, ATMs must tell you they charge a fee and the amount on or at the terminal screen before you complete the transaction. Check with your institution and at ATMs, you use for more information about these fees.

Direct deposit lets you authorize specific deposits—like paychecks, Social Security checks, and other benefits—to your account on a regular basis. You also may preauthorize direct withdrawals so that recurring bills—like insurance premiums, mortgages, utility bills, and gym memberships—are paid automatically. Be cautious before you preauthorize recurring withdrawals to pay companies you aren't familiar with; funds from your bank account could be withdrawn improperly. Monitor your bank account to make sure direct recurring payments take place and are for the right amount.

Pay-by-phone systems let you call your financial institution with instructions to pay certain bills or to transfer funds between accounts. You must have an agreement with your institution to make these transfers.

Personal computer banking lets you handle many banking transactions using your personal computer. For example, you may use your computer to request transfers between accounts and pay bills electronically.

Debit card purchase or payment transactions let you make purchases or payments with a debit card, which also may be your ATM card. Transactions can take place in-person, online, or by phone. The process is similar to using a credit card, with some important exceptions: a debit card purchase or payment transfers money quickly from your bank account to the company's account, so you have to have sufficient funds in your account to cover your purchase. This means you need to keep accurate records of the dates and amounts of your debit card purchases, payments, and ATM withdrawals. Be sure you know the store or business before you provide your debit card information to avoid the possible loss of funds through fraud. Your liability for unauthorized use and your rights for dealing with errors may be different for a debit card than a credit card.

Electronic check conversion converts a paper check into an electronic payment in a store or when a company gets your check in the mail.

When you give your check to a cashier in a store, the check is run through an electronic system that captures your banking information and the amount of the check. You sign a receipt and you get a copy for your records. When your check is given back to you, it should be voided or marked by the merchant so that it can't be used again. The merchant electronically sends information from the check (but not the check itself) to your bank or other financial institution, and the funds are transferred into the merchant's account.

When you mail a check for payment to a merchant or other company, they may electronically send information from your check (but not the check itself) through the system; the funds are transferred from your account into their account. For a mailed check, you still should get a notice from a company that expects to send your check information through the system electronically. For example, the company might include the notice on your monthly statement. The notice also should state if the company will electronically collect a fee from your account—like a "bounced check" fee—if you don't have enough money to cover the transaction.

Be careful with online and telephone transactions that may involve the use of your bank account information, rather than a check. A legitimate merchant that lets you use your bank account information to make a purchase or pay on an account should post information about the process on its website or explain the process on the phone. The merchant also should ask for your permission to electronically debit your bank account for the item you're buying or paying on. However, because online and telephone electronic debits don't occur face-to-face, be cautious about sharing your bank account information. Don't give out this information when you have no experience with the business, when you didn't initiate the call, or when the business seems reluctant to discuss the process with you. Check your bank account regularly to be sure that the right amounts were transferred.

Not all electronic fund transfers are covered by the EFT Act. For example, some financial institutions and merchants issue cards with cash value stored electronically on the card itself. Examples include prepaid phone cards, mass transit passes, general purpose reloadable cards, and some gift cards. These "stored-value" cards, as well as transactions using them, may not be covered by the EFT Act, or they may be subject to different rules under the EFT Act. This means you may not be covered for the loss or misuse of the card. Ask your financial institution or merchant about any protections offered for these cards.

Chapter 46

Finding and Applying for a Scholarship

Scholarships are gifts. They don't need to be repaid. There are thousands of them, offered by schools, employers, individuals, private companies, nonprofits, communities, religious groups, and professional and social organizations.

What Kinds of Scholarships Are Available?

Some scholarships for college are merit-based. You earn them by meeting or exceeding certain standards set by the scholarship-giver. Merit scholarships might be awarded based on academic achievement or on a combination of academics and a special talent, trait, or interest. Other scholarships are based on financial need.

Many scholarships are geared toward particular groups of people; for instance, there are scholarships for women or high school seniors. And some are available because of where you or your parent work, or because you come from a certain background (for instance, there are scholarships for military families).

A scholarship might cover the entire cost of your tuition, or it might be a one-time award of a few hundred dollars. Either way, it's worth applying for, because it'll help reduce the cost of your education.

How Do I Find Scholarships?

You can learn about scholarships in several ways, including contacting the financial aid office at the school you plan to attend and checking information in a public library or online.

About This Chapter: This chapter includes text excerpted from "Finding and Applying for Scholarships," Federal Student Aid, U.S. Department of Education (ED), February 2, 2017.

But be careful. Make sure scholarship information and offers you receive are legitimate; and remember that you don't have to pay to find scholarships or other financial aid.

Try these free sources of information about scholarships:

- The financial aid office at a college or career school

- A high school or TRiO counselor

- The U.S. Department of Labor's (DOL) FREE scholarship search tool

- Federal agencies

- Your state grant agency

- Your library's reference section

- Foundations, religious or community organizations, local businesses, or civic groups

- Organizations (including professional associations) related to your field of interest

- Ethnicity-based organizations

- Your employer or your parents' employers

When Do I Apply for Scholarships?

That depends on each scholarship's deadline. Some deadlines are as early as a year before college starts, so if you're in high school now, you should be researching and applying for scholarships during the summer between your junior and senior years. But if you've missed that window, don't give up!

How Do I Apply for Scholarships?

Each scholarship has its own requirements. The scholarship's website should give you an idea of who qualifies for the scholarship and how to apply. Make sure you read the application carefully, fill it out completely, and meet the application deadline.

How Do I Get My Scholarship Money?

That depends on the scholarship. The money might go directly to your college, where it will be applied to any tuition, fees, or other amounts you owe, and then any leftover funds given to you. Or it might be sent directly to you in a check. The scholarship provider should tell you what to expect when it informs you that you've been awarded the scholarship. If not, make sure to ask.

How Does a Scholarship Affect My Other Student Aid?

A scholarship will affect your other student aid because all your student aid added together can't be more than your cost of attendance at your college or career school. So, you'll need to let your school know if you've been awarded a scholarship so that the financial aid office can subtract that amount from your cost of attendance (and from certain other aid, such as loans, that you might have been offered). Then, any amount left can be covered by other financial aid for which you're eligible.

Chapter 47

Financial Aid for Studying Abroad

International Schools

Many students get federal student aid to help pay for their study at international schools, either at the undergraduate or graduate level.

Whether you plan to study abroad for a semester or get your entire degree outside the United States, you may be able to use federal student aid to pay your expenses. The type of aid you can get—and the process you must follow—will depend on the type of program (study-abroad or full degree) you plan to enter. Your status as an undergraduate or graduate student also affects the type of aid for which you're eligible, just as it does at schools in the United States.

Study Abroad for a Semester or Year

You may receive federal student aid for a study-abroad program if you meet the aid eligibility criteria. If you aren't already in the habit of filling out a *Free Application for Federal Student Aid* (FAFSA®) each year for college, be sure to learn about the federal student aid programs and the FAFSA® process. You'll need to fill out a FAFSA® before you can receive federal student aid to study abroad.

To determine which types of aid you'll be able to use for your study-abroad program, contact the financial aid office at your American school. (If your American school doesn't participate in the federal student aid programs, then you won't be able to get federal student aid to help pay for your study abroad.) Start early, because it's important to get all necessary paperwork done on time, both at your American school and at the international school.

About This Chapter: This chapter includes text excerpted from "International Schools," Federal Student Aid, U.S. Department of Education (ED), November 30, 2016.

Get a Degree from an International School

If you've decided to get your degree from a school outside the United States, congratulations.

How Can I Research Schools and Their Requirements?

First, don't panic. You're on your own, but if you're organized and determined, you'll be okay. In this chapter, we'll share some tips about preparing to study at an international school and some resources to help you learn about schools that participate in the American federal student aid programs.

Here are general tips:

- Start early. You've got more to do than your friends who are going to American schools, so don't think you can apply for financial aid this month and use it to pay your tuition next month.

- If you're interested in a particular school, check its website to find out about program availability (does it offer the degree you want?), cost, enrollment policies, and resources and programs for international students.

- Do your research and keep a to-do list. For instance, what paperwork needs to be done? (Visas? Housing forms? Registering with the police? Valid passport? Emergency contacts? Medical insurance?)

- Create a file to organize your documents and information from your school.

- Find out who at the school will be processing your financial aid. Get their email address, and contact them when you have questions. (If you're not sure where to start, try the school's office for international students.)

- Don't forget that you can get help filling out the FAFSA® either within the form itself at fafsa.gov (in the "Help and Hints" section on each page of the application) or by phone at 800-4-FED-AID (800-433-3243).

What Federal Student Aid Can I Receive for My Degree at an International School?

At many schools around the world, you can receive a federal student loan from the William D. Ford Federal Direct Loan (Direct Loan) Program. (Find out which international schools participate in the Direct Loan Program.) You may receive a Direct Subsidized Loan or Direct Unsubsidized Loan for your undergraduate education. Direct Unsubsidized Loans and Direct

PLUS Loans are available to graduate students. Your parent also might be able to borrow on your behalf; she or he should ask about getting a Direct PLUS Loan for parents. International schools do not participate in the U.S. Department of Education's grant programs, so you will not be able to obtain a Federal Pell Grant to get your degree at an international school.

How Much Can I Receive in Federal Student Loan Funds?

The annual limit for Direct Subsidized Loans plus Direct Unsubsidized Loans varies from $5,500 to $20,500, depending on a variety of factors (year in school, status as a dependent or independent student, etc.). Direct PLUS Loan amounts are determined by subtracting any other financial aid you're receiving from your total cost of attendance at the school.

How Do I Apply for a Federal Student Loan to Use at an International School?

Apply for student loans at your international school using the same process you use to apply for aid in the United States.

1. Fill out a FAFSA® at fafsa.gov as early as possible. The FAFSA® is available on October 1 for school attendance that begins any time from July 1 of the following year through June of the year beyond that. There is no special FAFSA® for students planning to attend international schools.

2. Make sure the school you plan to attend has your FAFSA® information. International schools have the ability to access your FAFSA® information electronically. When you fill out the FAFSA®, list the school you plan to attend in the question about Federal School Codes. (The FAFSA® site has a tool to let you search for your school's Federal School Code [https://fafsa.ed.gov/FAFSA/app/schoolSearch?].) Once it's listed on your FAFSA®, your school will then download your data.

3. Find out the next steps from your chosen school. Different schools proceed differently at this stage of the process. Ask your school how you will get your loan money—what paperwork do you need to fill out, what are the deadlines, etc. Keep track of everything that is required of you; make copies of paper documents (or scan them) and file them safely, and meet those deadlines! And if your parent plans to get a Direct PLUS Loan, she or he should keep a close eye on required documents and deadlines as well.

4. If you are a first-year student borrowing federal funds for the first time, you will have to complete entrance counseling. This means you'll be required to read text or watch a

video online, or attend an in-person presentation, in order to learn about the responsibilities of taking out a loan. Your entrance counseling might happen before you leave the United States or after you arrive at your school; it depends on the school.

How Will I Get Paid?

Your loan funds will be electronically transmitted from the U.S. Department of the Treasury to the international school's designated bank. First, the school will put the funds toward anything you owe them (tuition, fees, etc.). If there is any money left over after the funds are applied to your account at the school, the extra money will go to you.

Your funds might not be disbursed (paid out) before you leave the United States, so you will most likely have to come up with your travel expenses yourself.

When and How Do I Repay the Loan?

That depends on whether it's a subsidized or unsubsidized loan versus a PLUS loan. Repayment of a loan used to pay for international study works the same way as repayment of a loan used to pay for an American school.

Part Five
Planning for the Future

Chapter 48

Future Financial Goals

You might envision major changes, like moving to a new city for a new job, or starting a family.

You might anticipate smaller changes too, like starting a hobby or exercise program, upgrading your home appliances or technology, spending more time with friends or family, or volunteering more. Maybe you want to reduce your debt or save up for a purchase instead of charging it.

Goals, whether long term or short term, usually cost money to accomplish. That means when you have a life goal, you probably have a financial goal, too. Life goal—and financial goals—can be small or large, short-term, or long-term. Whatever your goals are, here are a few steps that can help you reach them:

- **Set a financial goal.** Let's say you want to go on a vacation next year, and you set a goal of saving $1,000.

- **Break it down into specific steps.** You could decide to save $1,000, for example, by bringing lunch from home instead of buying it for $5 a day. Or you could set aside $20 from your pay every week for 50 weeks. Or you could find additional income from an extra shift or side job.

- **Set up the system you need to make it work.** Sometimes we forget the small things that can get in our way—like making sure you have the right kitchen supplies and groceries to make lunch every day or opening a savings account to keep your vacation fund separate. Set up what you need in your life so that you don't have excuses to miss your goals.

About This Chapter: This chapter includes text excerpted from "You've Got Goals for Your Life—And Some of Them Take Money to Achieve," Federal Trade Commission (FTC), February 23, 2015.

- **Get help sticking to your plan.** You can set up automatic transfers at your bank, moving funds automatically from checking to savings. You can set a weekly alarm on your phone. You can ask a friend to remind you—or join you and save along with you.

Make your own list and then think about which goals are the most important to you. List your most important goals first. Decide how many years you have to meet each specific goal because when you save or invest you'll need to find a savings or investment option that fits your time frame for meeting each goal.

(Source: "Saving and Investing," U.S. Securities and Exchange Commission (SEC).)

When thinking about setting financial goals, consider what financial well-being means to you. Now is the time to think about how to achieve the changes you envision for yourself. Know what motivates you, then take action. By meeting your financial goals, you'll make a start on following your life goals.

Managing Expenditure to Keep up with Financial Goals

Managing spending and keeping up with your budget can be difficult tasks, but there are ways to make it easier to manage your spending and reach your financial goals—and improve your financial well-being.

Improving your financial well-being means you:

- Have more control over day-to-day, month-to-month finances
- Have a greater cushion to absorb a financial shock
- Are getting on track to meet your financial goals
- Have more financial freedom to make the choices that allow you to enjoy life

(Source: "Consumer Tips for Managing Spending," Federal Trade Commission (FTC).)

Chapter 49

How to Become an Entrepreneur

Are you a teenager or in your early 20s? Do you have a great business idea? Perhaps you're already making headway towards starting your own business.

But how do you get others to believe in you and your business idea?

Here are eight surefire ways that you can be taken seriously as a young entrepreneur:

1. Have a Plan

Having a plan means knowing where you want to be and what steps you are going to take to get there. If you can't communicate this to investors, vendors, distributors, employees, and so on, you will never be taken seriously.

Case in point—U.S. Small Business Administration (SBA) Young Entrepreneur of the Year in 2011—Mollie Breault-Binaghi. Now in her mid-20s, Mollie owns two successful graphic design and printing businesses in Vermont. With input from her boyfriend and her family, she spent considerable time working out the details of a business plan. "When you're going to be investing not only money but your time, you need to invest an equal amount of energy laying it out on paper before you jump in," Mollie said.

2. Be Serious about Your Passion

While Mollie's advice for other young entrepreneurs is simple: "Plan!" she also added: "And you have to be passionate about it. Otherwise, it's not worth doing. Owning your own business

About This Chapter: This chapter includes text excerpted from "8 Things You Can Do to Be Taken Seriously as a Young Entrepreneur," U.S. Small Business Administration (SBA), September 13, 2016.

is not easy and it's not going to make you rich quick. You're going to be in it for the long haul, so it's got to be something you love."

It's inevitable that you are going to come across people who are going to try and talk you out of your idea—put your earmuffs on and stand your ground. Be proud of your idea, innovation, or business and be ready to showcase what you've done to get this far and what your plans are for the next step.

A few sure-fire ways to demonstrate your commitment include:

- Work at it—Be prepared to put the hours and weekends into your business.

- Educate yourself and take educated risks!—Take advantage of free or low-cost business start-up workshops from your local business incubator, Small Business Development Center, Women's Business Centers and more. Check out free online courses such as those offered by SBA in the Learning Center accessible at www.sba.gov/tools/sba-learning-center/search/training. Learn about your industry but also what it takes to be a successful business leader/marketer/planner, and so on.

- Stick at it through adversity—Nothing says commitment better than sticking with something even when you feel like throwing in the towel.

- Identify what went wrong and learn from it.

3. Find a Mentor

Many young entrepreneurs struggle to succeed because they don't have a mentor. Whether it's a former boss, someone in your business network, or family friend, find a mentor who has experience in your field and has walked in your shoes before. Not only can a mentor provide valuable advice, they can also give you access to contacts, resources, and events that you might not otherwise have access to. If you can't pinpoint a mentor, check out SCORE—a network of over 13,000 volunteer business mentors who have helped over 10,000 Americans start and grow their businesses. SCORE is accessible on the Internet at www.score.org.

4. Surround Yourself with the Right People

Just as it's important to have a mentor, it's also important to work on being around the right people—as much as you can. Surround yourself with the kind of people who are living the life you want to live or exemplify—they will challenge you and probably tell you things you don't want to hear, but they'll also tell you the things you have to hear. Look to entrepreneurial groups, experts in your industry, college professors—those who are respected in your industry or community.

5. Put Yourself in Environments That Will Allow You to Grow

Just as surrounding yourself with the right people will challenge your way of thinking, push yourself to seek out new possibilities beyond your comfort zone. As a series of young entrepreneurs explain this as: "Putting yourself in an environment that causes you to be against the wall and maybe is a little uncomfortable, but being around it enough times you start to own it and you start to get a little bit more belief, in increments, in yourself and all that adds up to where you're comfortable in your own shoes…"

6. Don't Be Flash with Cash!

One of the surest ways to show you are serious about your business idea is to demonstrate that you can manage your cash and keep it flowing. Look for ways to keep costs low. Consider working part-time when you launch your company; this will help you build your business with less risk and provide you with a steady cash flow from another source. Once you've established a base, then transition to full-time business ownership.

You should also utilize technology and the resources around you to keep costs low—think of using garage space to store inventory instead of paying for a warehouse, or use social media to make the most of low-cost marketing.

7. Need Financing?—Do Your Homework

Securing financing as a young entrepreneur can be particularly challenging. Without a credit history or career history, finding someone who will entrust their money to you isn't going to be easy. But with a solid business plan and commitment to success, investors are out there ready to take you seriously. Here are just some of the options that young entrepreneurs can explore:

- Borrowing from Friends and Family
- Peer-to-Peer Lending and Crowdfunding
- Microloans

8. Look Like a Pro

It goes without saying, or does it? Try to look like you are serious about what you are doing. Whether you are meeting customers, potential partners, mentors or investors—clean up your act. No, you don't need to wear a suit all the time, but dress appropriately. "Remember, you might need to overcome some preconceived ideas about what teenagers are like, so be sure your looks and your language reflect the fact that you're serious about your business," advises Young entrepreneur, Adam Toren. "When communicating through email, use spell check and keep slang and abbreviations to a minimum. If you're polite, professional and knowledgeable, your potential customers are sure to take you seriously.

Check out These Famous Teen Entrepreneurs!

Nick D'Aloisio—founder of Summly, an application aimed at transforming how we consume news on mobile devices

Cory Nieves—founder and CEO of Mr. Corey's Cookies

Brian Wong—co-founder of Kiip, a mobile app rewards platform that lets brands and companies give real-world rewards for in-game achievements

Moziah "Mo" Bridges—CEO of Mo's Bows Handmade Bow Ties

Chapter 50

Deciding Your Career

Most people need some preparation before they're ready for the workforce, and planning should begin long before it's time to start a career. This could include taking technical courses during high school or, after graduating, attending a college or university to earn a certificate or a degree. Knowing what type of career preparation you need begins with thinking about what type of career you want.

This chapter helps high school students plan for careers. The first section talks about exploring your interests. The second section highlights the importance of internships, jobs, and other opportunities for getting experience. The third section describes some education or training options, both in high school and afterward. The fourth section offers some thoughts on pursuing your dream career.

Explore Your Interests

High school is a great time to start thinking about careers. "All your life you've been asked what you want to do when you grow up," says Steve Schneider, a school counselor at Sheboygan South High School in Sheboygan, Wisconsin. "In high school, you start to work towards making that happen."

Many high schoolers don't yet know what they want to do. And school counselors say that's perfectly fine. In fact, students are likely to change their minds multiple times, perhaps even after they enter the workforce. And some of tomorrow's careers might not exist today.

About This Chapter: This chapter includes text excerpted from "Career Planning for High Schoolers," U.S. Bureau of Labor Statistics (BLS), U.S. Department of Labor (DOL), January 2015.

Settling on just one occupation in high school isn't necessary. But looking into the types of careers you might like can help set you up for success. "My feeling is that high school students don't have to know the exact career they want," says Danaher, "but they should know how to explore careers and put time into investigating them and learning about their skills and interests."

Learn about Yourself

Understanding what you enjoy—and what you're good at—is the first step in exploring careers, say school counselors. "If you don't know what you want to do, the question is, 'What do you like to learn about?'" Schneider says. "If you really like science, what do you enjoy about it—the lab work, the research?"

Use the answers to those questions to identify careers that may have similar tasks. High school junior Kate Sours, for example, loves spending time with kids as a babysitter and enjoys helping people. So she focused on those two interests when she began considering potential careers.

It's important to think about what you like to do, say school counselors because work will eventually be a big part of your life. "The whole purpose of thinking about careers is so that when you go to the workforce, you wake up in the morning and look forward to going to work," says Julie Hartline, a school counseling consultant at Cobb County public schools in Smyrna, Georgia.

Identify Possible Careers

Once you've thought about the subjects and activities you like best, the next step is to look for careers that put those interests to use. If you love sports, for example, you might consider a career as a gym teacher, recreational therapist, or coach. If you like math, a career as a cost estimator, accountant, or budget analyst might be a good fit.

But those aren't the only options for people interested in sports or math. There are hundreds of occupations, and most of them involve more than one skill area. School counselors, teachers, and parents can help point you in the direction of occupations that match your interests and skills. School counselors, for example, often have tools that they use to link interests and skills with careers. Free online resources, such as My Next Move, also help with career exploration.

Another approach to identifying potential career interests is to consider local employers and the types of jobs they have. There are many jobs in manufacturing and healthcare near the high school where Schneider works, for example, so he often talks to students about the range of career options in those fields—from occupations that require a six-week course after high school to those that require a bachelor's or higher degree.

Exploring careers that combine working with children and helping people led Sours to nursing. She's now considering working in a hospital's neonatal intensive care unit or pediatrics department.

Sours notes the importance of broadening, rather than narrowing, possibilities when studying careers. "Keep an open mind," she says, "because, with some work, you might think, 'Oh, that's a nasty job.' But when you start exploring it, you might discover, 'This is cool. I might want to do this.'"

Do Your Research

After identifying possible occupations, you'll want to learn more about them. Resources such as *Career Outlook* and the *Occupational Outlook Handbook* can help you get started. Other sources of information include career-day programs, mentoring, and opportunities offered through your school to learn more about the world of work.

Talking directly to workers can help you get information about what they do. If you don't know workers in occupations that interest you, ask people such as parents, friends, or teachers for their contacts. Some schools have business liaisons or coordinators who help put students in touch with employers—and school counselors can assist, too. These networking efforts might pay off later, even if opportunities aren't available now.

After you've found workers who are willing to help, talk to them on the phone, by email, or through online forums. Meet with them in person for informational interviews to learn more about what they do. Or ask if you can shadow them on the job to see what their daily work is like.

To find out if you'll really like an occupation, school counselors say firsthand experience is indispensable. Sours, for example, shadowed her aunt, who works in a hospital as a physical therapist. Sours liked the hospital environment so much that she attended a week-long nursing camp, where she got to see the many tasks that nurses do. "I had so much fun, and I learned so much," she says about both experiences.

Get Experience

If job shadowing gives you a taste of what an occupation is like, imagine how helpful getting experience could be. Students can begin getting career-related experiences in high school through internships, employment, and other activities.

Taking part in different experiences is another step toward helping you to figure out what you like—and what you don't. These experiences may teach valuable job skills, such as the importance of arriving on time.

But, say school counselors, students need to remember that school takes priority over other pursuits. "It's a good idea to get experience while you're a student," says Hartline, "but not at the expense of academic success." Danaher agrees. "School should be your full-time job," he says.

Internships

Completing an internship is an excellent way to get experience. Internships are temporary, supervised assignments designed to give students or recent graduates practical job training. Sometimes, internships or other experiential learning positions are built into educational programs, and students receive academic credit for completing them.

At Lovely's school, for example, students have the option to fulfill an internship for credit during their junior or senior year. Lovely interned during her junior year for her high school theater director. "She gave us opportunities to do everything from contacting local newspapers for ads to writing program notes to directing the middle school production," says Lovely. The experience gave Lovely a feel for a director's work—and helped to cement her career goals.

At other schools, students seek out internships on their own. Academic credit may not be awarded, but gaining hands-on experience can still be worthwhile. Check with your school counselor to see if opportunities exist at your school.

Jobs

Summer or part-time employment is another way to get experience. Paid jobs allow you to earn money, which can help you learn how to budget and save for future goals or expenses.

For some students, summer is a great time to explore careers through employment. As the chart shows, young people worked in a variety of industries in July 2014, according to the Bureau of Labor Statistics (BLS).

The U.S. Department of Labor (DOL) has rules about youth employment. These rules differ depending on your age, but they often limit the types of jobs and number of hours you can work. States may have additional restrictions.

Hartline advises that students who work during the school year start with a few hours and build from there, once they find it won't interfere with their studies. "For some students, work is a motivator. For others, it's a distractor," she says.

Regardless of when or where they work, school counselors say, students who pursue employment can learn from it. "I think there's no substitute for any type of work experience," says Michael Carter, director of college counseling at St. Stephen's and St. Agnes School in Alexandria, Virginia. "Without experience, it's hard for students to appreciate what type of career they'd like to have because it's all hypothetical."

Other Activities

You can participate in other activities in high school that may spark a career interest. Examples include the yearbook committee, science club, and debate team.

By joining groups that involve community service and leadership opportunities, such as student government or honor societies, you can hone work-related skills or interests. Attending a camp in a subject area that interests you, such as engineering or writing, can help you focus on academic skills that may lead to a career.

Some student organizations aim to promote career readiness. SkillsUSA, DECA, and the Future Business Leaders of America are just a few of the national-level groups that might have student chapters at your high school.

Volunteering allows you to serve your community and bolster your experience. Religious institutions, local nonprofits, and government agencies are among the many organizations that use volunteers to fill a variety of roles.

In addition to encouraging you to meet like-minded people and develop your interests, these activities also show future employers and postsecondary schools that you are motivated and engaged. And the more you shape your thoughts about a career, the better you'll know how to prepare for it.

Train for a Career

Career preparation should start in high school, but it shouldn't end with graduation: Most occupations require some type of training or education after high school. On-the-job training, apprenticeships, certificates, nondegree awards, and various levels of college degrees are typically required for entry-level jobs.

Which type of training you need depends on the career you want to pursue. Your high school may offer opportunities for getting career training or college credits before you graduate. And after graduation, your training options expand even more. The closer you get to entering the workforce, the more you'll want to narrow your choices.

In High School

Getting a solid education is an important foundation for any career. Workers in many occupations use problem-solving, communication, research, and other skills that they first learned in high school. By doing well in classes and taking part in career-training or college-preparation programs, you demonstrate that you're ready to put these skills into action.

Plan and achieve. Make sure your high school course plan prepares you for entering the next phase of training or education in your desired career. To enter an electrician apprenticeship, for example, you may need a year of high school algebra. Your school counselor can help you plan your schedule to ensure that you take the required classes.

Employers and postsecondary schools often look to your high school record to gauge how you might perform on the job or in an educational program. And finishing high school shows that you can set goals and follow through. "Starting freshman year, do the absolute best you can in your classes," says Laura Inscoe, dean of counseling and student services at Wakefield High School in Raleigh, North Carolina. "Start strong and stay strong."

But school counselors also say not to worry too much if your grades aren't as good as you'd like. "School studies open doors if you do well, but they don't shut doors if you don't," says Danaher. "You might just take a different path."

Career programs. Your high school may offer options for exploring careers while earning credit toward graduation. Some of these options also allow you to earn industry certifications, licensure, or college credit.

In her high school, for example, Sours attends a career academy for health and medical sciences. She is learning about healthcare careers and will have a chance to apply some of her skills and knowledge as she continues in the program. By graduation, she'll have earned both certifications and credits toward an applied nursing degree program at the local community college.

Career academies and other types of technical education are available in many schools to provide hands-on career training. Classes in fields such as business and finance, culinary arts, and information technology are designed to prepare you for work or postsecondary school.

College prep. If you know your goal is college, school counselors usually recommend taking the most rigorous academic classes your school offers—and those that you can successfully handle. Doing so helps bolster both your college application credentials and your readiness for college-level study.

Some college-prep programs, such as Advanced Placement and dual enrollment, may help you get a head start on earning a postsecondary degree. Taking classes in these programs may allow you to waive some college course requirements, either by achieving a high score on exams or by completing a course for both high school and college credit.

Admission to a college is not based on coursework alone, however. Not all high schools offer advanced academics programs, and not all students take them. You may still have more options than you think, depending on your career goals.

After High School

About two-thirds of high school graduates from the class of 2013 enrolled in college that fall, according to BLS: 42 percent in baccalaureate (four-year) colleges and 24 percent in two-year schools. Of the remaining one-third of 2013 graduates, who opted not to go to college, 74 percent entered the labor force.

College-bound high school graduates may not know it, but BLS data show that wages are usually higher, and unemployment rates lower, for people who continue their education after high school.

Associate's and bachelor's degree programs range from accounting to zoology. But job training and vocational school programs may offer the type of career preparation you need for the occupation that interests you.

Job training. If you get a job or enter the military directly out of high school, you'll receive training specific to the job. Some employers may even pay for you to get related credentials, such as industry certification.

The type and length of on-the-job training you get depends on the occupation. For example, community health workers typically need 1 month or less of experience on the job and informal training, in addition to a high school diploma, to become competent in the occupation.

Apprenticeships are a form of job training in which a sponsor, such as an employer, pays a trainee to learn and work in a particular occupation. Some jobs in the military include apprenticeship training, but others involve different types of hands-on learning.

Vocational school. Also known as trade or technical schools, vocational schools have programs designed to give you hands-on training in a specific field. Many of these programs lead to nondegree credentials, such as a certificate or diploma. Occupations that you can prepare for at these types of schools include automotive mechanic and emergency medical technician (EMT).

Some vocational schools specialize in a certain occupation or career field, such as truck driving, culinary arts, or cosmetology. Others provide a diverse range of programs, such as medical assisting and precision production.

Earning a certificate allows you to prepare for a career in a relatively short amount of time: Nearly all certificate programs take fewer than two years to complete. For example, you may earn a nursing assistant certificate in less than one year.

Associate's degree. Associate's degrees, which may qualify you for occupations such as dental hygienist and funeral services manager, are available through public community colleges and other two-year schools. But some four-year schools also offer associate degrees that complement or lead into their bachelor's degree programs.

Associate's degrees are available in a variety of subject areas, but most degrees awarded in the past decade have been broadly focused. According to the National Center for Education Statistics, the most popular fields of study for associate's degree recipients between 2001–2 and 2011–12 were liberal arts and sciences, general studies, and humanities.

Earning an associate's degree and then transferring to a bachelor's degree program might make sense if you're unsure of what you want to study. It also allows you to save money on tuition because community colleges are usually less expensive than baccalaureate colleges and universities.

Bachelor's degree. If you plan to get a bachelor's degree, your school counselor can help you with the application processes for colleges and financial aid. But you should also have a plan for why you're pursuing a degree.

A good initial step is to think about what you might like to major in. If you've been considering your career interests throughout high school, declaring a major won't be difficult. "Your initial undergraduate program should be an outgrowth of your academic strengths in high school," says Carter.

Still not sure what you want to study? Look at some studies. For example, job opportunities and starting salaries vary by college major. Data may be helpful in narrowing your choices, but they shouldn't be the sole determinant of your future. "Don't let your decision be based on money alone," says Hartline. "Find something you're going to love to do."

To keep your options open as you choose a major, school counselors suggest entering a liberal arts program. Take classes in a broad range of subjects to help you figure out what you like best—and where that might lead in your future.

Be Flexible and Follow Your Dream

Everyone's career path is different, and there is no "right" way to start a career. For example, if you want to postpone your studies to discover your passion, you might decide to take a "gap year" after high school. A gap year gives you a chance to pursue meaningful volunteer, work, or travel experiences. But school counselors recommend that you have a plan to ensure that your time off is productive.

Whatever career path you choose, says Schneider, remember that you can change your mind at any time. "There's always the flexibility to shift course," he says. "A career is not a life sentence. If at some point you realize, 'I don't want to do this,' back up and ask yourself the same questions again: 'What am I good at? What do I like to do?'"

And have the confidence to work toward your ideal career, school counselors say, even if it seems out of reach. "Put a plan together and go for it," says Danaher, "even if everyone else says you're crazy, or you'll never make it. You may not make the NBA, but you might find a way to work within it doing work you really enjoy."

Chapter 51

Protecting Your Credit Score

Credit Reports

Credit reports contain information about your bill payment history, loans, current debt, and other financial information. They show where you work and live and whether you've been sued, arrested, or filed for bankruptcy.

Credit reports help lenders decide whether or not to extend you credit or approve a loan and determine what interest rate they will charge you. Prospective employers, insurers, and rental property owners may also look at your credit report.

It's important to check your credit report regularly to ensure that your personal information and financial accounts are being accurately reported and that no fraudulent accounts have been opened in your name. If you find errors on your credit report, take steps to have them corrected.

Free Credit Reports

You are entitled to a free credit report from each of the three credit reporting agencies (Equifax, Experian, and TransUnion) once every 12 months. You can request all three reports at once, or space them out throughout the year.

Request your free credit report:

- **Online**: www.annualcreditreport.com

About This Chapter: This chapter includes text excerpted from "Credit Reports and Scores," USA.gov, October 22, 2018.

- **By phone**: Call 877-322-8228. Deaf and hard of hearing consumers can access the text telephone (TTY) service by calling 711 and referring the relay operator to 800-821-7232.

- **By mail**: Complete the annual credit report request form (www.consumer.ftc.gov/articles/pdf-0093-annual-report-request-form.pdf) and mail it to:

Annual Credit Report Request Service

P.O. Box 105281

Atlanta, GA 30348-5281

If your request for a free credit report is denied then contact the credit reporting agency (CRA) directly to try and resolve the issue. The CRA should inform you of the reason they denied your request and explain what to do next. Often, you will only need to provide information that was missing or incorrect on your application for a free credit report.

If you are unable to resolve your dispute with the CRA, contact the Consumer Financial Protection Bureau (CFPB).

Credit Scores

A credit score is a number that rates your credit risk at one point in time. It can help creditors determine whether to give you credit, decide the terms you are offered or the rate you will pay for the loan. Having a high score can benefit you in many ways, including making it easier for you to obtain a loan, rent an apartment, and lower your insurance rate.

The information in your credit report is used to calculate your credit score. A credit score is calculated based on your:

- Payment history
- Balances outstanding
- Length of your credit history
- Applications for new credit accounts
- Types of credit accounts (mortgages, car loans, credit cards)

It's important to make sure your credit report is accurate because it can affect the accuracy of a credit score. You can have multiple credit scores, created by different companies or lenders that use their own credit scoring system.

Your free annual credit report does not include your credit score, but it's available, often for a fee. You can get your credit score, from several sources, such as your credit card statement or buying it from one of the three major credit reporting agencies. When you buy your score, you often get information on how you can improve it.

Credit Freeze

Placing a credit freeze allows you to restrict access to your credit report. This is important after a data breach or identity theft when someone could use your personal information to apply for new credit accounts. Most creditors look at your credit report before opening a new account. But if you've frozen your credit report, creditors can't access it, and probably won't approve fraudulent applications.

You have the right to place or lift a credit freeze for free. You can place a freeze on your own credit files and on those of your children age 16 or younger.

Place a Credit Freeze

Contact each CRA to place a freeze on your credit report. Each agency accepts freeze requests online, by phone, or by postal mail.

Experian

Online: Experian Freeze Center

Phone: 888-397-3742

By mail, write to:

Experian Security Freeze

P.O. Box 9554

Allen, TX 75013

Equifax

Online: Equifax Credit Report Services

Phone: 800-685-1111

By mail, write to:

Equifax Information Services LLC

P.O. Box 105788

Atlanta, GA 30348-5788

TransUnion

Online: TransUnion Credit Freezes

Phone: 800-909-8872

By mail, write to:

TransUnion LLC

P.O. Box 2000

Chester, PA 19016

Innovis

Online: Innovis Freeze Options

Phone: 800-540-2505

By mail, write to:

Innovis Consumer Assistance

P.O. Box 26

Pittsburgh, PA 15230-0026

Your credit freeze will go into effect the next business day if you place it online or by phone. If you place the freeze by postal mail, it will be in effect three business days after the credit agency receives your request. A credit freeze does not expire. Unless you lift the credit freeze, it stays in effect.

Lift a Credit Freeze

If you want lenders and other companies to be able to access your credit files again, you will need to lift your credit freeze permanently or temporarily. Contact each CRA. Some require you to use a PIN or password to lift your credit freeze. You can lift your credit freeze as often as you need to, without penalties.

It takes one hour for a lift request to take effect if you place it online or by phone. It can take three business days if you request the lift by mail.

Credit Reporting Agencies

A CRA is a company that collects information about where you live and work, how you pay your bills, whether or not you have been sued, arrested, or filed for bankruptcy. All of this information is combined together in a credit report. A CRA will then sell your credit report to creditors, employers, insurers, and others. These companies will use these reports to make decisions about extending credit, jobs, and insurance policies to you.

You are entitled to order (every 12 months) a free copy of your credit report from each of the major credit reporting agencies (Equifax, Experian, and TransUnion) through www.annualcreditreport.com. This website is the only one that is government authorized to provide you with free copies of your credit report.

You can also contact the credit agencies directly if you need to dispute information in your report, place a fraud alert or security freeze on your credit file, or have other questions.

Equifax by phone at 866-349-5191

Experian by phone at 888-397-3742

TransUnion by phone at 800-916-8800

File a Complaint

CRAs are not operated by the government, but you can still file a complaint about them to the federal government. Some reasons for filing a complaint include:

- Dissatisfaction with the outcome of a dispute with a CRA

- The CRA doesn't respond to your dispute request

- Credit report was used improperly

- Inability to get a copy of a credit report or score

- Problems with credit monitoring or identity protection services.

File a complaint about a CRA to the CFPB online or by phone at 1-855-411-2372.

Errors on Your Credit Report

If you find errors on your credit report, write a letter disputing the errors and send it (along with supporting documentation) to the following:

- CRA (Equifax, Experian, or TransUnion)

- Information provider (bank, credit card company, or other organization that provided the CRA with inaccurate information)

Find a sample dispute letter and get detailed instructions on how to report errors.

Under the Fair Credit Reporting Act (FRCA) both the CRA and the information provider are responsible for correcting inaccurate or incomplete information in your credit report.

If the errors have not been corrected after you've disputed them in writing, you can file a complaint with the CFPB.

Negative Information in a Credit Report

Negative information in a credit report can include public records—tax liens, judgments, bankruptcies—that provide insight into your financial status and obligations. A credit reporting company generally can report most negative information for seven years.

Information about a lawsuit or a judgment against you can be reported for seven years or until the statute of limitations runs out, whichever is longer. Bankruptcies can be kept on your report for up to ten years, and unpaid tax liens for 15 years.

Fixing Errors in a Credit Report

Anyone who denies you credit, housing, insurance, or a job because of a credit report must give you the name, address, and telephone number of the CRA that provided the report. Under the FCRA, you have the right to request a free report within 60 days if a company denies you credit based on the report.

You can get your credit report fixed if it contains inaccurate or incomplete information:

- Contact both the CRA and the company that provided the information to the CRA.

- Tell the CRA, in writing, what information you believe is inaccurate. Keep a copy of all correspondence.

Some companies may promise to repair or fix your credit for an upfront fee—but there is no way to remove negative information in your credit report if it is accurate.

File a Complaint

If you have a problem with credit reporting, you can file a complaint with the CFPB.

Equifax Data Breach

Equifax, one of the three major credit reporting agencies in the United States, announced a data breach that affects 143 million consumers. The hackers accessed Social Security numbers (SSNs), birthdates, addresses, and driver's license numbers.

Equifax has launched a tool that will let you know if you were affected by the breach. Check if you were impacted. You will need to provide your last name and the last six numbers of your Social Security number.

If you are impacted, Equifax offers you a free credit monitoring service, TrustedIDPremier. However, you won't be able to enroll in it immediately. You will be given a date when you can return to the site to enroll. Equifax will not send you a reminder to enroll. Mark that date on your calendar, so you can start monitoring your credit as soon as possible.

If you detect suspicious activity on your credit report due to the breach, report it immediately.

Chapter 52

Your Credit Score and Why It Matters

Why Your Credit Report Is Important

Businesses look at your credit report when you apply for:

- Loans from a bank
- Credit cards
- Jobs
- Insurance

If you apply for one of these, the business wants to know if you pay your bills. The business also wants to know if you owe money to someone else. The business uses the information in your credit report to decide whether to give you a loan, a credit card, a job, or insurance.

What "Good Credit" Means

Some people have good credit. Some people have bad credit. Some people do not have a credit history. Businesses see this in your credit report. Different things happen based on your credit history:

I have good credit.

- I pay my bills on time.

About This Chapter: This chapter includes text excerpted from "Your Credit History," Consumer.gov, Federal Trade Commission (FTC), September 28, 2012.

- I do not have big loans.

That means:

- I have more loan choices.
- It is easier to get credit cards.
- I pay lower interest rates.
- I pay less for loans and credit cards.

I have bad credit.

- I pay my bills late.
- I owe a lot of money.

That means:

- I have fewer loan choices.
- It is harder to get credit cards.
- I pay higher interest rates.
- I pay more for loans and credit cards.

I do not have credit.

- I never borrowed money from a bank or credit union.
- I never had a credit card.

That means:

- I have no bank loan choices.
- It is very hard to get credit cards.
- I pay high-interest rates.
- Loans and credit cards are hard to get and cost a lot.

All this information is in your credit report.

Why You Should Get Your Credit Report

An important reason to get your credit report is to find problems or mistakes and fix them:

- You might find somebody's information in your report by mistake.

- You might find information about you from a long time ago.

- You might find accounts that are not yours. That might mean someone stole your identity.

- You want to know what is in your report. The information in your report will help decide whether you get a loan, a credit card, a job or insurance.

If the information is wrong, you can try to fix it. If the information is right—but not so good—you can try to improve your credit history.

Where You Can Get Your Free Credit Report

You can get your free credit report from Annual Credit Report. That is the only free place to get your report. You can get it online: www.annualcreditreport.com/foreignLocation.action, or by phone: 877-322-8228.

You get one free report from each credit reporting company every year. That means you get three reports each year.

What You Should Do When You Get Your Credit Report

Your credit report has a lot of information. Check to see if the information is correct. Is it your name and address? Do you recognize the accounts listed?

If there is wrong information in your report, try to fix it. You can write to the credit reporting company. Ask them to change the information that is wrong. You might need to send proof that the information is wrong—for example, a copy of a bill that shows the correct information. The credit reporting company must check it out and write back to you.

How You Can Improve Your Credit

Look at your free credit report. The report will tell you how to improve your credit history. Only you can improve your credit. No one else can fix information in your credit report that is not good but is correct.

It takes time to improve your credit history. Here are some ways to help rebuild your credit.

- **Pay your bills by the date they are due.** This is the most important thing you can do.

- **Lower the amount you owe, especially on your credit cards.** Owing a lot of money hurts your credit history.

- **Do not get new credit cards if you do not need them.** A lot of new credit hurts your credit history.

- **Do not close older credit cards.** Having credit for a longer time helps your rating.

After six to nine months of this, check your credit report again. You can use one of your free reports from Annual Credit Report.

How Your Credit Score Works

Your credit score is a number related to your credit history. If your credit score is high, your credit is good. If your credit score is low, your credit is bad.

There are different credit scores. Each credit reporting company creates a credit score. Other companies create scores, too. The range is different, but it usually goes from about 300 (low) to 850 (high).

It costs money to look at your credit score. Sometimes a company might say the score is free. But usually, there is a cost.

What Goes into a Credit Score?

Each company has its own way to calculate your credit score. They look at:

- How many loans and credit cards you have

- How much money you owe

- How long you have had credit

- How much new credit you have

They look at the information in your credit report and give it a number. That is your credit score.

It is very important to know what is in your credit report. If your report is good, your score will be good. You can decide if it is worth paying money to see what number someone gives your credit history.

Chapter 53

How to Rebuild Your Credit Score

Your Rights

No one can legally remove accurate and timely negative information from a credit report. You can ask for an investigation—at no charge to you—of information in your file that you dispute as inaccurate or incomplete. Some people hire a company to investigate for them, but anything a credit repair company can do legally, you can do for yourself at little or no cost. By law:

- You're entitled to a free credit report if a company takes "adverse action" against you, like denying your application for credit, insurance, or employment. You have to ask for your report within 60 days of receiving notice of the action. The notice includes the name, address, and phone number of the consumer reporting company. You're also entitled to one free report a year if you're unemployed and plan to look for a job within 60 days; if you're on welfare; or if your report is inaccurate because of fraud, including identity theft.

- Each of the nationwide credit reporting companies—Equifax, Experian, and TransUnion—is required to provide you with a free copy of your credit report once every 12 months, if you ask for it. To order, visit annualcreditreport.com, or call 877-322-8228. You may order reports from each of the three credit reporting companies at the same time, or you can stagger your requests throughout the year.

About This Chapter: Text beginning with the heading "Your Rights" is excerpted from "Credit Repair: How to Help Yourself," Federal Trade Commission (FTC), November 2012; Text under the heading "Five Tips to Help Rebound from a Bad Credit History" is excerpted from "5 Tips to Help Rebound from a Bad Credit History," Federal Deposit Insurance Corporation (FDIC), August 21, 2014; Text under the heading "Changes Could Help Boost Credit Scores" is excerpted from "Changes Could Help Boost Credit Scores," Federal Deposit Insurance Corporation (FDIC), June 10, 2015.

- It doesn't cost anything to dispute mistakes or outdated items on your credit report. Both the credit reporting company and the information provider (the person, company, or organization that provides information about you to a credit reporting company) are responsible for correcting inaccurate or incomplete information in your report. To take advantage of all your rights, contact both the credit reporting company and the information provider.

Do It Yourself

Step 1: Tell the credit reporting company, in writing, what information you think is inaccurate. In addition to including your complete name and address, your letter should identify each item in your report that you dispute; state the facts and the reasons you dispute the information, and ask that it be removed or corrected. You may want to enclose a copy of your report and circle the items in question. Send your letter by certified mail, "return receipt requested," so you can document that the credit reporting company got it. Keep copies of your dispute letter and enclosures.

Credit reporting companies must investigate the items you question within 30 days—unless they consider your dispute frivolous. They also must forward all the relevant data you provide about the inaccuracy to the organization that provided the information. After the information provider gets notice of a dispute from the credit reporting company, it must investigate, review the relevant information, and report the results back to the credit reporting company. If the investigation reveals that the disputed information is inaccurate, the information provider has to notify the nationwide credit reporting companies so they can correct it in your file.

When the investigation is complete, the credit reporting company must give you the results in writing, too, and a free copy of your report if the dispute results in a change. If an item is changed or deleted, the credit reporting company cannot put the disputed information back in your file unless the information provider verifies that it's accurate and complete. The credit reporting company also must send you written notice that includes the name, address, and phone number of the information provider. If you ask, the credit reporting company must send notices of any correction to anyone who got your report in the past six months. You also can ask that a corrected copy of your report be sent to anyone who got a copy during the past two years for employment purposes.

If an investigation doesn't resolve your dispute with the credit reporting company, you can ask that a statement of the dispute be included in your file and in future reports. You also can ask the credit reporting company to give your statement to anyone who got a copy of your report in the recent past. You'll probably have to pay for this service.

Step 2: Tell the creditor or another information provider, in writing, that you dispute an item. Include copies (NOT originals) of documents that support your position. Many providers specify an address for disputes. If the provider reports the item to a consumer reporting company, it must include a notice of your dispute. And if the information is found to be inaccurate, the provider may not report it again.

If you pay with a credit card, pay your balance off every month

You'll build credit by using your credit card and paying on time, every time. Pay off your balances in full each month to avoid paying finance charges. Paying off your balance each month can also build better credit than carrying a balance.

(Source: "How to Rebuild Your Credit," Consumer Financial Protection Bureau (CFPB).)

Reporting Accurate Negative Information

When negative information in your report is accurate, only time can make it go away. A credit reporting company can report most accurate negative information for seven years and bankruptcy information for 10 years. Information about an unpaid judgment against you can be reported for seven years or until the statute of limitations runs out, whichever is longer. The seven-year reporting period starts from the date the event took place. There is no time limit on reporting information about criminal convictions; information reported in response to your application for a job that pays more than $75,000 a year, and information reported because you've applied for more than $150,000 worth of credit or life insurance.

The Credit Repair Organizations Act

The Credit Repair Organization Act (CROA) makes it illegal for credit repair companies to lie about what they can do for you, and to charge you before they've performed their services. The CROA is enforced by the Federal Trade Commission (FTC) and requires credit repair companies to explain:

- Your legal rights in a written contract that also details the services they'll perform
- Your three day right to cancel without any charge
- How long it will take to get results
- The total cost you will pay
- Any guarantees

What if a credit repair company you hired doesn't live up to its promises? You have some options. You can:

- Sue them in federal court for your actual losses or for what you paid them, whichever is more

- Seek punitive damages—money to punish the company for violating the law

- Join other people in a class action lawsuit against the company, and if you win, the company has to pay your attorney's fees

Report Credit Repair Fraud
State Attorneys General

Many states also have laws regulating credit repair companies. If you have a problem with a credit repair company, report it to your local consumer affairs office or, and your state attorney general (AG).

Federal Trade Commission

You also can file a complaint with the Federal Trade Commission (FTC). Although the FTC can't resolve individual credit disputes, it can take action against a company if there's a pattern of possible law violations. File your complaint online at ftc.gov/complaint or call 877-FTC-HELP (877-382-4357).

Where to Get Legitimate Help

Just because you have a poor credit history doesn't mean you can't get credit. Creditors set their own standards, and not all look at your credit history the same way. Some may look only at recent years to evaluate you for credit, and they may give you credit if your bill-paying history has improved. It may be worthwhile to contact creditors informally to discuss their credit standards.

If you're not disciplined enough to create a budget and stick to it, to work out a repayment plan with your creditors, or to keep track of your mounting bills, you might consider contacting a credit counseling organization. Many are nonprofit and work with you to solve your financial problems. But remember that "nonprofit" status doesn't guarantee free, affordable, or even legitimate services. In fact, some credit counseling organizations—even some that claim nonprofit status—may charge high fees or hide their fees by pressuring people to make "voluntary" contributions that only cause more debt.

Most credit counselors offer services through local offices, online, or on the phone. If possible, find an organization that offers in-person counseling. Many universities, military bases, credit unions, housing authorities, and branches of the U.S. Cooperative Extension Service (CES) operate nonprofit credit counseling programs. Your financial institution, local consumer protection agency, and friends and family also may be good sources of information and referrals.

If you're thinking about filing for bankruptcy, be aware that bankruptcy laws require that you get credit counseling from a government-approved organization within six months before you file for bankruptcy relief. You can find a state-by-state list of government-approved organizations at www.usdoj.gov/ust, the website of the U.S. Trustee Program. That's the organization within the U.S. Department of Justice (DOJ) that supervises bankruptcy cases and trustees. Be wary of credit counseling organizations that say they are government-approved, but don't appear on the list of approved organizations.

Reputable credit counseling organizations can advise you on managing your money and debts, help you develop a budget, and offer free educational materials and workshops. Their counselors are certified and trained in the areas of consumer credit, money and debt management, and budgeting. Counselors discuss your entire financial situation with you, and can help you develop a personalized plan to solve your money problems. An initial counseling session typically lasts an hour, with an offer of follow-up sessions.

Five Tips to Help Rebound from a Bad Credit History

1. **Order your free credit reports and look for errors.** Credit reporting companies, often referred to as "credit bureaus," maintain reports that show how an individual handles certain aspects of his or her finances. Your credit report includes information on how much credit you have available, how much credit you are using, whether you pay loans and other bills on time, your payment history on closed accounts, and any debt collections or bankruptcy filings. Credit bureaus and other companies use the information in your credit report to generate a credit score to predict, for example, how likely you are to repay your debts or how reliable you may be as a tenant.

    Federal law requires credit reporting companies to provide consumers with a free copy of their credit report once every 12 months if requested. You can easily obtain your free credit reports from each of the three major credit bureaus (Equifax, Experian, and TransUnion) or by calling 877-322-8228. Under other circumstances, such as being denied a loan or employment based on your credit report or if you believe you may be a fraud victim, you are also entitled to a free copy directly from the credit bureau that provided the initial report. Be cautious of costly subscriptions to additional credit-related services that you may be offered while requesting your credit report.

Because mistakes can happen, closely review your credit report(s) when you receive it. According to a study from the Federal Trade Commission (FTC), more than 25 percent of consumers surveyed identified errors on their credit reports that might affect their credit scores. "It is important to dispute inaccurate information, in writing, with both the credit reporting company as well as with the original source of the information so that the error does not show up again," said Jennifer Dice, a Federal Deposit Insurance Corporation (FDIC) Supervisory Consumer Affairs Specialist.

If you have a complaint about a credit reporting company, you can contact the Consumer Financial Protection Bureau (CFPB) or by calling 855-411-2372.

2. **Improve your credit history by paying your bills on time.** Paying on time is one of the biggest contributors to your credit score. If you have a history of paying bills late, find out if your bank will send you an e-mail or text message reminding you when a payment is due. You may also consider having your payments for loans or other bills automatically debited from your bank account.

   Once you become current on payments, stay current. "The more you pay your bills on time after being late, the more your credit score should increase," Dice added. "The impact of past credit problems on your credit score fades as time passes and as your current timeliness in paying bills is reflected on your credit report."

3. **Reduce the amounts you owe.** You can get on track toward a better score by paying down balances owed.

   It takes some discipline, so start by getting organized. Make a list of all of your accounts and debts (perhaps using your credit report, if it's accurate, and recent statements) to determine how much you owe and the interest rate you are being charged. You may be able to reduce your interest costs by paying off the debts with the highest interest rate first, while still making the minimum payments (if not more) on your other accounts.

   Also consider how to limit your use of credit cards in favor of cash, checks or a debit card. "While regular, responsible use of your credit card may help your credit score, it is best to keep your balance low enough so that you can pay the account balance in full, on time, every month," suggested Heather St. Germain, an FDIC Senior Consumer Affairs Specialist.

4. **Consider free or low-cost help from reputable sources.** Counseling services are available to help consumers budget money, pay bills, and develop a plan to improve their credit report. Be cautious of counseling services that advise you to stop making payments to your creditors or to pay the counselors instead (so they can negotiate on your behalf with the lender). These programs can be costly and may result in your credit score becoming even worse.

5. **Beware of credit repair scams.** Con artists lure innocent victims in with false promises to "erase" a bad credit history in a short amount of time, but there are no quick ways to remove credit problems on your record that are legitimate. "You'll also know you've encountered credit repair fraud if the company insists you pay upfront before it does any work on your behalf or it encourages you to give false information on your credit applications," said St. Germain. In general, before doing business with a for-profit credit repair company, learn how you can improve your own credit history at little or no cost.

Changes Could Help Boost Credit Scores

Your credit score, which is mainly based on your history of repaying loans, can determine your ability to borrow money and how much you will pay for it. Here is good news for some consumers: Your score may improve as a result of changes in how credit reports and scores are compiled.

In one development, Fair Isaac Corporation (FICO), a company that provides software used to produce many consumer credit scores, announced that unpaid medical debt will not have as big an impact on the new version of its most popular credit score.

The Consumer Financial Protection Bureau (CFPB) announced that it requires the major consumer reporting agencies to provide regular accuracy reports to the Bureau on how disputes from consumers are being handled. The CFPB said medical debt, in particular, is a source of numerous complaints because the billing process can be complicated and confusing to consumers. The CFPB noted that the accuracy reports will help it hold credit reporting companies accountable for ensuring that erroneous information does not damage a consumer's credit score.

Separately, as part of an agreement with the New York Attorney General's Office, the nation's three major credit reporting agencies—Equifax, Experian, and TransUnion—are taking steps that could help some consumers raise their scores. For example, they committed to conduct a more thorough review of documents provided by a consumer who is disputing information in a credit report. Also, they are clarifying how consumers can appeal the decision that the credit reporting company makes. In addition, medical debts will not appear on credit reports until they are at least 180 days past due.

These changes may help raise some consumers' credit scores and reduce their borrowing costs. In general, though, to build or maintain a good credit score, consumers need to manage their money carefully, and that includes using caution when taking on additional debt.

These Four Things Don't Help Rebuild Your Credit

1. Using a debit card or paying cash. These transactions don't help you prove you can repay debts.

2. Using a prepaid card. A prepaid card is your own money, loaded on to the card in advance.

3. Taking out a payday loan. Even making on-time repayments might not help your credit.

4. Taking an auto loan from a "buy here, pay here" car lot, unless they promise in writing to report your on-time payments.

(Source: "How to Rebuild Your Credit," Consumer Financial Protection Bureau (CFPB).)

Chapter 54

How to Dispute Credit Report Errors

Your credit report contains information about where you live, how you pay your bills, and whether you've been sued or arrested, or have filed for bankruptcy. Credit reporting companies sell the information in your report to creditors, insurers, employers, and other businesses that use it to evaluate your applications for credit, insurance, employment, or renting a home. The federal Fair Credit Reporting Act (FCRA) promotes the accuracy and privacy of information in the files of the nation's credit reporting companies.

Some financial advisors and consumer advocates suggest that you review your credit report periodically. Why?

- Because the information it contains affects whether you can get a loan—and how much you will have to pay to borrow money.

- To make sure the information is accurate, complete, and up-to-date before you apply for a loan for a major purchase like a house or car, buy insurance, or apply for a job.

- To help guard against identity theft. That's when someone uses your personal information—like your name, your Social Security number (SSN), or your credit card number—to commit fraud. Identity thieves may use your information to open a new credit card account in your name. Then, when they don't pay the bills, the delinquent account is reported on your credit report. Inaccurate information like that could affect your ability to get credit, insurance, or even a job.

About This Chapter: This chapter includes text excerpted from "Disputing Errors on Credit Reports," Federal Trade Commission (FTC), February 2017.

What Are Common Credit Report Errors That I Should Look for on My Credit Report?

When reviewing your credit report, check that it contains only items about you. Be sure to look for information that is inaccurate or incomplete.

- Identity errors
- Incorrect reporting of account status
- Data management errors
- Balance errors

(Source: "What Are Common Credit Report Errors That I Should Look for on My Credit Report?" Consumer Financial Protection Bureau (CFPB).)

How to Order Your Free Report

An amendment to the FCRA requires each of the nationwide credit reporting companies—Equifax, Experian, and TransUnion—to provide you with a free copy of your credit report, at your request, once every 12 months.

The three nationwide credit reporting companies have set up one website, toll-free telephone number, and mailing address through which you can order your free annual report. To order, visit annualcreditreport.com, call 877-322-8228, or complete the Annual Credit Report Request Form and mail it to:

Annual Credit Report Request Service

P.O. Box 105281

Atlanta, GA 30348-5281

Do not contact the three nationwide credit reporting companies individually.

You may order your reports from each of the three nationwide credit reporting companies at the same time, or you can order from only one or two. The FCRA allows you to order one free copy from each of the nationwide credit reporting companies every 12 months.

You need to provide your name, address, Social Security number, and date of birth. If you have moved in the last two years, you may have to provide your previous address. To maintain the security of your file, each nationwide credit reporting company may ask you for some information that only you would know, like the amount of your monthly mortgage payment. Each company may ask you for different information because the information each has in your file may come from different sources.

Other Situations Where You Might Be Eligible for a Free Report

You're also entitled to a free report if a company takes adverse action against you, such as denying your application for credit, insurance, or employment, based on information in your report. You must ask for your report within 60 days of receiving notice of the action. The notice will give you the name, address, and phone number of the credit reporting company.

You're also entitled to one free report a year if you're unemployed and plan to look for a job within 60 days; if you're on welfare; or if your report is inaccurate because of fraud, including identity theft.

Otherwise, a credit reporting company may charge you a reasonable amount for another copy of your report within a 12-month period. To buy a copy of your report, contact the three credit report companies:

Experian-888-397-3742

www.experian.com

TransUnion-800-916-8800

www.transunion.com

Equifax-800-685-1111

www.equifax.com

Correcting Errors

Under the FCRA, both the credit reporting company and the information provider (that is, the person, company, or organization that provides information about you to a credit reporting company) are responsible for correcting inaccurate or incomplete information in your report. To take advantage of all your rights under this law, contact the credit reporting company and the information provider.

Step One

Tell the credit reporting company, in writing, what information you think is inaccurate. Include copies (NOT originals) of documents that support your position. In addition to providing your complete name and address, your letter should clearly identify each item in your report you dispute, state the facts and explain why you dispute the information, and request that it be removed or corrected. You may want to enclose a copy of your report with the items in question circled. Send your letter by certified mail, "return receipt requested," so you can document what the credit reporting company received. Keep copies of your dispute letter and enclosures.

Credit reporting companies must investigate the items in question—usually within 30 days—unless they consider your dispute frivolous. They also must forward all the relevant data you provide about the inaccuracy to the organization that provided the information. After the information provider receives notice of a dispute from the credit reporting company, it must investigate, review the relevant information, and report the results back to the credit report-ing company. If the information provider finds the disputed information is inaccurate, it must notify all three nationwide credit reporting companies so they can correct the information in your file.

When the investigation is complete, the credit reporting company must give you the results in writing and a free copy of your report if the dispute results in a change. This free report does not count as your annual free report. If an item is changed or deleted, the credit reporting company cannot put the disputed information back in your file unless the information pro-vider verifies that it is accurate and complete. The credit reporting company also must send you written notice that includes the name, address, and phone number of the information provider.

If you ask, the credit reporting company must send notices of any corrections to anyone who received your report in the past six months. You can have a corrected copy of your report sent to anyone who received a copy during the past two years for employment purposes.

If an investigation doesn't resolve your dispute with the credit reporting company, you can ask that a statement of the dispute be included in your file and in future reports. You also can ask the credit reporting company to provide your statement to anyone who received a copy of your report in the recent past. You can expect to pay a fee for this service.

Step Two

Tell the information provider (that is, the person, company, or organization that provides information about you to a credit reporting company), in writing, that you dispute an item in your credit report. If the provider listed an address on your credit report, send your letter to that address. If no address is listed, contact the provider and ask for the correct address to send your letter. If the information provider does not give you an address, you can send your letter to any business address for that provider.

If the provider continues to report the item you disputed to a credit reporting company, it must let the credit reporting company know about your dispute. And if you are correct—that is, if the information you dispute is found to be inaccurate or incomplete—the information provider must tell the credit reporting company to update or delete the item.

About Your File

Your credit file may not reflect all your credit accounts. Although most national department store and all-purpose bank credit card accounts will be included in your file, not all creditors supply information to credit reporting companies: some local retailers, credit unions, travel, entertainment, and gasoline card companies are among the creditors that don't.

When negative information in your report is accurate, only the passage of time can assure its removal.

Chapter 55

Educational Goals and Responsibilities

Postsecondary education is important for future economic stability for the individual and the nation. Unfortunately, the high cost to attend a two- or four-year institution of higher education can keep lower and middle-income students from achieving an academic degree. A student must make a number of financial decisions to make higher education a possibility.

Prospective college students need to think about where they will go for college, how they will pay for it, and how they will manage their finances during school and beyond. Institutions of higher education, both two- and four-year, can help young people and other students gain financial capability.

Things to Consider before Applying for Student Loan

Don't Ignore Your Student Loans

Everyone can agree that student loans are no fun to pay back, but ignoring them can have serious consequences (and it won't make them go away.) If you're worried about your student loans or don't think you can afford your payments, contact for help. No matter what your financial situation is, Department of Education (DOL) can help you find an affordable repayment option. For many, that could mean payments as low as $0 per month.

About This Chapter: Text in this chapter begins with excerpts from "Financing Higher Education," Youth.gov, April 28, 2016; Text under the heading "Things to Consider before Applying for Student Loan" is excerpted from "8 Student Loan Tips for Recent College Grads," U.S. Department of Education, April 27, 2016.

Set a Budget

Life after graduation gets real, real fast. To make a plan to tackle your student loans, you need to understand what money you have coming in, and what expenses you have going out. If you haven't already, it's important that you create a budget. This will help determine your repayment strategy. Here are some budgeting tips to help you get started.

Choose an Affordable Payment Amount

There is no one-size-fits-all approach to paying back student loans. The key question you need to answer is: Do you want to get rid of your loans quickly or do you want to pay the lowest amount possible per month?

With the Standard Repayment Plan, the plan you'll enter if you don't take any action, you'll have your loans paid off in 10 years. If you can't afford that amount or if you need or want lower payments because you haven't found a job, aren't making much money, or want to free up room in your budget for other expenses and goals, you should apply for an income-driven repayment plan. Your monthly payments will likely be lower than they would on the standard plan—in fact they could be as low as $0 per month—but you'll likely be paying more and for a longer period of time. If you choose an income-driven plan, you must provide documentation of your income to your loan servicer each year (even if your income hasn't changed) so that your payment can be recalculated. To compare the different repayment options based on your loan debt, family size, and income, use the repayment calculator.

Research Forgiveness Options

There are legitimate ways to have your loans forgiven, but there are often very specific requirements you must meet in order to qualify. Research forgiveness programs ASAP, as it may affect your repayment strategy. For example, if you're interested in Public Service Loan Forgiveness, you'll want to make sure you have the right type of loans from the get-go (which may mean you have to consolidate), and you'll want to make sure to get on an income-driven repayment plan.

Sign Up for Automatic Payments

If you don't like thinking about your student loans, this is a great solution! Ok, ok, so you'll still have to think about your loans and make sure you have the money in your account to cover your monthly payments, but you won't have to worry about missing payments, writing checks, or logging into websites every month to pay your loans manually. Sign up for automatic debit through your loan servicer and your payments will be automatically taken from your bank account each month. As an added bonus, you get a 0.25 percent interest rate deduction when you enroll!

Make Extra Payments Whenever You Can

Pay early. Pay often. Pay extra. If you want to ensure that your loan is paid off faster, tell your servicer two things. First, tell them that the extra you pay is not intended to be put toward future payments. Second, tell them to apply the additional payments to your loan with the highest interest rate. By doing this, you can reduce the amount of interest you pay and reduce the total cost of your loan over time.

Don't Postpone Payments Unless You Really Need To

One of the flexible repayment options offered is the ability to temporarily stop (postpone) your student loan payments. This is called a deferment or forbearance. While they can be helpful solutions if you're experiencing a temporary hardship, these are not good long-term solutions. Why? Because in most cases, interest will continue to accrue (accumulate) on your loan while you're not making payments and may be capitalized (cause interest to accrue on interest). When you resume repayment (which you will have to do eventually) your loan balance will probably be even higher than it was before. If you're having financial trouble, why set yourself back even further by doing this? There are often better solutions available. Before choosing deferment or forbearance, ask about enrolling in an income-driven repayment plan. Under those plans, if you make little or nothing, you pay little or nothing. Additionally, with the income-driven repayment plans, you're working toward loan forgiveness while making a lower payment. Before postponing your payments, consider your other options.

Take Advantage of the Free Federal Student Loan Assistance

Each federal student loan borrower is assigned to a loan servicer (some borrowers may have more than one servicer, depending on the types of loans you have). Your loan servicer is a company that collects your student loan payments and provides customer service on behalf of the U.S. Department of Education. This is a FREE service. There are many companies out there who offer to help you with your student loans for a fee. Do not trust these companies.

Remember: You never have to pay for help with your student loans. If you need advice, assistance, or help applying for one of repayment programs, contact your loan servicer. They can help you for free. Just remember to keep your contact information up to date so they can reach you when they need to.

Student loans can seem overwhelming at first, but by taking this advice and setting up a repayment strategy that works for you, you'll master your student loans in no time!

Chapter 56

How to Have a Higher Earning Potential

You might want to earn a master's degree for the potential increase in earnings it may deliver. But there's more to going to graduate school than the chance for extra income, especially because the payoff varies by occupation.

In 2013, the median annual wage for full-time workers ages 25 and over whose highest level of education was a master's degree was $68,000, compared with $56,000 for those whose highest level was a bachelor's degree—a $12,000 a year wage premium. Not all workers earn a premium. In some occupations, workers with a master's degree earned about the same as, or even less than, those with a bachelor's degree.

Potential wages are just one of the factors to consider before embarking on a graduate education. In addition to showing how much more—or less—workers who had a master's degree earned compared with workers who had a bachelor's degree, this article highlights other questions to think about when deciding whether to pursue a master's degree.

Wage Premiums for a Master's Degree

In some occupations, you're likely to need a master's degree to qualify for entry-level jobs. In others, a master's degree may not be required, but having one might lead to advancement or higher pay.

There could be lots of reasons why workers with a master's degree had higher or lower wages than did those who had a bachelor's degree. Master's degree holders, for example, might

About This Chapter: This chapter includes text excerpted from "Should I Get a Master's Degree?" U.S. Bureau of Labor Statistics (BLS), U.S. Department of Labor (DOL), September 2015.

have qualified for better-paying jobs and have earned more than their counterparts who had a bachelor's degree. Or bachelor's degree holders—especially in occupations in which minimum educational requirements are increasing—might have had more years of experience and, as a result, might have had higher wages than workers with a master's degree.

Business

More master's degrees were awarded in business than in any other field, during 2012–13. And among all occupations in 2013, business, financial, and sales occupations had some of the highest wage premiums for workers with a master's degree.

Securities, commodities, and financial services sales agents had the biggest wage premium of any of these occupations: workers who had a master's degree earned a wage that was nearly 90 percent higher than that for workers with a bachelor's degree. Many of these sales agents earned a master's degree in business administration (MBA), which may be required for high-level jobs.

Other business occupations not shown in the table had wage premiums for a master's degree, including accountants and auditors, general and operations managers, and human resources workers.

However, in some business occupations, having a master's degree may not pay a premium. Training and development managers with a master's degree, for example, had a six-percent lower median wage than did these workers with a bachelor's degree.

Education

More than one out of every five master's degrees was awarded in education in 2012–13. And the payoff for these degrees was usually relatively high.

Education administrators had the highest percentage wage premium, with 44 percent higher wages for master's degree holders than for bachelor's degree holders. The wage premium for preschool and kindergarten teachers was nearly as high, at 43 percent.

The lowest wage premiums were for postsecondary teachers, who frequently needed a Ph.D. to qualify for entry-level jobs. About 30 percent of these workers had a master's degree, about 13 percent had a bachelor's degree, and nearly all remaining workers had a doctoral degree. Postsecondary teachers without a doctoral degree might work as a graduate teaching assistant or qualify to teach a subject such as nursing (with a master's degree) or vocational education (with a bachelor's degree).

Healthcare and Social Service

The fast-growing fields of healthcare and social service were common for master's degree awarded during 2012–13. Many occupations in these fields had wage premiums for a master's degree.

Chapter 57

Day Trading

What Is Day Trading?

Day trading is the practice of buying and selling stocks, commodities, securities, or options very quickly, usually by making many buy/sell transactions in a single day. Day traders are people who make their living by rapidly trading stocks with the goal of earning small profits on each one of a large number of trades. Because the value of individual stocks tends to change throughout a single day, day traders try to maximize their stock purchases by selling stocks at a higher price than they paid to buy the stocks. Day traders closely watch the fluctuating prices of stocks they own, and sell their stocks when the price reaches a certain value. As a result, day traders often hold the stocks they buy for very short periods of time, sometimes selling stocks a few seconds or minutes after they bought them. Day traders rarely hold stocks for long periods of time.

Quick Note

Day trading is extremely risky and can result in substantial financial losses in a very short period of time. Day traders must be able to tolerate this risk without losing confidence in their ability to make successful trades.

Who Are Day Traders?

In general, there are two kinds of day traders: those who work alone and those who work for a large financial institution. Day traders who work for a financial institution usually have

---

About This chapter: "Day Trading," © 2017 Omnigraphics.

extensive resources at their disposal, including the most advanced trading technology and software, access to large amounts of money for making stock purchases, and support staff that may assist with analysis of financial news in real time. Day traders who work alone sometimes manage money on behalf of other people and/or use their own money for trading. Individual day traders often do not have access to the robust resources and support that are available to institutional day traders. All day traders are typically well-educated and informed about the trading markets so that they can leverage information to maximize numerous transactions in a very short amount of time.

Day trading is a high-stress, fast-paced business that requires patience, intense focus, dedication, and quick reaction time. Each day trader will likely have a different approach or personal style when making short-term trades, but there are some characteristics that are generally shared by all successful day traders. The most successful day traders have extensive in-depth knowledge of the trading marketplace. Day trading requires a deep level of understanding of financial basics and stock market fundamental concepts. Day traders also need money that they can afford to lose, which is called capital. The use of capital for day trades helps to ensure that day traders minimize their risk. Every successful trader also works with a strategy that guides each of their trading decisions. A good strategy, informed by thorough analysis and plenty of real-time information, helps day traders achieve consistent profits and limit losses to acceptable levels. Perhaps the most important characteristic of a successful day trader is discipline. Adhering to a strategy and not allowing oneself to become overwhelmed by excitement or emotion requires an exceptional amount of discipline.

> The most common factor that causes day traders to quickly lose large amounts of money is failure to follow a strategy. A well-planned trading strategy typically outlines specific trading criteria and the discipline to follow the strategy. Most people simply do not have the money, time, or personality to become successful day traders.

How Does Day Trading Work?

Like all stock market transactions, day trading is governed by the U.S. Securities and Exchange Commission (SEC). The SEC defines day trading and publishes certain rules and guidelines that apply to short-term transactions. In general, day traders are defined as anyone who executes four or more buy/sell transactions within five business days, where the number of day trades exceeds six percent of that person's total number of trades for that same five-day period.

The SEC's definition is a minimum requirement, and some brokerage firms use a definition that is either more restrictive or broader in its view of day trading. Many brokerages require day traders to maintain $25,000 worth of minimum equity with which to execute rapid buy/sell transactions. This minimum equity deposit is usually required to be maintained at all times. If a trader's equity account falls below the minimum amount, they will not be allowed to make any more trades until the minimum deposit is restored.

Conversely, some brokerages place limits on the amount of trades each day trader can make. For example, some brokerages limit trades to a maximum of four times the value of the equity amount. If a day trader exceeds this limitation, their ability to execute day trades will be restricted for a period of time during which the trader must meet certain requirements. This practice is known as a margin call.

Pros and Cons of Day Trading

Day trading is considered a somewhat controversial activity. Some financial experts believe that day trading provides important benefits to the stock market in that day trades help the market operate with more efficiency while also providing a necessary amount of liquidity in stock values. (The term "liquidity" refers to money that is easily accessible or easily converted to cash.)

By contrast, some other financial experts find fault with day trading because it can be easily used to cheat vulnerable stock market investors. Critics of day trading typically view the practice as a suspicious get-rich-quick scheme that does more harm than good. For this reason, many professional money managers and financial advisors do not participate in or recommend day trading to their clients.

Did You Know?

Day trading is highly controversial but it is neither illegal nor unethical. Questioned by critics and praised by practitioners, day trading is one of the most hotly debated topics on Wall Street.

Day Trading Tools

Like most other professions, day trading requires access to and knowledge of specific tools and technology. Some common tools required for day trading include:

- Stock screening software programs that help traders focus on specific stocks and compare them against a set of criteria. The software performs the analysis based on criteria chosen by the trader and produces a list of potential stocks that meet the specified goal.

- Streaming quote software that acts as important analytic tools for day traders. Real-time information on stock values and other criteria help traders quickly react to changing market conditions.

- Watch lists that allow traders to constantly and automatically monitor the performance and value of specific stocks.

- Trading strategy building software that helps traders define the most appropriate criteria for buy/sell transactions in order to meet specific trading goals. Strategy building software typically includes functions such as market forecasting, risk prioritizing, market simulations, and advanced analysis.

- Multiple news sources that help day traders maximize real-time information that is related to the stock market. Successful day traders strive to be among the first to know when something happens in the world that will ultimately affect stock values. This requires constant monitoring and analysis of various sources of financial and current events news. Many different software programs exist to help traders keep up with the constant flow of information.

References

1. "An Introduction to Day Trading," Investopedia, January 10, 2017.

2. "What Is Day Trading?" Dummies.com, n.d.

3. "Margin Rules for Day Trading," U.S. Securities and Exchange Commission (SEC), Office of Investor Assistance and Education (OIAE), February 2011.

4. "Day Trading: Your Dollars at Risk," U.S. Securities and Exchange Commission (SEC), April 20, 2005.

5. "Pros and Cons of Day Trading vs Swing Trading," Investopedia, September 27, 2016.

6. "What Are the Pros and Cons of Day Trading?" Fox Business, March 28, 2012.

7. "The Four Best Tools for Day Trading," Day Trade Warrior Blog, February 27, 2017.

8. "Top Day Trading Tools," Advisory HQ, n.d.

Chapter 58

Ways to Make Money Online

Money is tight. It always is. Many high-school students are saving for college, need to help pay expenses, or just want extra cash for movies, video games, or other incidentals. College students have to think about tuition, books, lab fees, and other education-related costs, as well as spending money for entertainment, snacks, and miscellaneous expenses that give them a greater degree of independence.

And, sure, there are a lot of traditional jobs for teens—such as waiting tables, working at a grocery store, mowing lawns, or working at a fast-food restaurant—and these kinds of activities still provide good opportunities for millions of students every year. But enterprising, creative young people have a wealth of other opportunities available to them in the online world. And this kind of work has a number of advantages:

- You can work from home, a dorm room, or a nearby cafe, so there are no transportation issues.

- The Internet provides a level playing field; there, you're not seen as a kid earning pocket change, but are judged on the quality of your work, like everyone else.

- You're also paid the same as everyone else.

- You can make money with skills learned from a hobby or special area of interest.

- Most often, your time is your own, and you can schedule work in between classes, sports, and other activities.

So, although there's nothing wrong with bussing tables or working in a convenience store, if that's what you'd like to do, consider a few of the following examples of ways to earn money online.

About This Chapter: "Ways to Make Money Online," © 2017 Omnigraphics.

> At one time, teens looking to earn extra money had relatively few, poor-paying jobs available to them. But now, online sources provide a wide variety of opportunities to earn a good income.

Taking Surveys

A really easy way to begin making some cash on the Internet is to take online surveys. Each individual survey may not pay much, but there are a lot of survey sites out there, and working with them gives you a chance to express your opinion about various topics or products and perhaps influence others. However, some of these sites can be scams trying to get personal information, so it pays to be careful. Some of the better-known survey sites include GlobalTestMarket, InBoxDollars, i-Say, MySurvey, and Toluna.

Starting a Blog or Video Blog

One way to begin is to create a website, blog, or video blog focused on something you're passionate and knowledgeable about—a hobby, sport, school subject, or other areas of interest. If you're not up to building your own website, there are a number of existing sites that will host your written blog for free, including Tumblr, Weebly, Blogger, and WordPress. Video blogs can be uploaded to sites like YouTube or Vimeo. Turning your blog into a money-making operation may take time since you'll need to build a following, which translates into ad dollars. But once you get enough people reading or viewing your blog, platforms like Google's AdSense can help funnel money your way.

> At age 14, Ashley Qualls started Whateverlife.com, an informational website for teens. Through advertising sales, she made $1 million by the time she was 17. This success has allowed her to pursue new online interests that benefit other people and her community.

Selling Products Online

The advent of sites like eBay, Amazon, and Etsy has opened up a world of opportunity for people to sell things online. Global markets are no longer just the domain of multinational corporations. Everyone, including students, can now find worldwide buyers for everything from junk to collectibles to crafts. Even stuff that's been in your closet for years—old toys, video games, clothing, obsolete electronics—likely has value to someone, somewhere.

Testing Websites

Web developers, designers, and companies with their own sites are always looking for feedback from users, and some are willing to pay for it. If you have a good eye for detail, can identify poor navigation, design, and content, and are able to express your opinions in a clear and logical fashion, you could be an excellent candidate for testing websites. The best way to get started is to sign up at an online service that specializes in providing testers for many websites. One of the best known is UserTesting. Others include TryMyUI, Userlytics, and UserZoom. The best strategy is to sign up with as many services as possible to maximize income.

Writing for a Website

Site owners want their content refreshed regularly to keep users coming back, and that translates into opportunity for students who have the ability to write clearly and concisely on a variety of topics. A good way to begin is to approach the owners of sites you visit regularly for school, a hobby or other area of interest and ask if they need writers. Or, better yet, propose an article on a particular topic. Another option is to sign up as a writer at an online service that provides content for websites. Some of these include Iwriter, Scripted, and Writerbay. There are also sites like Articlesale that allow you to upload your own articles and make them available for sale.

Reviewing Music

Everyone has opinions about the music they listen to, so it makes sense to try to make some money reviewing songs. And since young people comprise a large segment of the listening audiences, many websites welcome the opinions of younger reviewers. At sites like MusicXray, Slicethepie, Radioloyalty, and Hitpredictor you can sign up to give a rating or write a review of songs by a variety of artists in many genres. Most don't pay much per song, but if you listen to a lot of music, the income can add up.

Programming

If you're good at programming, there are numerous opportunities for online work. Sites like Freelancer and Upwork allow you to see available projects on their sites and bid on them. In order to win a project, you'll either need to be known to the client or submit a very low bid. But by bidding low you'll gain experience and make contacts, which will help get future jobs. There are also programming contests for various languages, in which you compete against others for prizes. Companies and web developers watch these contests to scout for new talent, so the competition can lead to money-making opportunities. And if you can develop interesting apps for mobile devices, there are many online avenues for selling them.

Data Entry

Okay, so maybe you're not a programmer, but almost anyone can key, and there are online services that pay people for data entry. This area is rife with scams, so be careful. But if you're a reasonably fast, accurate keyer there are a number of reputable services you can sign up for, including VirtualBee, SmartLocating, and Microworkers.

Selling Photography

Students who take a lot of photos for their enjoyment may not think of their pictures as a money-makers, but there are a number of online outlets that regularly buy photographs, And, as a rule, they generally don't care if the photographer is a professional or an amateur as long as the quality is good and the subject matter fits into their agenda. Some of the better-known sites include Shutterstock, iStockPhoto, 500pxPrime, SmugMugPro, and Dreamstime.

Tutoring Online

If you have an outstanding skill or excel at a particular subject, you can sign up to be an online tutor. Even if you don't have formal training or an education degree, there are sites where you can register to share your knowledge. Some of these include Tutor.com, HomeworkTutoring, MyTutor24, Homeworkhelp, and Tutorvista. Many online tutoring jobs take place via video chat, so a reliable webcam may be required, but others are handled by sending documents back and forth. Almost all of them offer flexible hours and the ability to pick the jobs you're interested in.

These are just some of the ways it's possible for students to make money online. Once you start thinking about it, many more are likely to occur to you. The main thing is to be creative, be persistent, and concentrate on areas where you have the most interest. That way the work you find will be both profitable and enjoyable. Just be sure to use common sense when it comes to online security. As with almost anything else in the cyber world, online money-making opportunities present a lot of ways for unscrupulous people to take advantage of others.

> In addition to making money, working online also gives you the chance to try different things, make contacts for possible future work, and build your résumé.

References

1. Ahmad, Basheer. "The Best Online Jobs for College Students in 2017," CollegeStudentJobs.com, n.d.

2. Clarke, Oliver. "18 Legit Ways to Make Real Cash as a Teenager (Online)," 101Geek.com, 2016.

3. Dube, Ryan. "Best Websites for Teens to Earn Money Online," MakeUseOf.com, October 22, 2015.

4. Joseph, Frank. "How to Make Money Online for Teenagers in 2017," MoneyHomeBlog.com, January 22, 2017.

5. Satpathy, Sweta, "30 Secrets for Teens and Adults to Make Money Quickly Sitting at Home," Fedobe.com, n.d.

6. VanDerLaan, John. "12 Easy Ways for Teens to Make Money Online," Jvanderlaan.com, July 28, 2016.

Chapter 59

Things You Can Do to Avoid Fraud

Crooks use clever schemes to defraud millions of people every year. They often combine new technology with old tricks to get people to send money or give out personal information. Here are some practical tips to help you stay a step ahead.

1. **Spot imposters.** Scammers often pretend to be someone you trust, like a government official, a family member, a charity, or a company you do business with. Don't send money or give out personal information in response to an unexpected request—whether it comes as a text, a phone call, or an email.

2. **Do online searches.** Type a company or product name into your favorite search engine with words like "review," "complaint" or "scam." Or search for a phrase that describes your situation, like "IRS call." You can even search for phone numbers to see if other people have reported them as scams.

3. **Don't believe your caller ID.** Technology makes it easy for scammers to fake caller ID information, so the name and number you see aren't always real. If someone calls asking for money or personal information, hang up. If you think the caller might be telling the truth, call back to a number you know is genuine.

4. **Don't pay upfront for a promise.** Someone might ask you to pay in advance for things like debt relief, credit and loan offer, mortgage assistance, or a job. They might even say you've won a prize, but first, you have to pay taxes or fees. If you do, they will probably take the money and disappear.

About This Chapter: This chapter includes text excerpted from "10 Things You Can Do to Avoid Fraud," Federal Trade Commission (FTC), February 2014.

5. **Consider how you pay.** Credit cards have significant fraud protection built in, but some payment methods don't. Wiring money through services like Western Union or MoneyGram is risky because it's nearly impossible to get your money back. That's also true for reloadable cards like MoneyPak, Reloadit or Vanilla. Government offices and honest companies won't require you to use these payment methods.

6. **Talk to someone.** Before you give up your money or personal information, talk to someone you trust. Con artists want you to make decisions in a hurry. They might even threaten you. Slow down, check out the story, do an online search, consult an expert—or just tell a friend.

7. **Hang up on robocalls.** If you answer the phone and hear a recorded sales pitch, hang up and report it to the Federal Trade Commission (FTC). These calls are illegal, and often the products are bogus. Don't press 1 to speak to a person or to be taken off the list. That could lead to more calls.

8. **Be skeptical about free trial offers.** Some companies use free trials to sign you up for products and bill you every month until you cancel. Before you agree to a free trial, research the company and read the cancellation policy. And always review your monthly statements for charges you don't recognize.

9. **Don't deposit a check and wire money back.** By law, banks must make funds from deposited checks available within days, but uncovering a fake check can take weeks. If a check you deposit turns out to be a fake, you're responsible for repaying the bank.

10. **Sign up for free scam alerts from the FTC at** ftc.gov/scams. Get the latest tips and advice about scams sent right to your inbox.

If you spot a scam, report it at ftc.gov/complaint. Your reports help the FTC and other law enforcement investigate scams and bring crooks to justice.

Tips to Protect Yourself from Scams

- **Don't share numbers or passwords for accounts, credit cards, or Social Security.**
- **Never pay up front for a promised prize.** It's a scam if you are told that you must pay fees or taxes to receive a prize or other financial windfall.
- **After hearing a sales pitch, take time to compare prices.** Ask for information in writing and read it carefully.

- **Too good to be true?** Ask yourself why someone is trying so hard to give you a "great deal". If it sounds too good to be true, it probably is.

- **Watch out for deals that are only "good today" and that pressure you to act quickly.** Walk away from high-pressure sales tactics that don't allow you time to read a contract or get legal advice before signing. Also, don't fall for the sales pitch that says you need to pay immediately, for example by wiring the money or sending it by courier.

- **Put your number on the National Do Not Call Registry.** Go to www.donotcall.gov or call 1-888-382-1222.

(Source: "Bank Accounts and Services," Consumer Financial Protection Bureau (CFPB).)

Part Six
If You Need More Information

Chapter 60

Online Money Management Tools

BizKid$

A companion site for the public TV series that teaches kids and teens about money and business.
Website: www.bizkids.com

College Savings Plans Network

A nonprofit association dedicated to making a college education affordable and accessible.
Website: www.collegesavings.org

Compound Interest Calculator

Determine how much your money can grow using the power of compound interest. You can find out if you're dealing with a registered investment professional with a free search on Investor.gov's homepage.
Website: www.investor.gov/additional-resources/free-financial-planning-tools/compound-interest-calculator

Cost of Raising a Child Calculator

With this calculator you can estimate how much it will annually cost to raise a child. This may help you plan better for overall expenses including food or to purchase adequate life insurance.
Website: www.cnpp.usda.gov/calculatorintro

Dollars from Sense

Funded by the FINRA Investor Education, this interactive site instructs young adults in the basics of personal finance and investing.
Website: www.dollarsfromsense.com

About This Chapter: The tools/resources listed in this chapter were excerpted from various sources deemed reliable. Inclusion does not constitute endorsement, and there is no implication associated with omission. All website information was verified and updated in November 2018.

Estimation Calculators

This tool helps approximate the future value of your savings bonds and show how much and how long it will take to reach your goals.

Website: www.treasurydirect.gov/indiv/tools/tools_estimationcalc.htm

FastWeb

Fastweb is one of the oldest and largest scholarship sites. It offers connection to scholarships, colleges, financial aid, and student loan options.

Website: www.fastweb.com

GenIRevolution

Developed for middle school and high school students, this online game gives students the chance to learn important personal finance skills as they play and compete against fellow classmates. Online personal finance game for high school students developed by the Council for Economic Education.

Website: www.genirevolution.org

Growth Calculator

Use this calculator to see how your savings add up.

Website: www.savingsbonds.gov/BC/SBCGrw

Investor.gov: Invest Wisely

The resources you need to learn the basics, protect yourself, and stay informed.

Website: www.investor.gov

IRS Withholding Calculator

This Withholding calculator works for most taxpayers. You can use your results from this calculator to help you complete a new Form W-4, Employee's Withholding Allowance Certificate.

Website: www.irs.gov/individuals/irs-withholding-calculator

Jumpstart Coalition for Personal Financial Literacy

Coalition of organizations dedicated to improve financial literacy of pre-K through college-age youth.

Website: www.jumpstart.org

The Mint

Money management tips, games, and tools for kids, teens, and parents.

Website: www.themint.org

Moneytopia

Online interactive game to help teens learn to save and manage money.
Website: apps.finra.org/moneytopia

National Foundation for Credit Counseling

It is a nonprofit organization dedicated to improving people's financial well-being. It connects the consumers with local credit counseling services.
Website: www.nfcc.org

Savings Bond Calculator

This calculator will price Series EE, Series E, and Series I savings bonds, and Savings Notes. Features include current interest rate, next accrual date, final maturity date, and year-to-date interest earned.
Website: www.savingsbonds.gov/indiv/tools/tools_savingsbondcalc.htm

Savings Planner

Use this planner to find out how you can reach your savings goals.
Website: www.savingsbonds.gov/BC/SBCPln

SBA Teen Business Link

Ideas and advice for teen entrepreneurs.
Website: www. sba.gov/teens

Tax Advantage Calculator

This calculator is used to see how tax advantages factor into your savings bond earnings.
Website: www.savingsbonds.gov/BC/SBCTax

Teens and Money: Money 101

Resources, games, and activities for sound money management from the FINRA Investor Education Foundation.
Website: www.saveandinvest.org/educate-youth

Treasury Direct Kids®

Excellent introduction to public debt, treasury securities, and saving money.
Website: www.treasurydirect.gov/kids/kids.htm

U.S. Mint for Kids

Fun money facts and activities for kids, also includes financial literacy links for parents and teachers.
Website: www.usmint.gov/learn/kids

Chapter 61

Financial Independence Information for Disabled Teens

Self-Determination Resources

The Collaboration to Promote Self Determination (CPSD)
1667 K St. N.W.
Ste. 640
Washington, DC 20006
Phone: 202-350-0128
Website: www.thecpsd.org
E-mail: thecpsd@gmail.com

Office of the State Superintendent of Education (OSSE)
Division of Elementary, Secondary, and Specialized Education
810 First St. N.E.
Ninth Fl.
Washington, DC 20002
Phone: 202-727-6436
Website: osse.dc.gov

About This Chapter: Resources in this chapter were compiled from several sources deemed reliable; all contact information was verified and updated in November 2018.

Community Resources for IEP Meetings

Advocates for Justice and Education (AJE)

We Educate. We Advocate. We Empower.
25 E St. N.W.
Third Fl.
Washington, DC 20001
Phone: 202-678-8060
Website: www.aje-dc.org
E-mail: information@aje-dc.org

Disability Support Services

Department of Behavioral Health (DBH)

64 New York Ave. N.E.
Third Fl.
Washington, DC 20002
Toll-Free: 888-7WE-HELP (888-793-4357)
Phone: 202-673-2200
TTY: 202-673-7500
Fax: 202-673-3433
Website: dbh.dc.gov
E-mail: dbh@dc.gov

Department on Disability Services (DDS)

250 E St. S.W.
Washington, DC 20024
Phone: 202-730-1700
TTY: 202-730-1516
Fax: 202-730-1843
Website: dds.dc.gov
E-mail: dds@dc.gov

Office on Disability Rights (ODR)

441 Fourth St., N.W., Ste. 729 N.
Washington, DC 20001
Phone: 202-724-5055
TTY: 202-727-3363
Fax: 202-727-9484
Website: odr.dc.gov
E-mail: odr@dc.gov

Employment Resources

DC Rehabilitation Services Administration (RSA)

250 E St. S.W.
Washington, DC 20024
Phone: 202-730-1700
TTY: 202-730-1516
Website: dds.dc.gov
E-mail: dds@dc.gov

Department of Employment Services (DOES)

4058 Minnesota Ave. N.E.
Washington, DC 20019
Phone: 202-724-7000
TTY: 202-698-4817
Fax: 202-673-6993
Website: www.does.dc.gov
E-mail: does@dc.gov

DOES Office of Youth Programs (OYP)

Second Fl.
Phone: 202-698-3492
TTY: 202-741-5876
Fax: 202-698-5693
Website: www.does.dc.gov/service/youth-services
E-mail: does@dc.gov

Additional Employment Resources

Columbia Lighthouse for the Blind (CLB)

1825 K St. N.W.
Ste. 1103
Washington, DC 20006
Phone: 202-454-6400
Website: www.clb.org

Goodwill of Greater Washington (GGW)

2200 S. Dakota Ave. N.E.
Washington, DC 20018
Phone: 202-636-4225
Website: www.dcgoodwill.org

Montgomery Works

South Office Building
11002 Veirs Mill Rd.
First Fl.
Wheaton, MD 20902
Phone: 301-946-1806
Website: www.montgomeryworks.com

National Youth Employment Coalition (NYEC)

1836 Jefferson Place, N.W.
Washington, DC 20036
Phone: 202-659-1064
Website: www.nyec.org
E-mail: nyec@nyec.org

Supported Employment and Day Programs

Developmental Disabilities Administration (DDA)

250 E St. S.W.
Washington, DC 20024
Phone: 202-730-1700
TTY: 202-730-1516
Fax: 202-730-1843
Website: dds.dc.gov
E-mail: dds@dc.gov

Saint John's Community Services (SJCS)

2201 Wisconsin Ave. N.W.
Ste. C-120
Washington, DC 20007
Phone: 202-274-3459
Website: www.sjcs.org

United Cerebral Palsy (UCP) of Washington DC and Northern Virginia

3135 Eighth St. N.E.
Washington, DC 20017
Phone: 202-269-1500
Website: www.ucpdc.org

Government Benefits

U.S. Social Security Administration (SSA)

Toll-Free: 800-772-1213
Toll-Free TTY: 800-325-0778
Website: www.ssa.gov

College and Adult Education Resources

American University

Academic Support and Access Center
4400 Massachusetts Ave. N.W.
Mary Graydon Center, Rm. 243
Washington, DC 20016
Phone: 202-885-3360
Website: www.american.edu/ocl/asac
E-mail: asac@american.edu

The Catholic University of America (CUA)

620 Michigan Ave. N.E.
127 Pryzbyla Center
Washington, DC 20064
Phone: 202-319-5211
Website: www.dss.cua.edu

DC Tuition Assistance Grant Program (DCTAG)

810 First St. N.E.
Third Fl.
Washington, DC 20002
Toll-Free: 877-485-6751
Phone: 202-727-2824
Toll-Free TDD: 800-752-6096
Website: osse.dc.gov/service/dc-tuition-assistance-grant-dc-tag

DC College Savings Plan

P.O. Box 11466
Washington, DC 20008
Toll-Free: 800-987-4859
Website: www.dccollegesavings.com

District of Columbia College Access Program (DC CAP)

1400 L St. N.W.
Ste. 400
Toll-Free: 866-729-2025
Phone: 202-783-7933
Fax: 202-783-7939
Website: www.dccap.org

Free Application for Federal Student Aid (FAFSA®)

U.S. Department of Education (ED)
Toll-Free: 800-4-FED-AID (800 433-3243)
Phone: 319-337-5665
Toll-Free TTY: 800-730-8913
Website: www.fafsa.ed.gov

Gallaudet University

Jordan Student Academic Center (JSAC) 1220
800 Florida Ave. N.E.
Washington, DC 20002
Phone: 202-651-5256
Website: www.gallaudet.edu/oswd-the-office-for-students-with-disabilities.html

George Mason University (GMU)

Student Union Building I (SUB)
4400 University Dr.
Rm. 2500 MSN 5C9
Fairfax, VA 22030
Phone: 703-993-2474
Website: ods.gmu.edu

Georgetown University

Leavey Center
P.O. Box 571235
Ste. 335
Washington, DC 20057
Phone: 202-784-7366
Website: academicsupport.georgetown.edu/academic

Howard University

Howard Center
2225 Georgia Ave. N.W.
Ste. 725
Washington, DC 20059
Phone: 202-238-2420
Website: www.howard.edu/specialstudentservices/DisabledStudents.htm

Trinity Washington University (Trinity DC)

Main Bldg.
Second Fl., Office Number 212
Phone: 202-884-9358
Website: www.trinitydc.edu/disability

The University of Maryland (UMD), College Park

0106 Shoemaker Bldg.
4281 Chapel Ln.
College Park, MD 20740
Phone: 301-314-7682
Website: www.counseling.umd.edu/dss

University of the District of Columbia (UDC)

Disability Support Services Office
4200 Connecticut Ave. N.W.
Bldg. 44, Rm. A-39
Washington, DC 20008
Phone: 202-274-6417
TTY: 202-274-5579
Website: www.udc.edu/drc

Healthcare Resources

Advocates for Justice and Education (AJE)

Serving as the DC Health and Information Center and Family Voices for the District of Columbia
25 E St. N.W.
Third Fl.
Washington, DC 20001
Phone: 202-678-8060
Website: www.aje-dc.org
E-mail: information@aje-dc.org

Children's National Medical Center

111 Michigan Ave. N.W.
Washington, DC 20010
Phone: 202-476-5000
Website: www.childrensnational.org

DC Department of Health Care Finance (DHCF)

441 Fourth St. N.W. 900S
Washington, DC 20001
Phone: 202-442-5988
Fax: 202-442-4790
Website: dhcf.dc.gov
E-mail: dhcf@dc.gov

The George Washington University Hospital

900 2Third St. N.W.
Washington, DC 20037
Phone: 202-715-4000
Website: www.gwhospital.com

Hospital for Sick Children

1731 Bunker Hill Rd., N.E.
Washington, DC 20017
Phone: 202-832-4400
Website: www.hscpediatriccenter.org

Howard University Hospital

2041 Georgia Ave. N.W.
Washington, DC 20060
Phone: 202-865-6100
Website: www.huhealthcare.com

The HSC Foundation

2013 H St. N.W.
Ste. 300
Washington, DC 20006
Phone: 202-454-1220
Website: www.hscfoundation.org

MedStar Georgetown University Hospital

3800 Reservoir Rd., N.W.
Washington, DC 20007
Phone: 202-444-2000
Website: www.medstargeorgetown.org

MedStar National Rehabilitation Hospital

102 Irving St. N.W.
Washington, DC 20010
Phone: 202-877-1000
Website: www.medstarnrh.org

MedStar Washington Hospital Center

110 Irving St. N.W.
Washington, DC 20010
Phone: 202-877-7000
Website: www.medstarwashington.org

The National Alliance to Advance Adolescent Health

1615 M St. N.W.
Ste. 290
Washington, DC 20036
Phone: 202-223-1500
Website: www.TheNationalAlliance.org

Providence Hospital

1150 Varnum St. N.E.
Washington, DC 20017
Phone: 202-269-7000
Website: www.provhosp.org

Sibley Memorial Hospital

5255 Loughboro Rd., N.W.
Washington, DC 20016
Phone: 202-537-4000
Website: www.sibley.org

Housing Rights

District of Columbia Field Office

820 First St. N.E.
Ste. 300
Washington, DC 20002
Phone: 202-275-9200
TTY: 202-275-6388
Fax: 202-275-6381
Website: www.hud.gov

Residential Resources

District of Columbia Housing Authority

1133 N. Capitol St. N.E.
Washington, DC 20002
Phone: 202-535-1000
Website: www.dchousing.org

Independent Living Resources

DC Center for Independent Living, Inc. (DCCIL)

1400 Florida Ave. N.E.
Ste. 3A
Washington, DC 20002
Phone: 202-388-0033
TTY: 202-470-1534
Website: www.dccil.org

Transportation Resources

Washington Metropolitan Area Transit Authority (WMATA)

600 Fifth St. N.W.
Washington, DC 20001
Phone: 202-637-7000
TTY: 202-638-3780
Website: www.wmata.com

Recreation, Social, and Arts Programs

The Art and Drama Therapy Institute
327 S St. N.E.
Washington, DC 20002
Phone: 202-635-1576
Website: www.adtinet.com

Art Enables
2204 Rhode Island Ave. N.W.
Washington, DC 20018
Phone: 202-554-9455
Website: www.art-enables.org
E-mail: staff@art-enables.org

ArtStream, Inc.
620 Pershing Dr.
Silver Spring, MD 20910
Phone: 301-565-4567
Website: www.art-stream.org

DC Center for Therapeutic Recreation
DC Parks and Recreation
3030 G St. S.E.
Washington, DC 20019
Phone: 202-698-1794
TTY: 023-345-6789
Website: dpr.dc.gov/service/therapeutic-recreation

John F. Kennedy Center for the Performing Arts
2700 F St. N.W.
Washington, DC 20566
Toll-Free: 800-444-1324
Phone: 202-467-4600
Website: www.kennedy-center.org/education/vsa

Lifeline Partnerships, Inc.
309 E St. N.W.
Washington, DC 20001
Phone: 202-628-4819
Website: www.LifelinePartnership.org

Additional Recreation Resources

Best Buddies Program Washington, D.C.
1875 Connecticut Ave.
10th Fl.
Washington, DC 20009
Toll-Free: 800-892-8339
Phone: 703-533–9420
Website: www.ebuddies.org

Imagination Stage
4908 Auburn Ave.
Bethesda, MD 20814
Phone: 301-961-6060
Website: www.imaginationstage.org

Keen Greater DC
P.O. Box 341590
Bethesda, MD 20827
Phone: 301-770-3200
Website: www.keengreaterdc.org

Serve DC
Frank D Reeves Municipal Center
2000 14th St. N.W.
Ste. 101
Washington, DC 20009
Phone: 202-727-7925
TTY: 202-727-8421
Website: www.serve.dc.gov

Technology Resources

Assistive Technology Program for the District of Columbia (ATPDC)
220 I St. N.E.
Ste. 130
Washington, DC 20002
Phone: 202-589-0288
Website: www.atpdc.org

DC Public Library

DC Regional Library for the Blind and Physically Handicapped (Center for Accessibility)
901 G St. N.W.
Rm. 215
Washington, DC 20001
Phone: 202-727-2142
Website: www.dclibrary.org/services/accessibility

Advocacy Resources

Advocates for Justice and Education (AJE)

We Educate. We Advocate. We Empower.
25 E St. N.W.
Third Fl.
Washington DC 20001
Phone: 202-678-8060
Website: www.aje-dc.org
E-mail: information@aje-dc.org

Children's Law Center

616 H St. N.W.
Ste. 300
Washington, DC 20001
Phone: 202-467-4900
Website: www.childrenslawcenter.org

Quality Trust for Individuals with Disabilities

4301 Connecticut Ave. N.W.
Ste. 310
Washington, DC 20008
Phone: 202-448-1450
Fax: 202-448-1451
Website: www.dcqualitytrust.org

University Legal Services (ULS)

Protection and Advocacy Program
220 I St. N.E., Ste. 130
Washington, DC 20002
Phone: 202-547-0198
Fax: 202-547-2662
Website: www.uls-dc.org

Youth Advocates Program, Inc.

2007 N. Third St.
P.O. Box 950
Harrisburg, PA 17102
Phone: 717-232-7580
Website: www.yapinc.org

National Resources

AmeriCorps VISTA

1201 New York Ave. N.W.
Washington, DC 20525
Toll-Free: 800-833-3722
Phone: 202-606-5000
Website: www.americorps.gov

The Arc

1825 K St. N.W.
Ste. 1200
Washington, DC 20036
Toll-Free: 800-433-5255
Website: www.thearc.org

Institute for Community Inclusion (ICI)

University of Massachusetts, Boston
100 Morrissey Blvd.
Boston, MA 02125
Phone: 617-287-4300
TTY: 617-287-4350
Fax: 617-287-4352
Website: www.communityinclusion.org

Job Accommodation Network (JAN)

Toll-Free: 800-526-7234
Toll-Free TTY: 877-781-9403
Website: askjan.org

National Collaborative on Workforce and Disability (NCWD/Youth)

Toll-Free: 877-871-0744
Toll-Free TTY: 877-871-0665
Website: www.nwcd-youth.info

National Youth Leadership Network (NYLN)

P.O. Box 5908
Bethesda, MD 20824
Phone: 301-915-0353
Website: www.nyln.org

United Cerebral Palsy (UCP) of Washington DC and Northern Virginia

3135 Eighth St. N.E.
Washington, DC 20017
Phone: 202-269-1500
Website: www.ucpdc.org

Chapter 62

Resources for Financial Independence

ACA International
P.O. Box 390106
Minneapolis, MN 55439
Phone: 952-926-6547
Website: www.acainternational.org

American Association of Individual Investors (AAII)
625 N. Michigan Ave.
Chicago, IL 60611
Toll-Free: 800-428-2244
Phone: 312-280-0170
Fax: 312-280-9883
Website: www.aaii.com
E-mail: techsupport@aaii.com

American Bankers Association (ABA)
1120 Connecticut Ave. N.W.
Washington, DC 20036
Toll-Free: 800-BANKERS (800-226-5377)
Website: www.aba.com
E-mail: cutserv@aba.com

About This Chapter: Resources in this chapter were compiled from several sources deemed reliable; all contact information was verified and updated in November 2018.

American Consumer Credit Counseling (ACCC)

130 Rumford Ave.
Ste. 202
Auburndale, MA 02466-1371
Toll-Free: 800-769-3571
Phone: 617-559-5700
Fax: 617-244-1116
Website: www.consumercredit.com
E-mail: info@consumercredit.com

American Council of Life Insurers (ACLI)

101 Constitution Ave. N.W.
Ste. 700
Washington, DC 20001-2133
Toll-Free: 877-674-4659
Phone: 202-624-2000
Website: www.acli.com
E-mail: webadmin@acli.com

American Financial Services Association (AFSA)

919 18th St. N.W.
Ste. 300
Washington, DC 20006
Website: www.afsaonline.org
E-mail: info@afsamail.org

American Institute of Certified Public Accountants (AICPA)

Personal Financial Planning Division
1455 Pennsylvania Ave. N.W.
Washington, DC 20004-1081
Toll-Free: 888-777-7077
Phone: 202-737-6600
Fax: 202-638-4512
Website: www.aicpa.org
E-mail: service@aicpa.org

338

Asset Builders of America

1213 N. Sherman Ave.
Ste. 195
Madison, WI 53704
Phone: 608-663-6332
Website: www.assetbuilders.org
E-mail: info@assetbuilders.org

Bankrate.com

Toll-Free: 855-733-0700
Website: www.bankrate.com

BetterInvesting

711 W. 13 Mile Rd.
Ste. 900
Madison Heights, MI 48071
Phone: 248-583-6242
Fax: 248-583-4880
Website: www.betterinvesting.org
E-mail: service@betterinvesting.org

Certified Financial Planner (CFP)

Board of Standards
1425 K St. N.W.
Ste. 800
Washington, DC 20005
Toll-Free: 800-487-1497
Phone: 202-379-2200
Fax: 202-379-2299
Website: www.cfp.net
E-mail: mail@cfpboard.org

Choose to Save®

Employee Benefit Research Institute's Education and Research Fund (EBRI-ERF)
1100 13th St. N.W.
Ste. 878
Washington, DC 20005
Phone: 202-659-0670
Fax: 202-775-6312
Website: www.choosetosave.org
E-mail: info@choosetosave.org

Consolidated Credit, Inc.
5701 W. Sunrise Blvd.
Fort Lauderdale, FL 33313
Toll-Free: 800-320-9929
Website: www.consolidatedcredit.org

Consumer Action
1170 Market St.
Ste. 500
San Francisco, CA 94102
Phone: 415-777-9635
Fax: 415-777-5267
Website: www.consumer-action.org

Consumer Federation of America (CFA)
1620 I St. N.W.
Ste. 200
Washington, DC 20006
Phone: 202-387-6121
Website: consumerfed.org
E-mail: cfa@consumerfed.org

Consumers' Checkbook
1625 K St. N.W.
Eighth Fl.
Washington, DC 20006
Toll-Free: 800-213-7283
Website: www.checkbook.org

Council for Economic Education (CEE)
122 E. 42nd St.
Ste. 2600
New York, NY 10168
Phone: 212-730-7007
Fax: 212-730-1793
Website: www.councilforeconed.org

Credit Union National Association (CUNA)
5710 Mineral Pt. Rd.
Madison, WI 53705
Toll-Free: 800-356-9655
Website: www.cuna.org
E-mail: hello@cuna.coop

Credit.org
4351 Latham St.
Riverside, CA 92501
Toll-Free: 800-431-8157
Website: www.credit.org
E-mail: ClientHelp@credit.org

CreditSmart
1551 Park Run Dr. MS D5O
McLean, VA 22102
Toll-Free: 800-FREDDIE (800-373-3343)
Website: www.freddiemac.com/creditsmart

CuraDebt
4000 Hollywood Blvd.
Ste. 555-S
Hollywood, FL 33021
Toll-Free: 877-850-3328
Fax: 754-333-5510
Website: www.curadebt.com
E-mail: counselors@curadebt.com

Debtors Anonymous (DA)
1116 Great Plain Ave.
Needham, MA 02492
Toll-Free: 800-421-2383
Phone: 781-453-2743
Fax: 781-453-2745
Website: debtorsanonymous.org

Dominion Bond Rating Service (DBRS)

333 W. Wacker Dr.
Ste. 1800
Chicago, IL 60606
Phone: 312-332-3429
Fax: 312-332-3492
Website: www.dbrs.com
E-mail: info@dbrs.com

Employee Benefit Research Institute (EBRI)

1100 13th St. N.W.
Ste. 878
Washington, DC 20005-4051
Phone: 202-659-0670
Fax: 202-775-6312
Website: ww.ebri.org
E-mail: info@ebri.org

Equifax, Inc.

P.O. Box 740241
Atlanta, GA 30374-0241
Toll-Free: 866-349-5191
Website: www.equifax.com/personal

Experian Information Solutions, Inc.

475 Anton Blvd.
Costa Mesa, CA 92626
Phone: 714-830-7000
Website: www.experian.com

Federal Deposit Insurance Corporation (FDIC)

Division of Finance
3501 N. Fairfax Dr. Bldg. E
Fifth Fl.
Arlington, VA 22226
Toll-Free: 800-759-6596
Website: www.fdic.gov
E-mail: assessments@fdic.gov

Federal Reserve Education
Board of Governors of the Federal Reserve System
20th St. and Constitution Ave. N.W.
Washington, DC 20551
Phone: 202-452-3000
TDD: 202-263-4869
Website: www.federalreserveeducation.org

Federal Trade Commission (FTC)
600 Pennsylvania Ave. N.W.
Washington, DC 20580
Phone: 202-326-2222
Website: www.ftc.gov
E-mail: webmaster@ftc.gov

Financial Planning Association (FPA)
7535 E. Hampden Ave.
Ste. 600
Denver, CO 80231
Toll-Free: 800-322-4237
Phone: 303-759-4900
Website: www.onefpa.org
E-mail: info@onefpa.org

InCharge Debt Solutions
5750 Major Blvd.
Ste. 300
Orlando, FL 32819
Toll-Free: 877-906-5599
Website: www.incharge.org

Insurance Information Institute (III)
110 William St.
New York, NY 10038
Phone: 212-346-5500
Website: www.iii.org
E-mail: info@iii.org

Internal Revenue Service (IRS)
1111 Constitution Ave. N.W.
Washington, DC 20224
Phone: 267-941-1000
Fax: 267-466-1055
Website: www.irs.gov

Investment Company Institute (ICI)
1401 H St. N.W.
Ste. 1200
Washington, DC 20005
Phone: 202-326-5800
Website: www.ici.org
E-mail: webmaster@ici.org

Investor Protection Trust (IPT)
1020 19th St. N.W.
Ste. 890
Washington, DC 20036-6123
Website: www.investorprotection.org
E-mail: iptinfo@investorprotection.org

Iowa State University (ISU) Cooperative Extension
2150 Beardshear Hall
Ames, IA 50011-2031
Toll-Free: 800-262-3804
Website: www.extension.iastate.edu

Jump$tart Coalition
1001 Connecticut Ave. N.W.
Ste. 640
Washington, DC 20036
Phone: 202-846-6780
Website: www.jumpstart.org
E-mail: info@jumpstart.org

Junior Achievement USA®
One Education Way
Colorado Springs, CO 80906
Phone: 719-540-8000
Website: www.juniorachievement.org

Kiplinger

1100 13th St. N.W.
Ste. 750
Washington, DC 20005
Toll-Free: 800-544-0155
Phone: 202-887-6400
Website: www.kiplinger.com

Morningstar

22 W. Washington St.
Chicago, IL 60602
Phone: 312-696-6000
Website: www.morningstar.in
E-mail: productinfo@morningstar.com

Motley Fool

2000 Duke St.
Fourth Fl.
Alexandria, VA 22314
Fax: 703-254-1999
Website: www.fool.com

Nasdaq

One Liberty Plaza
165 Bdwy.
New York, NY 10006
Phone: 212-401-8700
Website: www.nasdaq.com

National Association of Personal Financial Advisors (NAPFA)

8700 W. Bryn Mawr Ave.
Ste. 700N
Chicago, IL 60631
Toll-Free: 888-FEE-ONLY (888-333-6659)
Phone: 847-483-5400
Website: www.napfa.org
E-mail: info@napfa.org

National Association of Professional Insurance Agents (PIA)

419 N. Lee St.
Alexandria, VA 22314
Phone: 703-836-9340
Fax: 703-836-1279
Website: pianet.com
E-mail: web@pianet.org

National Association of Real Estate Investment Trusts (NAREIT)

1875 I St. N.W.
Ste. 600
Washington, DC 20006
Toll-Free: 800-362-7348
Phone: 202-739-9400
Fax: 202-739-9401
Website: www.reit.com/nareit

National Consumer Law Center, Inc. (NCLC)

7 Winthrop Sq.
Boston, MA 02110-1245
Phone: 617-542-8010
Fax: 617-542-8028
Website: www.nclc.org
E-mail: consumerlaw@nclc.org

National Consumers League (NCL)

1701 K St. N.W.
Ste. 1200
Washington, DC 20006
Phone: 202-835-3323
Website: www.nclnet.org
E-mail: info@nclnet.org

National Endowment for Financial Education (NEFE)

1331 17th St.
Ste. 1200
Denver, CO 80202
Toll-Free: 866-460-5586
Phone: 303-741-6333
Website: www.nefe.org

National Futures Association (NFA)

300 S. Riverside Plaza, Ste. 1800
Chicago, IL 60606-6615
Toll-Free: 800-621-3570
Phone: 312-781-1300
Fax: 312-781-1467
Website: www.nfa.futures.org

National Institute of Food and Agriculture (NIFA)

U.S. Department of Agriculture (USDA)
1400 Independence Ave. S.W.
Washington, DC 20250
Toll-Free: 877-622-3056
Phone: 202-720-2791
Website: nifa.usda.gov

Navient Solutions, Inc.

P.O. Box 9500
Wilkes-Barre, PA 18773-9500
Phone: 570-821-6585
Website: www.navient.com

New York Stock Exchange, Inc. (NYSE)

Website: www.nyse.com

North American Securities Administrators Association (NASAA)

750 First St. N.E.
Ste. 1140
Washington, DC 20002
Phone: 202-737-0900
Fax: 202-783-3571
Website: www.nasaa.org

Plan Sponsor Council of America (PSCA)

200 S. Wacker Dr.
Ste. 3100
Chicago, IL 60606
Phone: 312-419-186
Fax: 703-516-9308
Website: www.psca.org
E-mail: psca@psca.org

Practical Money Skills

900 Metro Center Blvd.
MS-M1-11NE
Foster City, CA 94404-2172
Website: www.practicalmoneyskills.com
E-mail: info@practicalmoneyskills.com

Rutgers Cooperative Extension

New Jersey Agricultural Experiment Station (NJAES)
88 Lipman Dr.
New Brunswick, NJ 08901-8525
Phone: 848-932-9126
Website: njaes.rutgers.edu

Securities Industry and Financial Markets Association Foundation for Investor Education (SIFMA)

120 Bdwy.
35th Fl.
Phone: 212-313-1200
Website: www.sifma.org
E-mail: inquiry@sifma.org

Society of Financial Service Professionals (FSP)

3803 W. Chester Pike
Newtown Square, PA 19073-2334
Phone: 610-526-2500
Website: national.societyoffsp.org

TransUnion LLC

Website: www.transunion.com

TSX Inc.

TMX Group Limited
Toll-Free: 888-873-8392
Website: www.tmx.com
E-mail: businessdevelopment@tmx.com

USAA Educational Foundation (USAAEF)

9800 Fredericksburg Rd.
San Antonio, TX 78288-0026
Website: usaaef.org
E-mail: edfoundation_info@usaa.com

U.S. Commodity Futures Trading Commission (CFTC)

Three Lafayette Centre
1155 21st St. N.W.
Washington, DC 20581
Phone: 202-418-5000
Website: www.cftc.gov

U.S. Department of the Treasury (USDT)

1500 Pennsylvania Ave. N.W.
Washington, DC 20220
Toll-Free: 800-826-9434
Phone: 202-622-2000
Website: home.treasury.gov

U.S. Securities and Exchange Commission (SEC)

100 F St. N.E.
Washington, DC 20549
Toll-Free: 800-SEC-0330 (800-732-0330)
Phone: 202-551-6551
Website: www.sec.gov
E-mail: webmaster@sec.gov

U.S. Trustee Program

Website: www.justice.gov/ust

Index

Index

Page numbers that appear in *Italics* refer to tables or illustrations. Page numbers that have a small 'n' after the page number refer to citation information shown as Notes. Page numbers that appear in **Bold** refer to information contained in boxes within the chapters.

A

"About Ticket to Work" (SSA) 31n
adjustable-rate mortgage (ARM), mortgage loan 164
adverse action
    background check 195
    described 213
    free report 289
    your rights 279
adverse action notice, background check 195
advertising
    plan ahead 23
    traditional marketing tools 123
Advocates for Justice and Education (AJE), contact 322, 327, 333
afterschool program, financial confidence 25
age of majority, emancipation laws 27
allowance, formal instruction on money matters 5
alternative financial services, people with disabilities 32
American opportunity tax credit (AOTC), tax benefits for education 179
American University, contact 325
Americans with Disabilities Act (ADA), job banks and other resources 56
AmeriCorps
    contact 334
    volunteer experience 74
AmeriCorps VISTA, contact 334

annual percentage rate (APR)
    borrowing money 177
    getting good deals 170
    money mistakes 136
antivirus software, secure your computer 163
apartment cosigner service, described 222
apprenticeship
    career preparation 261
    defined 263
    high school course plan 262
    transition to adulthood and careers **57**
APR *see* annual percentage rate
The Arc, contact 334
"Are You A Teen Worker" (CDC) 111n
The Art and Drama Therapy Institute, contact 331
Art Enables, contact 331
Articlesale, online content writing service 307
ArtStream, Inc., contact 331
"Assessing Yourself and Your Future" (Omnigraphics) 7n
assessment tools, described 9
assets
    banks 141
    fiduciary **184**
    loan programs **122**
    poor credit history 35
Assistive Technology Program for the District of Columbia (ATPDC), contact 332
associate's degree, described 264

athlete, career path 55
ATM *see* automated teller machine
ATM card, described 237
attorney fees
    closing costs 15
    security deposit 215
auto insurance, late payments 137
automated deposits, saving money 172
automated teller machine (ATM)
    charges **138**
    money management **153**
automatic debit
    checking account 153
    electronic banking 237
    school-preferred products 295
automatic transfer
    future financial goals 252
    individual retirement account (IRA) 173
    savings 161
awards, other qualifications 75

B

bachelor's degree
    after high school 263
    described 264
    higher earning potential 297
    specific entry requirements 119
background check
    job application 176
    landlord requirements 211
    renting an apartment 194
    reputable creditors 121
bad credit
    background check 194
    tips to help rebound 283
balance
    credit card *281*
    credit report errors *288*
    mortgage payment 15
    reducing debt 284
    repayment plan 295
    work–life balance 101
bank *see* banking; bankruptcy
bank accounts, described 174
bank statement
    financial records 163
    landlords requirements 222
    review bills 139

banking
    choosing account 174
    facts 141
    savings accounts 138
banking practices, financial illiteracy 5
banking system, retail banks 142
bankruptcy
    credit record 137, 267
    credit reporting agencies (CRA) 270
    filing 283
    negative information 281
    private student loans 168
banks
    avoiding fraud 312
    overview 141–6
    savings account choices 162
barriers, financial capability 36
"Basic Facts about Banks and Banking"
    (Omnigraphics) 141n
"Being an Effective Parent—Helping Your Child
    through Early Adolescence" (USA.gov) 19n
benefit rolls, Ticket to Work 33
Best Buddies Program Washington, D.C., contact 332
bill payment history, credit report 267
bills
    budget 128, 282
    credit report 275
    debt 233
    expenses 235
    late payment 136
    rebuilding credit history 284
BizKid$, website 317
blog, described 306
bonds
    financial planning services 184
    savings 138
borrow
    costs and responsibilities 177
    credit score 285
    described 164
    equity 17
    federal student loan 247
    higher education loans 167
    interest 15
borrowers, federal student loan 295
borrowing money
    described 167
    mortgage payment 15
    serious debt problem 136

budgeting
    credit counseling organizations 283
    overview 127–33
    tips 294
"Budgeting Tips" (ED) 127n

C

calculators
    auto loans 170
    financial goals 148
capacity, financial capability 3
car loan
    credit score 268
    poor credit history 35
career clusters, school and community-based
    programs 114
career counselor, effective self-assessment assistance 10
career development, Ticket to Work program 32
career development services, Ticket to Work
    program 32
"Career Planning for High Schoolers" (BLS) 257n
career preparation, overview 257–65
career-related experiences, getting experience 259
cash
    banks 142
    credit card rewards programs 165
    electronic banking 237
    limiting credit card use 136, 284
    liquidity 303
    savings 129
cash flow, banks 142
The Catholic University of America (CUA),
    contact 325
Centers for Disease Control and Prevention (CDC)
    publications
        teens with disabilities 31n
        workers' rights 111n
        workplace stress 97n
        young workers' safety 107n
central bank, defined 142
certificate
    apprenticeships 80
    education 74
    savings accounts 143
certificates of deposit (CDs), retail bank services 143
certification, career programs 262
"Changes Could Help Boost Credit Scores"
    (FDIC) 279n

chartered financial analyst, financial planning
    services 185
"Checklist for Opening a Bank or Credit Union
    Account" (CFPB) 151n
checking accounts
    bank services 143
    credit unions 145
checklists, checking account 152
checks
    checking account 143
    electronic fund transfer (EFT) 237
child labor laws, safe work 108
"Child Labor Provisions of the Fair Labor Standards
    Act (FLSA) for Nonagricultural Occupations"
    (DOL) 39n
Children's Law Center, contact 333
Children's National Medical Center, contact 328
chore
    gaining experiences 56
    taking responsibility 20
coins, history 141
college
    bachelor's degree 264
    career preparation 257
    college-prep programs 262
    making money online 305
    scholarship sources 242
    statistics 263
    study-abroad program 245
    transportation costs 231
college degrees, career preparation 261
college-prep programs, described 262
College Savings Plans Network, website 317
Columbia Lighthouse for the Blind (CLB), contact 323
commercial banks, bank types 142
commodities
    biggest wage premium 298
    day trading 301
communication skills
    social media 66
    soft skills 85
community career services, described 68
community college
    associate's degree 264
    continuous learning options 58
community service, work-related skills 261
comparison shopping
    defined 133
    financial capability 4

complaints, work organization 99
compound interest, defined 138
Compound Interest Calculator, website 317
compulsory school attendance, hours' standards 47
computers
    business etiquette 85
    vocational programs 56
consumer culture, responsible financial habits 23
Consumer Financial Protection Bureau (CFPB)
    publications
        banking basics 151n
        financial independence and disabled teens 31n
        money management 23n
        teen financial independence 23n
consumer protection, tabulated *158*
consumer report, described 212
consumer reporting agency
    borrowing 164
    credit scores 285
    landlord requirements 212
contributions, credit repair fraud 282
corporations, credit unions 145
correcting errors
    credit report accuracy 164
    credit report errors 289
cosigner
    adverse action 213
    overview 221–3
"Cosigning Requirements for Young Renters"
    (Omnigraphics) 221n
Cost of Raising a Child Calculator, website 317
counseling, credit score rebuilding 285
cover letter, overview 77–9
Coverdell education savings account (ESA), savings
    plans 180
credentials
    financial planner 185
    job training 263
credit accounts
    credit file 291
    credit scores 268
credit bureaus
    bad credit 283
    credit reports 164
    defined 136
credit card
    budgeting 129
    cosigner 222
    credit file 291

credit card, *continued*
    credit report 275
    debit card 238
    good credit record 171
    savings and investing 149
    scams **312**
    tabulated *156*
credit card balance
    debt 165
    interest 139
    risks **156**
credit card debt, financial capability 4
credit check, apartment renting 192
credit counselor, credit score rebuilding 283
credit freeze, described 269
credit history
    borrowing 164
    cosigner 222
    credit scores 268
    financing 255
    security deposit 12
credit limit
    credit record **171**
    tabulated *156*
credit record, money management 136
"Credit Repair: How to Help Yourself" (FTC) 279n
credit report
    borrowing 164
    consumer report 212
    credit check 195
    credit score 279
    described 267
    errors **288**
    leasing 12
credit reporting agencies
    described 270
    free credit report 268
    credit scores 285
"Credit Reports and Scores" (USA.gov) 267n
credit score
    borrowing 164
    cosigner 222
    described 268
    overview 275–8
    rebuilding 284
    self-employment 121
credit union account
    disabled teens 32
    saving and investing 149

credit unions
    account 152
    credit file 291
    credit scores 283
    described 145
criminal history, landlord requirements 211
currency, central banks 142
customer service
    credit unions 145
    disabled teens 33
    federal student loan assistance 295
    self-employment 119

D

data entry, described 308
"Day Trading" (Omnigraphics) 301n
DC Center for Independent Living, Inc. (DCCIL), contact 330
DC Center for Therapeutic Recreation, contact 331
DC College Savings Plan, contact 325
DC Department of Health Care Finance (DHCF), contact 328
DC Public Library, contact 333
DC Rehabilitation Services Administration (RSA), contact 323
DC Tuition Assistance Grant Program (DCTAG), contact 325
debit card transactions, fees 138
debit cards
    bank account 174
    money management 177
    retail banks 142
debt
    cosigner 222
    credit card *156*
    credit record **171**
    credit report 267
    credit score 283
    eviction 199
    financial literacy 5
    foster care teens 35
    interest payment 165
    money management 136
    renting 16
    savings **148**
    student loan 294
debt collection agencies, student loan 168
debt overload, money management 136

decision-making
    assessment tools 9
    self-employment 117
    workplace ethics 95
deduction
    landlord responsibilities 215
    security deposit 199
    tax 180
Department of Behavioral Health (DBH), contact 322
Department of Employment Services (DOES), contact 323
Department on Disability Services (DDS), contact 322
dependence
    disabled teens 34
    workplace stress 98
deposit account, banks 174
deposits
    electronic fund transfers (EFT) 237
    mobile banking **143**
    renting 12
Developmental Disabilities Administration (DDA), contact 324
direct debit, tabulated *155*
direct deposit
    defined 238
    student aid 168
    wages 157
direct recurring payments, direct deposit 238
disability
    career exploration 56
    defined 31
    federal employee assistance **82**
    insurance 162
    landlord discrimination 195
    rights 112
    workplace stress 98
disability benefits, Ticket to Work program 33
"Disability Overview" (CDC) 31n
disclosure
    financial privacy **165**
    investment **184**
    landlord 215
discrimination
    employment 40
    housing 222
    landlord 195
    workers' rights 108

disputes
    credit score 281
    landlord 198
    roommate agreement 210
"Disputing Errors on Credit Reports" (FTC) 287n
District of Columbia College Access Program (DC CAP), contact 326
District of Columbia Field Office, contact 330
District of Columbia Housing Authority, contact 330
dividend, saving 149
DOES Office of Youth Programs (OYP), contact 323
Dollars from Sense, website 317
Dreamstime, photography 308
due date
    expenses 235
    loan payments 169
    money mistakes 135

E

earnings
    budget 128
    disabled teens 34
    emancipation 29
    potential 297
    savings 176
    self-employment 81
    student loan 167
economic stability
    education 293
    financial capability 4
economically vulnerable population, disabled teens 32
education credit, tax benefits 179
education loans, described 167
educational assistance benefits, tax benefits 181
"8 Things You Can Do to Be Taken Seriously as a Young Entrepreneur" (SBA) 253n
electronic banking, overview 237–9
"Electronic Banking" (FTC) 237n
electronic check conversion, electronic banking 238
electronic fund transfer (EFT), electronic banking 239
Electronic Fund Transfer Act (EFTA), electronic banking 239
electronic payment, electronic check conversion 238
emancipation laws, minors 27
"Emancipation Laws" (Omnigraphics) 27n
emergency fund, budgeting 133
emergency medical technician (EMT), vocational school 263

emergency savings fund
    expense management 235
    money management 162
    saving money 173
employment
    career 259
    credit report errors 287
    credit score 279
    disabled teens 32
    minimum age 40
    internship 64
    limitation of liability 217
    networking 84
    rules 49
    teen workforce 52
"Employment and Unemployment among Youth Summary" (BLS) 51n
employment network (EN), disabled teens 33
employment-support services, disabled teens 33
entry-level jobs
    career training 261
    education 298
Equifax
    bad credit 283
    consumer report 212
    credit freeze 269
    credit report 197
    credit scores 164
Equifax data breach, described 272
"Essential Skills to Getting a Job" (DOL) 83n
Estimation Calculators, website 318
ethical behaviors, workplace 93
eviction notice, renters guide 199
expenses
    budget 128
    career 260
    cosigner 222
    financial aid 245
    management 233
    planning 13
    roommate 210
    savings 148, 172
    spending 163
    student loan 294
Experian
    borrowing 164
    consumer report 212
    credit report 137
    credit score rebuilding 279
    free credit reports 267

"Exploring Your Career Path" (OWH) 55n
extracurricular activities
    self-assessment 8
    teamwork 91
    work-life balance 101

F

"Facts about Youth Financial Knowledge and
    Capability" (Youth.gov) 3n
Fair Credit Reporting Act (FCRA), credit report
    dispute 287
Fair Labor Standards Act (FLSA)
    employment 39
    penalties 43
FastWeb, website 318
Federal Deposit Insurance Corporation (FDIC)
    bak regulations 144
    money mistakes 136
    publications
        bad credit repair 279n
        credit scores rebuilding 279n
        common money mistakes 135n
        financial checkup 161n
        money management for teens 167n, 293n
        renting 11n
    student loan 168
federal loans, students 168
federal minimum wage
    teens 48
    workers' rights 112
federal student loans, college 168
Federal Trade Commission (FTC)
    publications
        budgeting 127n
        consumer reports and landlords 211n
        credit history 275n
        credit repair 279n
        credit report error dispute 287n
        electronic banking 237n
        future financial goals 251n
        landlord requirements 211n
        protection against fraud 311n
        renting an apartment or house 191n
federally-guaranteed consumer protections, bank
    accounts 174
fees
    auto loans 170
    budgeting 129

fees, *continued*
    Credit Repair Organization Act (CROA) 282
    credit unions 145
    electronic banking 237
    financial planner **185**
    money mistake 138
    scholarship 242
    school 168
    security deposit 12
fellowship, tax benefits 180
fiduciary, financial advisor **184**
finance charges
    credit cards **281**
    credit union 145
financial advice, financial professional 185
financial advisor
    credit report errors 287
    day trading 303
    financial planning 185
    investing 149
    money management 176
financial capability
    foster care teens 36
    overview 3–6
    educational goals 293
financial choices, financial literacy 4
financial common sense, preteens 24
financial decisions
    banking 141
    education 293
financial education
    financial capability 3
    foster care teens 36
"A Financial Empowerment Toolkit for Youth and
    Young Adults in Foster Care" (HHS) 35n
financial foundation, financial independence 23
financial freedom, financial goals **252**
financial future
    financial capability 3
    saving and investing 147
financial goals
    financial literacy 5
    future 251
    money management 161
    personal financial advisors 183
    saving and investing 147
financial habits, independence 23
financial institutions
    ATM fees 138
    credit unions 145

financial institutions, *continued*
    electronic banking 237
    financial privacy **165**
financial interest, financial capability **3**
financial knowledge, financial literacy **3**
financial life, preteens 24
financial literacy, teens 4
"Financial Literacy" (Youth.gov) 3n
financial literacy exam, high-school 4
financial management, financial capability 5
financial marketplace
    foster care teens 35
    youth 3
financial plan
    financial planners 184
    saving and investing 147
financial planners, described 184
financial planning services, financial planners 184
financial privacy, described **165**
financial reliability, debt 136
financial resources
    financial capability 3
    self-employment 118
financial skills, financial capability 4
financial status
    credit report 272
    savings and investing 148
financial transaction, financial planning **185**
financial well-being
    financial confidence 24
    financial literacy 3
    managing expenses **252**
"Financing Higher Education" (Youth.gov) 293n
"Find a Job" (USA.gov) 79n
"Find Job Openings" (DOL) 65n
"Finding and Applying for Scholarships" (ED) 241n
firewall, privacy protection 163
500pxPrime, photography 308
529 Plans
    college expenses 173
    savings 180
"5 Tips to Help Rebound from a Bad Credit History" (FDIC) 279n
flexible repayment plans, federal loans 168
flood insurance
    described 226
    renters insurance 14
"For Young Adults and Teens: Quick Tips for Managing Your Money" (FDIC) 167n, 293n
Form ADV, financial professional 186

fraud
    credit repair 282
    credit report agencies 271
    debit card 238
    fiduciary standard **184**
    finance 139
    protection 311
fraud alert, credit score 271
Free Application for Federal Student Aid (FAFSA®), contact 326
free credit reports
    bad credit history 283
    borrowing 164
    described 267
freelancer, self-employment 119
frugality, parent's role 23
Future Business Leaders of America (FBLA), student organizations 261

G

Gallaudet University, contact 326
GenIRevolution, website 318
George Mason University (GMU), contact 326
The George Washington University Hospital, contact 328
Georgetown University, contact 326
"Get a Job" (OWH) 73n
gift cards, electronic banking 239
GlobalTestMarket, making money online 306
good credit
    borrowing money 169
    credit score 286
    described 275
    renting an apartment or house 193
Goodwill of Greater Washington (GGW), contact 323
Google's AdSense, making money online 306
grace period, credit card bills 139
grade point average, creating a résumé 74
grants
    borrowing money 167
    Employment and Training Administration (ETA) **57**
    minor emancipation 27
    self-employment 121
    student loan 294
guidance counselor
    choosing a Career 58
    résumés **75**
    self-assessment 10

H

hands-on career training, choosing a career 262
hands-on training, choosing a career 263
hazardous occupations, jobs for different age
   groups 45
health savings account, saving money 173
high-deductible health insurance plans, saving
   money 173
high-interest-rate loans, financial capability and
   literacy 5
high school course plan, training for a career 262
higher education
   borrowing money 167
   educational goals and responsibilities 293
   financial capability and literacy 4
   self-employment 119
higher education loans, financial empowerment 167
Hitpredictor, making money online 307
Homeworkhelp, making money online 308
HomeworkTutoring, making money online 308
Hospital for Sick Children, contact 328
Howard University Hospital, contact 327, 328
The HSC Foundation, contact 328

I

i-Say, making money online 306
identity theft
   credit freeze 269
   credit report errors 287
   credit score 279
   financial empowerment 176
   foster care teens 35
   money management 164
"If at First You Don't Succeed: Common Mistakes
   Young Adults Make with Money and How to
   Avoid Them" (FDIC) 135n
Imagination Stage, contact 332
impairment, Financial Lives of People with
   Disabilities 32
impulse buying, common mistakes with money 135
InBoxDollars, making money online 306
income
   cosigning requirements for young renters 222
   educational goals and responsibilities 294
   financial capability and literacy 5
   financial empowerment 167
   making money online 307

income, *continued*
   planning for financial independence 13
   saving and investing 148
   self-employment 118
   taxes and tax benefits for education 181
income taxes
   financial empowerment 173
   planning for financial independence 17
individual retirement account (IRA), foster care
   teens 36
Individual Taxpayer Identification Number (ITIN),
   money management 152
inflation, financial capability and literacy 5
influential adults, financial capability and literacy 5
informational interviews, deciding a career 259
Institute for Community Inclusion (ICI), contact 334
insurance
   common mistakes with money 136
   credit report errors 287
   credit score 275
   financial empowerment 174
   foster care teens 35
   managing renters' insurance 225
   money management 161
   planning for financial independence 14
   tips for tenants 198
insured deposit account, financial empowerment 174
interest, financial capability and literacy 5
interest rate, planning for financial independence 17
Internal Revenue Service (IRS)
   publication
      cover letter 77n
internal yardstick, self-control 24
"International Schools" (ED) 245n
internships
   deciding a career 259
   overview 61–4
   workplace skills 90
"Internships: Previewing a Profession" (BLS) 61n
intervention, role of parents in teen spending 23
investing strategies, financial capability and literacy 5
investment
   banks and banking 145
   common mistakes with money 138
   financial empowerment 173
   personal financial advisors 183
   planning for financial independence 17
   saving and investing 149
   spending smart **236**

investment account
  money management 163
  saving and investing 147
investment banks, banks and banking 142
investment decisions, saving and investing 150
investment portfolios, personal financial
  advisors 183
investment products
  financial planners 184
  money management 162
Investor.gov: Invest Wisely, website 318
invoice, financial capability and literacy 4
IRS Withholding Calculator, website 318
"Is It Time for Your Financial Checkup?"
  (FDIC) 161n
iStockPhoto, making money online 308
Iwriter, making money online 307

J

Job Accommodation Network (JAN), contact 334
job bank, job opportunities 66
job fairs, job opportunities 67
job openings
  finding a job 79
  job opportunities 67
job opportunities
  jobs for disabled teens 84
  overview 65–8
  work–life balance 103
  workers' rights and safety 114
job-related injury, workplace hazards 107
job search
  finding a job 79
  job opportunities 68
  jobs for disabled teens 84
job shadow
  choosing a career 56, 259
  job opportunities 68
job training
  choosing a career 260
  Employment and Training Administration
  (ETA) **57**
  finding a job 80
jobs
  deciding a career 258
  disabled teens 84
  finding a job 82
  job opportunities 67

jobs, *continued*
  making money online 305
  work and age restrictions 42
  work–life balance 102
  workers' rights and safety 111
  workplace skills 90
John F. Kennedy Center for the Performing Arts,
  contact 331
Jumpstart Coalition for Personal Financial Literacy,
  website 318

K

Keen Greater DC, contact 332

L

landlord
  cosigning requirements for young renters 221
  planning for financial independence 12
  renter's guide 198
  renting an apartment or house 192
  responsibilities 215
  sharing rooms and related agreements 201
"Landlord–Tenant Handbook" (OHCD) 215n
landlord's insurance policy, renter's guide 198
late payments
  common mistakes with money 137
  cosigning requirements for young renters 222
lease
  cosigning requirements for young renters 222
  financial empowerment 170
  landlord requirements 212
  minor emancipation laws 29
  planning for financial independence 12
  renter's guide 197
  renting an apartment or house 191
  sharing rooms and related agreements 201
lease agreement, sharing rooms and related
  agreements 201
lease obligations
  cosigning requirements for young renters 223
  renting an apartment or house 194
lease payments, financial empowerment 170
leasing
  cosigning requirements for young renters 221
  financial empowerment 171
  sharing rooms and related agreements 209

legitimate
    educational goals and responsibilities 294
    electronic banking 239
    financial empowerment 176
    finding and applying for a scholarship 242
    rebuilding credit score 282
lenders
    common mistakes with money 136
    financial empowerment 170
    money management 165
    mortgage payment 15
    protecting your credit score 268
    rebuild your credit score 285
    self-employment 122
lending
    banks and banking 141
    financial capability and literacy 5
life map, exploring a career path 56
Lifeline Partnerships, Inc., contact 331
lifetime learning credit (LLC), taxes and tax benefits
    for education 179
lift a credit freeze, protecting credit score 269
loan forgiveness, financial empowerment 169
loans
    balance a job and school **101**
    banks and banking 142
    common mistakes with money 136
    credit score 276
    educational goals and responsibilities 294
    financial aid for studying abroad 247
    financial empowerment 168
    foster care teens 35
    protecting your credit score 268
local housing counseling agency, renting an apartment
    or house 195
long-term financial goals
    financial capability and literacy 5
    money management 161
long-term goals
    common mistakes with money 137
    working with financial professionals 184
long-term savings
    common mistakes with money 137
    financial empowerment 173
low-income individuals, financial capability and literacy 5

M

"Making a Budget" (FTC) 127n
"Managing Expenses" (Omnigraphics) 233n

manual dexterity, self-assessment 8
Matricula Consular, essential money management 152
median credit card debt, financial capability 4
MedStar Georgetown University Hospital,
    contact 329
MedStar National Rehabilitation Hospital,
    contact 329
MedStar Washington Hospital Center, contact 329
migrant teens, financial capability 6
minimum balance requirement, essential money
    management **151**
The Mint, website 318
mobile apps
    budgeting 132
    online and mobile banking 143
mobile banking, retail bank services 143
"Module 8: A Roof over Your Head" (FDIC) 11n
monetary system, bank regulation 144
money
    budgeting 127
    credit report 275
    credit score 285
    day trading 302
    developing financial confidence 25
    enforcement and penalties 43
    financial capability 5
    financial empowerment 167
    financial planners 184
    job opportunities 67
    managing expenses 233
    managing renters' insurance 226
    mortgage payment 15
    renting 191
    saving and investing 147
    scholarships 242
    security deposits 215
    self-employment 117
    teens with disabilities 33
    work-at-home scams 82
    work ethics and values 91
    work–life balance **101**
    workers' rights and safety 111
money management
    financial planners 184
    overview 151–9
Moneytopia, website 319
Montgomery Works, contact 324
monthly payment
    borrowing money 167
    credit card *156*

monthly payment, *continued*
 educational goals and responsibilities 294
 managing expenses 234
monthly statements, financial privacy **166**
mortgages
 borrowing 164
 credit report errors 288
 credit score 268
 electronic fund transfer (EFT) 238
 savings and loans 142
move-in statement, tips for tenants 199
MusicXray, making money online 307
mutual funds
 financial empowerment 173
 financial planners 184
 saving and investing 149
Myers–Briggs Type Indicator, assessment tools 9
MySurvey, making money online 306
MyTutor24, tutoring online 308

N

The National Alliance to Advance Adolescent Health,
 contact 329
National Collaborative on Workforce and Disability
 (NCWD/ Youth), contact 335
National Foundation for Credit Counseling,
 website 319
National Institute for Occupational Safety and
 Health (NIOSH)
  publication
   workplace safety 111n
National Longitudinal Survey of Youth (NLSY),
 financial capability 5
National Youth Employment Coalition (NYEC),
 contact 324
National Youth Leadership Network (NYLN),
 contact 335
network
 cover letter **78**
 internships 63
 jobs for disabled teens 84
 overview 69–71
 self-employment 122
"Networking for Teens" (Omnigraphics) 69n
new credit
 credit report 278
 credit scores 268
nondegree credentials, vocational school 263
nonfatal injuries, workplace hazards 107

O

occupational opportunities, self-assessment 7
Occupational Safety and Health Administration
 (OSHA)
  publication
   workplace hazard and workers' rights 107n
occupations
 borrowing money 168
 career preparation 261
 educational goals and responsibilities 294
 internships 63
 self-assessment **8**
 self-employment 119
 work and age restrictions 40
Office of Housing and Community Development
 (OHCD)
  publication
   landlord–tenant responsibilities 215n
Office of the State Superintendent of Education
 (OSSE), contact 321
Office on Disability Rights (ODR), contact 322
Office on Women's Health (OWH)
  publications
   career exploration 55n
   getting a job 73n
Omnigraphics
  publications
   assessing yourself and your future 7n
   basic facts about banks and banking 141n
   cosigning requirements for young
    renters 221n
   day trading 301n
   emancipation laws 27n
   managing expenses 233n
   networking for teens 69n
   savings and investing 147n
   sharing rooms and related agreements 201n
   transportation needs 229n
   ways to make money online 305n
   working with financial professionals 183n
   workplace ethics 101n
   workplace skills 89n
online banks, defined 142
online savings calculators, saving and investing 148
online surveys, making money online 306
on-the-job training
 apprenticeship **57**, 80
 career preparation 261

overdraft costs, financial empowerment 175
overdraft fees, essential money management 153
overdraft protection, common mistakes 139

P

paper paychecks, described 157
parenting teens, financial capability 5
pay-by-phone systems, electronic fund transfer (EFT) 238
paychecks
    budgeting 127
    electronic banking 237
    essential money management 157
    saving money 172
payments
    borrowing 165
    commercial banks 142
    credit cards 133
    credit history 284
    credit reports 267
    educational goals and responsibilities 293
    essential money management 151
    financial empowerment 170
    landlord responsibilities 215
    managing expenses 234
    residential sublease agreement 202
payroll card, described 158
personal bankruptcies
    bank regulation 144
    financial capability and literacy 4
personal computer banking, electronic fund transfer (EFT) 238
personal financial advisors, described 183
personal information
    credit freeze 269
    financial empowerment 177
    financial privacy **165**
    fraud 311
    résumé 74
"Planning for Your Future" (OWH) 55n
positive attitude, workplace ethics 94
predatory lending practices, financial illiteracy 5
premiums
    borrowing 164
    business 298
    electronic fund transfer (EFT) 238
    mortgage payment 15

prepaid cards
    described 159
    financial empowerment 174
principal
    borrowing 165
    mortgage payment 15
privacy notices, financial privacy **165**
privacy rights
    financial privacy **165**
    tips for tenants 198
private loans, borrowing money 168
probation, financial capability and literacy 5
problem-solving
    jobs for disabled teens 83
    teens with disabilities 32
    workplace skills 89
profits
    credit unions 145
    day trading 301
"Property Insurance" (USA.gov) 225n
Providence Hospital, contact 329
public records, credit report 272
punctuality, workplace ethics 93

Q

qualification
    apprenticeship **57**, 80
    job fairs 67
    résumé 75
qualified education expenses, deductions 180
qualified student loan, deductions 180
Quality Trust for Individuals with Disabilities, contact 333
quarters, managing renters' insurance 225

R

radio frequency identification (RFID), electronic banking 237
realistic goal setting, described 102
reasonable accommodations, career path 57
refinancing opportunities, loan 169, 296
refund
    bank accounts 175
    budget 132
    cosigning 222
    renter's guide 199
    taxes 179

registration
  financial planners 185
  loan 170
  transportation needs 231
regular commitments, debt 137
regulation
  banking 144
  business plan 121
  employment 40
  loan 169
  tenant responsibilities 218
relaxation activities, career 104
relaxation time, described 104
rent
  apartment or house 191
  bills 153
  budget 130
  business 123
  cosigning requirements 223
  credit score 267
  expenses 234
  landlord requirements 212
  rooms 201
"Renter's Guide: Ten Tips for Tenants" (HUD) 197n
renters' insurance
  overview 225–8
  renter's guide 198
"Renting an Apartment? Be Prepared for a
  Background Check" (FTC) 211n
"Renting an Apartment or House" (FTC) 191n
repayment
  borrowing money 167
  credit score 282
  educational goals 293
  loan 248
repayment plans
  borrowing money 167
  student loan 295
Residential Landlord and Tenant Act, landlord
  responsibilities 216
responsible financial habits, journey to
  independence 23
résumé
  balance job and school **101**
  cover letter 77
  internship 63
  job fairs 68
  overview 73–5
retail banks, defined 142

retail trade, employment 52
retirement
  common mistakes 138
  financial planners 184
  managing personal finances 36
  saving money 172
  self-employment 118
  spending smart **236**
rewards
  borrowing 165
  entrepreneurs **256**
  self-employment 118
  Ticket to Work 33
right financial records, money management 163
"The Right Shoes and Common Sense Can Help
  Your Preteen Gain Financial Ground" (CFPB) 23n
rights
  apprenticeships 80
  credit report 272
  credit score 279
  electronic banking 237
  emancipation status 28
  fraud 312
  landlord requirements 211
  privacy notices **165**
  renting 195
  roommate agreement 202
  workplace hazards 108
risks
  borrowing 164
  cosigning 221
  credit scores 268
  day trading **301**
  entrepreneur 254
  fraud 312
  personal financial advisors 183
  saving and investing 149
  saving money 173
  self-employment 118
  tabulated *155*
  teen drivers 231
  Ticket to Work 33
  workplace hazards 107
  workplace stress 98
roadmap
  assessment of future 7
  business plan 121
role model
  foster care 36
  guidance 20

S

safety
    bank accounts 174
    foster care 36
    landscape expectations 209
    renter's guide 199
    teen drivers 231
    workplace hazards 107
    workplace stress 97
Saint John's Community Services (SJCS), contact 324
sales
    business 298
    business plan 122
    fraud 312
    limitation of liability 217
    planning for independence 11
    website 307
saving money
    budgeting 128
    financial capability 5
    overview 172–3
    survey **150**
savings
    budgeting 128
    common mistakes 137
    financial capability 4
    financial empowerment 172
    foster care 36
    future financial goals 251
    jobs for disabled teens 87
    managing expenses 233
    money management 151, 161
    money management tools 317
    online earning 309
    renting 194
    sharing rooms 208
    student loan 294
    taxes 180
    see also investing
savings accounts
    banking 142
    budget 129
    expenses **136**
    financial empowerment 173
    foster care 36
    money management 162
    save and invest 150
    taxes 180

"Savings and Investing" (Omnigraphics) 147n
Savings Bond Calculator, website 319
savings bonds
    common mistakes 138
    online money management 318
    saving money 173
Savings Planner, website 319
savings plans
    described 180
    financial empowerment 172
    online money management 317
    save and invest 147
savings rates, financial capability 4
SBA Teen Business Link, website 319
scammers
    fraud 311
    money management 163
    self-employment 81
scams
    common mistakes 136
    credit history 285
    financial capability 5
    fraud 311
    job banks 67
    self-employment 81
    taking surveys 306
    work ethics 91
scholarships
    described 180
    educational goals 294
    financial empowerment 167
    overview 241–3
    teen networking 69
Scripted, make money online 307
securities
    assessing future 9
    bank accounts 176
    credit freeze 269
    credit report 287
    electronic fund transfer (EFT) 238
    job banks 67
    landlord requirements 211
    money management 157
    renting 192
    roommate agreement 203
    save and invest 149
    saving money 128
    scams **312**
    self-employment 81
    Ticket to Work 32

security deposit
  bills 153
  described 12
  landlord–tenant responsibilities 215
  renter's guide 198
  saving money 128, 192
security freeze, credit score 269
self-assessment, assessing yourself 7
self-control, journey to independence 23
"Self-Employment: What to Know to Be Your Own
  Boss" (BLS) 117n
selling photography, make money online 308
Serve DC, contact 332
"Sharing Rooms and Related Agreements"
  (Omnigraphics) 201n
shopping
  auto loans 170
  budget 133
  financial capability 4
  journey to independence 23
  managing expenses 235
  roommate agreement 206
short-term goals, financial capability 5
"Should I Get a Master's Degree?" (BLS) 297n
Shutterstock, selling photography 308
Sibley Memorial Hospital, contact 329
SkillsUSA, career 261
Slicethepie, reviewing music 307
SmartLocating, data entry 308
smartphone
  financial empowerment 176
  money management 163
social media
  described 66
  entrepreneur 225
  money management 163
  technology skills 92
  teen networking 71
social media accounts, job opportunities 66
social networking sites, money management 163
Social Security card, money management 158
Social Security disability, employment **82**
Social Security Disability Insurance (SSDI), Ticket to
  Work 32
software
  credit scores 285
  day trading 302
  internships 62
  résumé 75

software, *continued*
  saving 163
  self-employment 119
  technology skills 92
spending
  budget 128
  career path 59
  common mistakes 135
  financial capability 5
  financial goals 251
  financial status 148
  money management 163
  online earning 305
  tabulated *157*
state vocational rehabilitation (VR) agency,
  disabilities 33
statistics
  borrowing money 168
  jobs 260
  part-time jobs 104
  self-employment 117
  workforce 51
stocks
  common mistakes 138
  day trading 301
  financial planners 184
  saving and investing 149
StrengthsQuest, assessment tools 9
"Stress at Work" (CDC) 97n
strong interest inventory, assessment tools 9
stubs
  budget 128
  cosigner 222
  renting 195
student aid
  financial empowerment 167
  scholarship 243
student loan interest, taxes 180
student loans
  educational goals 293
  financial aid 246
  financial empowerment 167
  job and school **101**
  taxes 180
student organizations, deciding a career 261
students
  deciding a career 260
  educational goals and responsibilities 293
  financial aid for studying abroad 246

students, *contonued*
    financial capability and literacy 4
    financial empowerment 176
    internships 61
    jobs for disabled teens 85
    making money online 305
    teen participation in the workforce 51
subsidized apartment, renting an apartment or house 193
summer jobs
    financial empowerment 176
    teen participation in the workforce 51
Supplemental Security Income (SSI)
    exploring a career path 59
    teens with disabilities 34
surveys
    credit history 284
    disabled teens 83
    financial capability 4
    internships 64
    online money making 306
    self-employment 120

T

"Talking Safety" (NIOSH) 111n
take-home pay, financial empowerment 173
Tax Advantage Calculator, website 319
tax-advantaged retirement accounts, saving money 172
tax benefits
    saving money 173
    overview 179–81
tax credit, education benefits 181
"Tax Credits and Deductions" (USA.gov) 179n
tax-free
    income exclusions 181
    savings plans 180
tax information, self-employment 81
tax liens, credit report 272
tax return
    financial capability 5
    taxes 179
tax return form, financial capability 5
taxes
    escrow 15
    financial empowerment 170
    self-employment 81
    spending 163
    overview 179–81

team player
    described 94
    teamwork 86
technology
    career 262
    day trading 302
    defined 92
    electronic banking 237
    financial goals 251
    transportation needs 230
    workplace skills 89
"The Teenage Years Are for Practicing Money Decisions in a Safe Space" (CFPB) 23n
Teens and Money: Money 101, website 319
telephone banking, common mistakes with money 138
Ticket to Work program, described 32
time management
    described 119
    internships **61**
    workplace ethics 93
timely progress, teens with disabilities 34
"Tips for Building an Effective Résumé" (U.S. Department of the Treasury) 73n
Toluna, online surveys 306
"Transportation Needs" (Omnigraphics) 229n
TransUnion
    credit reporting agencies (CRA) 271
    credit reports 267
    credit scores 285
    renter's guide 197
Treasury Direct Kids®, website 319
Trinity Washington University (Trinity DC), contact 327
TryMyUI, website testing 307
tuition
    credits 179
    expenses 235
    financial planners 184
    scholarship 241
    studying abroad 248
    work–life balance **101**
tuition and fees deduction, taxes 180
Tumblr, blog 306
Tutor.com, online money making 308
tutoring online, described 308
Tutorvista, online tutoring 308

U

unauthorized charges, common mistakes with money 139

unauthorized use, electronic banking 238
undergraduate program, career 264
unemployment
    described 53
    saving and investing 149
    teen participation 51
unemployment rate
    career 263
    teens 51
United Cerebral Palsy (UCP) of Washington DC and
    Northern Virginia, contact 324. 335
university
    career 257
    education 74
University Legal Services (ULS), contact 333
The University of Maryland (UMD), College Park,
    contact 327
University of the District of Columbia (UDC),
    contact 327
unnecessary expenses, financial status 149
unpaid experience, résumé 74
unpaid tax liens, credit report 272
unplanned expenses, budget 130
unsolicited offers, financial privacy **166**
upfront fee
    credit report 272
    planning for independence 13
Upwork, make money online 307
USA.gov
    publications
        credit reports and scores 267n
        finding a job 79n
        guiding teens 19n
        property insurance 225n
        tax credits and deductions 179n
Userlytics, website testing 307
UserTesting, website testing 307
UserZoom, website testing 307
"Using Consumer Reports: What Landlords Need to
    Know" (FTC) 211n
U.S. Bureau of Labor Statistics (BLS)
    publications
        career planning 257n
        earning potential 297n
        employment and unemployment among
        youth 51n
        internships 61n
        self-employment 117n

U.S. Department of Education (ED)
    publications
        budgeting tips 127n
        financial aid 245n
        scholarships 241n
U.S. Department of Homeland Security (DHS)
    publication
        flood insurance 225n
U.S. Department of Housing and Urban
    Development (HUD)
    publication
        tips for tenants 197n
U.S. Department of Labor (DOL)
    publications
        employment regulations 45n
        Fair Labor Standards Act (FLSA) 39n
        job opportunities 65n
        job skills 83n
U.S. Department of the Treasury
    publication
        résumé writing 73n
U.S. Mint for Kids, website 319
U.S. Savings Bond
    common mistakes with money 138
    saving money 173
U.S. Small Business Administration (SBA)
    publication
        entrepreneurship 253n
U.S. Social Security Administration (SSA)
    contact 325
    publication
        assistance for disabled teen 31n
utilities
    budget 130
    described 13
    lease 191
    paying bills 153
    roommate agreement 203

V

video blogs, make money online 306
Vimeo, video blog 306
VirtualBee, data entry 308
vocational rehabilitation counselor, career
    path 56
vocational rehabilitation services, work program 32
vocational school, defined 263

vocational training
 career path 57
 jobs 80
volunteer experience, work experience 74
volunteering
 career path 56
 enthusiasm 85
 network 123
 financial goals 251

W

wages
 financial empowerment 168
 higher earning potential 297
 internships **61**
 tabulated *157*
Washington Metropolitan Area Transit Authority
 (WMATA), contact 330
"Ways to Make Money Online"
 (Omnigraphics) 305n
"Ways to Pay Your Bills" (CFPB) 151n
"Ways to Receive Your Money" (CFPB) 151n
Weebly Blogger, video blog 306
"What Should I Know before Writing a Cover Letter
 for the Federal Government?" (IRS) 77n
WordPress, blog 306
work experience
 jobs 261
 résumé 74
 workplace hazards 107
work–life balance, overview 101–5
"Work–Life Balance" (Omnigraphics) 101n
work mentoring program, career path 56
work-related benefits, financial capability 5
work-study
 student loan 167
 working hours 47

working online, tutoring **308**
"Working to Improve the Financial Lives of People
 with Disabilities" (CFPB) 31n
"Working with Financial Professionals"
 (Omnigraphics) 183n
workplace ethics, overview 93–5
"Workplace Ethics" (Omnigraphics) 93n
workplace harassment, employees 95
workplace hazards
 overview 107–9
 workers' rights and safety 112
"Workplace Skills" (Omnigraphics) 89n
"Workplace Stress" (CDC) 97n
Writerbay, make money online 307

Y

"Yes, Renters Can Buy Flood Insurance" (DHS) 225n
"You've Got Goals for Your Life—And Some of
 Them Take Money to Achieve" (FTC) 251n
"Young Workers—Hazard" (OSHA) 107n
"Young Workers Safety and Health" (CDC) 107n
"Young Workers—You Have the Rights"
 (OSHA) 107n
"Your Credit History" (FTC) 275n
Youth Advocates Program, Inc., contact 334
Youth.gov
 publications
  financial literacy 3n
  financing higher education 293n
youth labor force, labor force 52
"Youth Rules—Know the Rules" (DOL) 45n
YouTube, video blog 306

Z

zoning permit, self-employment 122